Interpreting Disciples

Interpreting
DISCIPLES
Practical Theology
in the
DISCIPLES OF CHRIST

Edited by

L. Dale Richesin *and* Larry D. Bouchard

Texas Christian University Press
Fort Worth

Copyright © 1987 by Texas Christian University Press

Library of Congress Cataloging-in-Publication Data

Interpreting Disciples.

1. Christian Church (Disciples of Christ)—Doctrines—History—19th century.
2. Christian Church (Disciples of Christ)—Doctrines—History—20th century.
I. Richesin, L. Dale. II. Bouchard, Larry D., 1952–
BX7321.2.I57   1987   253'.088266   86-30072
ISBN 0-87565-072-4 (pbk.)

Designed by Whitehead & Whitehead

THIS BOOK IS PRINTED ON AND BOUND WITH ACID-FREE MATERIALS.

Contents

In memory of
TOMMIE M. BOUCHARD
and
HUGH and KITTIE RICHESIN

Foreword

MARTIN E. MARTY

KIBITZERS AND EAVESDROPPERS on the Christian Church (Disciples of Christ) usually come prepared to point out ironies in their tradition. These are familiar to the point of being obvious, but newcomers have to be made aware of them. This ecclesial movement born on the American frontier wanted to be primitive, and yet it has produced a sophisticated tradition, some of whose evidences are present in this volume. It desired to be restorationist, yet it inevitably acquired the burden of history from times which intervened between the New Testament and the nineteenth century. Some of its leaders thought they were able to interpret the Bible head-on, yet today scholars are able to discern many levels of nineteenth-century philosophy and interpretation theory in their efforts.

More ironies, this most ironic of all: the Disciples of Christ and Christian movements wanted to be simply ecumenical. Run up a banner and see who salutes, the pioneers seemed to say. Who would salute? All believers who were of good will, since they had good reason to be tired of Christian division. Enough churches, sects, and denominations, they tried to say. So they helped produce what others, if not they, immediately began to call churches, sects, and denominations. They added to the number of Christian connections instead of subtracting. Then, by getting disconnected from each other, they multiplied the divisions. Few religious clusters today are more maddening to the sorter or mapmaker than the members of this tradition. Disciples of Christ? Christian? Church of Christ? Which branch? Have you a headquarters?

Whoever traces the Disciples of Christ patterns will find more ironies in the matter of polity and governance. The found-

ers thought they could reproduce simple New Testament patterns. Yet it takes no great perceptive skill to see that their heirs
creatively improvised to meet new situations. One can be cruel
and say that modern adaptations move as much by the norms of
Max Weber—who spoke of *Rationalität*, in this case bureaucratic
rationality—as by New Testament norms. There is more im-
provising to come.

The founders wished to be mainstream, yet some branches
of the stream have the highest banks on the landscape, are rigidly
bordered, and make their own way. Others have liberalized themselves into a bankless flatness that seems to meander over the same
scape, blending with other groups, barely making its own bed,
sometimes blending with sand.

Then there are the rites and orders of the church. Most Disciples of Christ would have called themselves sacramentally low
church, underordered if not disordered. Yet when Vatican II came
along and Catholics looked for fresh company, some theologians—I remember George Tavard among them—looked over
the Catholic wall and found surprising connections. Catholics
shouldn't only notice sacramentally high Anglicans and Lutherans,
he urged. Here are the Disciples of Christ, who make so much of
baptism and are really exciting because, no matter quite what they
mean by the communion, they at least celebrate it every week.

Name the topic and the observer will name the irony. The
Disciples of Christ would be nontheological, yet through the
decades the movement has generated notable theologians. The
Disciples of Christ would be nonhistorical in their primitiveness
or primitivism, yet they run impressive archives in Nashville,
have scholarly gleanings in Chicago, and find even the more mil-
itantly antihistorical wings of the Church of Christ arguing that
since they have been around and have a history, they would do
well to know it. Watch for more excitements on that front.

In the case of this volume, I have to remove a bit of fun from
the ironist or the irony-discerner. The authors know all about
these twists and turns in Disciples of Christ fates. They have, to
use a barbaric term for a good process, internalized them. They

begin where the traditional critic or observer leaves off. They all seem a bit nervous about coherence weighing too heavily on what should be a pluralist lineage. Then they enjoy finding coherences while celebrating pluralism. Meanwhile, they seem to be suffering no strain from the discovery that they are embodying and even touting a tension between the two. The reader should enjoy the creativity of that tension.

The issue here is: have we a tradition? Yes. Is it pluralist? Yes. Is there some coherence? Yes. So what do we do with the pluralist and cohering tradition *today*, here, now? These essays, addressing such questions in the context of various pastoral practices and theological disciplines, make urgent reading for all Disciples and enjoyable and helpful reading for those who are not of the movement but who are seeking coherences of their own.

The theologians and ministerial thinkers in this book are uncommonly alert to the contexts of theological and ministerial work in the 1980s. This alertness does not lead them into over-attention to code words or jargon. It certainly does not lead them into zones of impracticality. Some of the gutsy authors even conclude with enumerated "how to" lists, and they become vulnerable for being so explicit. Good for them. No, what is more evident is their ability to reckon with the broad issues and tools of the day, many of which come from beyond the Disciples of Christ or their Chicago niche. Ours is a hermeneutical era. The authors here all know that, but they are interested in how interpretation theory works in their sphere. They are aware of *praxis* and informed by liberation theology. But they bend and stretch until the reader can see something of "what's in it for us?" for Disciples, American Christians, and the like.

Literate, informed, balanced, and still provocative these authors and essays are. In editorial circles we sometimes complain that the newest generation of theologians has not taken shape. The last generational flowering emerged in the mid-sixties. It's about time for another cohort. Perhaps the near-emergences have been too isolated and lonely: they blossom for a moment but receive no encouragement and disappear. Now here, suddenly, are provokers who in modest ways demand to be taken seriously. They are effective because they interact. Let that be the last irony in this ecumenically and academically plotless era. From the least denominational orbit in Protestantism—or so it was intended to be—we have evidence of vitality made possible, made necessary we might even say, by the survival of the denomination, the movement, called Disciples of Christ.

MARTIN E. MARTY is the Fairfax M. Cone Distinguished Service Professor and Professor of History of Modern Christianity at the Divinity School of the University of Chicago. The author of many books and articles, he is also on the editorial staff of *The Christian Century*, *The Journal of Religion*, and other journals.

Introduction

DON S. BROWNING

THE ESSAYS in *Interpreting Disciples* were born out of a special inspiration and a special opportunity.

The inspiration, I believe, arises from a sense among many Disciples that the time is ripe for reinterpretation. The authors represented here each reflect an apologetic perspective on the Christian Church (Disciples of Christ) that deeply respects the resources for Christian living and thinking found within their tradition. They discover in the Stone-Campbell movement not merely a treasure to be dusted off now and then, but an important and usable resource in which Disciples can find continuity and new direction. What is needed is reinterpretation, especially interpretation that shows what the Disciples heritage continues to offer to discussions of issues alive in the contemporary church. The authors, in other words, see the Disciples tradition as providing a basis for practical theology. Some of their essays use this tradition as a starting point from which to address topics central to the practice of ministry and theology. Others move in the opposite direction, from issues of religious, moral, or social concern to aspects of Disciples history and practice that are distinctively illuminating and enriching. Each paper is intended not only to describe a Disciples perspective on the issue in question, but also to exemplify the perspective by interpreting it anew.

The special opportunity that occasioned these essays was associated with a seminar on Disciples history and thought that has been conducted twice a quarter for several years at the Disciples Divinity House of the University of Chicago. Led by historian C. Harvey Arnold, the seminar has involved Disciples graduate students preparing for careers in ministry or higher education and from time to time has included other Disciples scholars and clergy. In reading basic texts, hearing lectures, and sharing papers, the participants discussed and quite frequently debated a variety of issues pertaining to the history and thought of this American religious movement. During my tenure as dean of Disciples House (1977–1983), I hoped that stimulating several years of ongoing discussion would have a cumulative impact upon the consciousness of Disciples. To the extent that this book is a product of those discussions, the seminars succeeded beyond our fondest dreams.

At the urging of editors Dale Richesin and Larry Bouchard, certain Disciples House scholars and recent graduates prepared papers both appreciative and critical of the tradition that will shape their careers in ministry and teaching. The theme that became evident at many points in their projects was interpretation. Not only are the authors interpreting the Disciples of Christ, but in each area of practical concern they discover that the Disciples place prime importance on the activity of interpretation. Thus, the title of this volume is a double entendre: the essays interpret the Disciples, and the Disciples are a people especially called to be Christian interpreters.

It is not without precedent that these alumni of Disciples Divinity House make this contribution to the history and thought of the Christian Church (Disciples of Christ). Winfred E. Garrison, the second dean of the house, was one of our denomination's foremost historians. He combined his talents with those of Alfred T. DeGroot, who received his Ph.D. through Disciples House in 1940, to write *The Disciples of Christ: A History* (St. Louis: Christian Board of Publication, 1948). W. B. Blakemore, who was dean from 1945 to 1975, made innumerable contributions to Disciples history and thought, especially through his vigorous leadership as general editor of *The Renewal of Church: The Panel of Scholars Reports* (3 vols., St. Louis: Bethany Press, 1963). The authors of the papers in this volume have been inspired by this history of scholarship, and their work presented here adds to the tradition. They offer new insights into our shared past and new hope for a vigorous future. Realizing that the papers they were developing deserved to be shared with a larger community, I asked that several be presented on March 23, 1983, under sponsorship of the William Henry Hoover Lectures on Christian Unity at Disciples Divinity House. The response by the audience was unusually positive, adding to my conviction that these papers constitute an important new perspective on our denomination that should be shared with an even wider public.

DON S. BROWNING served as Dean of Disciples Divinity House from 1977 to 1983. He is the Alexander Campbell Professor of Religion and Psychological Studies at the Divinity School of the University of Chicago.

The Interpretation Principle: A Foundational Theme of Disciples Theology

LARRY D. BOUCHARD

Jesus said, "What is written in the Law? What is your reading [*anaginōskeis*] of it?"
—Luke 10:26 (New English Bible)

"What hypocrites you are! You know how to interpret the appearance of the earth and sky; how is it you cannot interpret [*dokimazein*] this fateful hour?"
—Luke 12:56

WHEN ASKED ABOUT their theology, it is not uncommon for good Disciples of Christ to pat their volumes of Alexander Campbell confidently and say, "No, we have no theology. We have only our biblical texts and our reasonable minds with which to interpret them." Didn't Campbell, after all, ban the teaching of theology from the Bethany College curriculum? Aren't we, after all, "reasonable, empirical, pragmatic," as W. B. Blakemore has said, but not "theological"? On the other hand—and sometimes in the same breath—it is not uncommon for Disciples to admit that Campbell's alleged antitheological position was itself a theology, and a sophisticated one at that. In fact, we may well ask, aren't *all* Christians—whether squirming in their pews or squirming in their pulpits—doing "theology" as soon as they begin thinking about their faith or thinking about what they are doing in the world in light of their faith?

Thinking is doing, and so is theology. Theology is an activity, just as all thought is activity. It is practical; it has consequences. For purposes here, we define Christian theology as the concerned and thoughtful inquiry into the foundations of faith, the meaning of beliefs, and the implications of both for human experience and action in the world. Every time a Christian (or a Jew in the context of Judaism, or a Hindu in the context of Hinduism) thinks about what he or she believes or cannot believe, or must do or refuse to do, in the context of faithful concern, then that person has engaged in theology. Every time a man or woman ponders the world of experience and the meaning of the Christian faith in the same moment, then Christian theology has happened. The thoughts may be affirmative or negative; they may say yes in a thoughtful and concerned way, or no. For theology itself is neither faith nor belief, but *thought* about faith and belief and about the tradition of others who have listened to the Christian message and have considered it carefully and critically. Insofar as thought is a human activity, so too is theology; it is an activity that can lead or relate to many other activities. Theology is a way of getting something done.

Disciples think about Christian faith, and in so doing they do theology. If an aspect of their collective theologizing is distinctive, it is the "foundational theology" that is implicit in the way Disciples have understood their relation to the Christian tradition as a whole. By "foundational theology," I generally mean thought about the very bases of Christian faith and thought— what makes theology possible. Such a concern is important among Disciples and is worth communicating to Disciples themselves and to others.

Few of us identified with the Disciples of Christ consider this allegiance to be the pivotal fact of our human or Christian identities. Before we are Disciples we are Christians, and we are not always sure what we mean when we say that. But in various ways we found ourselves in a church community that has provided a context for our Christianness and for our Christian thinking. To the extent that this community has formed and informed our thought in distinctive and perhaps strange ways, then the question naturally arises as to what we think as Disciples, and why and how.

Is there a distinctive Disciples theology? Are there assumptions in Disciples thought about the Christian faith that are distinctive among Christians? Those are both the right and the wrong questions. In a certain sense—certainly the most important sense—there can be no Disciples theology, only Christian theology. The whole force of the Stone-Campbell movement leads us to say as much. Our most distinctive claim is the plea that we have no corner and that there should be no corner on any doctrinal market. Yet as anyone who studies the old Disciples "plea" quickly discovers, that claim itself is a corner. And although it is not a unique claim, it has enabled generations of Disciples to find a degree of distinctiveness and identity within their religious community. Oftentimes flustered when asked who we are as Disciples, we have been able to begin with the notion that while "we are Christians only, we are not the only Christians." To be sure, it is hard to claim both inclusive unity with all Christians and distinctiveness among Christians as a basis for one's communal identity. But Disciples do just that, and when they begin to think about the assumptions behind that claim, a kind of "Disciples" Christian theology is happening.

The Pluralistic Setting

Paul Tillich taught that theology always happens in a setting or situation—a place in history, culture, and geography. Theological thinking always involves, in one way or another, thinking about the situation in terms of faith and about faith in terms of the situation. As situations change—and they are always changing—theology must rethink itself anew. Many have characterized the situation for theological thinking today as an acute awareness of change[1] and as a pluralism of interests, purposes, and methods in all aspects of science and culture[2]—to the extent that the many disciplines of discovery and human self-interpretation remain in states of flux.

When theology is done well today, it generally takes into account these many dimensions of change and pluralism, and it works along interdisciplinary lines. Any distinctively "Disciples" theology will also have to interpret this contemporary situation and address itself to the multiple methods of self-interpretation. The Disciples tradition is especially suited to this task and always has been; the churches, after all, comprise plural constituencies, occupations, points of view, and the like. But more importantly, pluralism now also characterizes the broader cultural horizons Disciples live and work within, and this fact affects how the Disciples interpret both their historical past and their present.

By pluralism in a cultural context, I mean the coexistence of genuinely different ways of looking at and thinking about things. This includes significantly, even radically different expectations for what life should offer individuals and communities: different religions, philosophies, ethical stances, lifestyles, and cultural orientations. Pluralism in a broad sense is nothing new. There have always been genuinely different ways of looking at things. Students of the Bible begin by studying the confluence of Hebraic, Greek, and Roman worlds in what was essentially a pluralistic environment in Palestine. And we know that every human being has a way of looking at things that is distinctly—not to say uniquely—his or her own. Interpersonal relationships become either superficially shallow or oppressively dominating if such pluralism is not acknowledged.

At times, however, pluralism becomes a predominant cultural factor. The worldwide cultural pluralism emerging today is in reality a pluralism of cultures. There are few places on earth today where critical thought is not dominated by competing systems of interpretation and conflicting political, religious, and ideological perspectives. This fact gives rise to tremendous cross-cultural understanding and enrichment within the so-called global village. But it also gives rise to violent eruptions in the midst of polarizing conflicts.

In a genuinely pluralistic environment there are no easy resolutions or grand syntheses that can turn truly different ways of understanding into one global perspective. The first norms of a pluralistic world seem to be distance and difference. So often we expect one another to be absolutely unique, embodying a subjective reality that is impenetrable and self-authenticating, even if in fact we have much in common. We tolerate each other not so much out of a sense of mutual understanding but out of a melancholy suspicion that such understanding is an impossible illusion. And on the global scale we more often than not, it frequently appears, fail to tolerate each other. In this global village mistrust and resentment, anxiety and natural defensiveness, ill-will and exclusivist strategies of self-preservation abound. We have little confidence that there can be a hidden creed or common set of assumptions about reality that can give such diverse viewpoints a shareable point of reference. There is a tragic dimension to pluralism that makes for a future far more uncertain than in past cultural experiences, where a religious consensus or shared set of cultural values might be assumed.

My point here is not to complain or even to urge change but simply to acknowledge that the mixed blessing of cultural and intellectual pluralism is our reality. It is also the reality we must think in; it is our setting, our theological situation. The problem of thinking critically and creatively in a pluralistic setting is acute. On the one hand, the honest thinker cannot deny the fact that other ways of thinking authentically confront different aspects of reality. These genuinely different frames of reference can, at different times and to various extents, be fruitful. That is, they disclose distinctive and meaningful claims to truth. But they do so in ways that are not mutually inclusive; they are really different. On the other hand, the honest thinker must make committed claims of his or her own, claims that are precise and inevitably different, but important. And these claims must not ignore pluralism dogmatically, dissolve pluralism into a premature or unrealistic synthesis, or deny real commitment to truth.[3]

This is the setting in which Disciples thinkers, like other

thinkers, find themselves today. The Disciples of Christ have something distinctive to say to Christianity as it tries to be a transformative voice in a pluralistic world. But this claim itself involves the Disciples in the same pluralistic problem.

Pluralism and the Disciples of Christ

It may be said that the Disciples began as a response to the failure of Protestant Christianity to think and live pluralistically. In similar ways the Campbells, Stone, and Scott became appalled by the sectarian divisions within their communities and so developed notions of Christian unity around the scriptural authority of Christ. By 1832 they had joined in a movement that enjoyed considerable growth in the midwestern United States during the middle decades of the nineteenth century. To understand the theological character of this movement and the themes, forces, and normative ideas or symbols that shaped the movement's history and still shape the way it understands itself in the present, it is helpful to have an historical text to start from and interpret. Propositions 1, 3, 4, and 6 of Thomas Campbell's *Declaration and Address* (1809) correspond fairly well with the movement's essential purposes as understood by the other founders.[4]

> PROP. 1. THAT the church of Christ upon earth is essentially, intentionally, and constitutionally one; consisting of all those in every place that profess their faith in Christ and obedience to him in all things according to the scriptures, and that manifest the same by their tempers and conduct, and of none else as none else can be truly and properly called christians.
>
> 3. That in order to this, nothing ought to be inculcated upon christians as articles of faith; nor required of them as terms of communion; but what is expressly taught and enjoined upon them, in the word of God. Nor ought any thing be admitted, as of divine obligation, in their church constitution and managements, but what is expressly enjoined by the authority of our

Lord Jesus Christ and his Apostles upon the New Testament church; either in expressed terms, or by approved precedent.

4. That although the scriptures of the Old and New Testament are inseparably connected, making together but one perfect and entire revelation of the Divine will, for the edification and salvation of the church; and therefore in that respect cannot be separated; yet as to what directly and properly belongs to their immediate object, the New Testament is as perfect a constitution for the worship, discipline and government of the New Testament church, and as perfect a rule for the particular duties of its members; as the Old Testament was for the worship, discipline and government of the Old Testament church, and the particular duties of its members.

6. That although inferences and deductions from scripture premises, when fairly inferred, may be truly called the doctrine of God's holy word: yet they are not formally binding upon the consciences of christians farther than they perceive the connection, and evidently see that they are so; for their faith must not stand in the wisdom of men; but in the power and veracity of God—therefore no such deduction can be made terms of communion, but do properly belong to the after and progressive edification of the church. Hence it is evident that no such deductions or inferential truths ought to have any place in the church's confession.[5]

Contained in these propositions are two themes that run explicitly through most nineteenth-century Disciples texts: the restoration of the Church to those foundations laid for it in the New Testament and the New Testament alone, and the essential unity of the Church based on those foundations. The first theme has long been known as the *restoration principle,* while the theme of unity might be termed the *ecumenical principle*. A third, implicit theme in the propositions also runs through most Disciples documents, namely, the freedom of the Christian individual to interpret the scriptures according to reason and conscience. This theme I am calling the *interpretation principle*. Later, the implications of these three principles must be brought together. But presently, it is enough to observe that early Disciples thought can be characterized by a polarity of restoration and unity, with freedom of interpretation being a supposition that needs further elaboration.

The two poles, restoration and unity, are deeply related.[6] For the early Disciples, unity did not mean that all the sects should join each other but that Christians should join in dropping all doctrinal and creedal prescriptions for church membership, except those explicit in the New Testament. This did not mean the abolition of creeds and doctrines—for their inferences could be fair and helpful to some—only that they were not to be held as essential to being a Christian.[7] That is, creeds and doctrines could not be used as tests of faith and fellowship. Likewise, unity was not to be realized by watering down doctrines to a lukewarm compromise of mutual acceptability. Rather, unity meant all Christians uniting around the restoration principle.

Tensions among the Stone-Campbell movement are at least partially understandable in terms of distortions of one pole or the other. Restoration, on the one hand, was never intended to be the shibboleth of yet another iconoclastic group arrogantly claiming to be the one true Church. At its best, the restoration principle expressed what Disciples believed all Christians could affirm, namely, the lordship of Jesus Christ based on the authoritative testimony of New Testament scripture. But the first divisions within the movement came from narrowing understanding of the restoration principle so that the scriptural text itself came to be treated as a creed and test of fellowship, as in the matters of baptism by immersion and the use or nonuse of instrumental music in worship. The movement, at its worst, could become as sectarian as any other. The other pole is also liable to distortion. Liberal Disciples' emphasis on unity with little regard to restoration as a founding principle may have contributed to the crisis of corporate identity that has been perceived in recent decades. Disciples, in my judgment, have not adequately reinterpreted the restoration principle in terms of a modern, critical consciousness, although they have so interpreted other dimensions of faith.[8]

Throughout this century, for example, the Disciples of Christ intentionally redefined themselves along liberal and ecumenical lines, culminating in *The Panel of Scholars Reports* (1963) and the completion of Restructure under the Provisional Design (1968) of the Christian Church (Disciples of Christ). This process of redefinition involved the more-or-less complete rejection of the restoration principle and the biblical literalism it fostered. The rejection was based on the fact that modern biblical and historical scholarship came to show that the basic propositional claims of restorationism are untenable. As Ralph Wilburn summarized the matter, there is no reasonable basis to consider the New Testament "ancient faith and order" as an exact, literal, and sufficient basis for today's faith and order: the texts are not infallible, the early churches were not of a single unified character, and the church was then as now as changeable as any historical institution.[9] The notion that the New Testament is a set of bylaws for worship and organization is untrue to the nature of the texts and promotes the very sectarianism that Disciples founders had risen to oppose. Wilburn did affirm that there were "elements of truth" in the "basically false concept of restoration," namely, (1) that Christ is the ground of Christian unity, (2) that revelation has a historical character by virtue of the Holy Spirit at work in the Church, (3) that the Church should be motivated by love, (4) that the restoration principle fostered a rebirth of freedom of inquiry and biblical interpretation, and (5) that restorationism provided a principle by which unity could be comprehended. But Wilburn redefined this unifying principle in such a way as to rob the old restoration principle of its focus. Unity was to be understood in terms of the "transhistorical, transrelative norm" of the Gospel, the "Christological motif."

The Christological motif is simply the affirmation that we as Disciples have "no creed but Christ." The Panel of Scholars saw in that slogan one of our most positive values, along with that of Christian unity. Our faith, the panelists repeat, is faith in a person, Christ; faith is not assent to propositions about that person, imposed in creeds and other doctrinal formulas. But, it should be noted, while the Panel of Scholars affirmed and reinterpreted "no creed but Christ" in light of modern consciousness and in dialogue with contemporary theology, the restoration principle was not so reinterpreted. Rather, it was rejected on basically nineteenth-century grounds. Modern Disciples cannot accept the restoration principle as propositionally true, because that would imply literal interpretations of scripture and church tradition that fail Alexander Campbell's own test of exact correspondence between words and realities:

> What, then, is truth? Momentous question! She is *Reality* herself! 'Tis not merely the exact correspondence of words with ideas. This is but *verbal* truth. 'Tis not the mere agreement of the terms of any proposition with logical arrangement.—This is *logical* truth. But it is the correspondence, the exact agreement of our ideas with things as they are. So that the representations of truth are exact pictures of all the realities about which we are conversant, or in which we are interested.[10]

Today, such a propositional model of truth leads to rejection of the restoration principle, since modern biblical and historical learning challenges the notion that Bible words correspond literally to biblical things or matters of faith and reason. But modern Disciples have been aware of other models of truth when they have interpreted other aspects of Christian tradition and the Disciples movement.

Among the modern interpretive models, for instance, Frank N. Gardner uses some basic tenets of analytical philosophy to understand the Disciples Confession of Faith in Christ.[11] In effect, Gardner treats the Confession as "performative speech." Disciples have never agreed on the propositional content of the Confession of Faith. When nervous little Disciples affirm before the congregation on some Palm Sunday morning that Jesus is the Christ, the Son of the living God and their savior, the minister does not ask them what they mean. Why? Not because they do not "understand," but because the truth of the Confession of Faith is in the relationship it establishes and discloses, not in the statement it makes. Its propositional content cannot be verified or falsified. It is more performative than propositional, more akin to making a promise than to relating an idea. Its symbolic disclosure of truth gives rise to many interpretations, a point to which I will return.[12]

The problem for a pluralist theology is to articulate clear, formal, normative meanings without denying the validity of material pluralism, with all its benefits and difficulties. In nineteenth-century Disciples thought, the formal norm of restoration became an oppressive, exclusivistic, material norm that denied the legitimacy of other material points of view and closed off authentic conversation in the midst of difference. But modern, liberal Disciples find that without the embarrassing restoration principle, the norm of Christian unity has no clear meaning or limits. What is needed is a foundational theology that can retrieve some advantages from the dialectic of restoration and unity. I believe this can be done by reinterpreting the third principle, that of free, reasonable, conscientious interpretation, in the context of Christian tradition and contemporary pluralistic experience.

Interpretation and Truth

Besides pluralism, another aspect of our theological setting should be considered here, namely, that thinking is often conceived today as an essentially interpretive activity. An anthropological conviction has taken hold that has important relevance for theology: *Homo sapiens* is the slightly furry animal that goes about interpreting itself and its world. So closely are the ideas of understanding and interpretation linked that in some circles the terms have become nearly synonymous.

An act of interpretation involves both the interpreter and what is being interpreted. In Paul Ricoeur's view, interpretation is an affair of shared or at least shareable meaning.[13] We make real connections between ourselves, others, and the world. And these connections are multiple. When we interpret different kinds of expressions—such as letters, laundry lists, poems, and scriptures—we find that they project many different dimensions of meaning. They mean more than they say. Even a precise scientific paper about insect population also projects meanings concerning the nature and values of scientific inquiry, meanings not so precise or univocal. When we read a letter from home—or a letter from St. Paul for that matter—we are attuned to all sorts of implicit or explicit meanings, nuances, and conventions that relate to letter-writing. We do not anticipate the kinds of meaning associated with newspapers, physics books, or novels. All these aspects of meaning are real, and it is a task of interpretation to sort them out. Some forms of expression, such as poetry, fiction, and parables, function primarily to create many resonances of meaning simultaneously—what Ricoeur calls a "surplus of meaning." This multifaceted expression creates a kind of world, projected by the text, that invites the reader or hearer to enter and interpret it. The interpreting act is guided by the meanings of the text and is informed by the interpreter's own body of experience; the result will be deeper understanding that leads to still more paths of interpretation. A multifaceted discourse does not easily become exhausted, and that the scriptures themselves present different dimensions of meaning has been variously recognized since the time of Augustine and Philo before him.

The plurality of meaning and the many aspects of interpretation raise the question of the truth of these meanings and the truth of our interpretations of them. These issues are too complex to be reviewed here, but I do hold that a person's interpretation can be more-or-less true to the text being interpreted. The issue can be clarified in terms of four kinds of truth claims or models of truth, which here are ordered as we usually apply them to different things we interpret:

1. *Artifactual truth* applies to the concrete leavings of culture and history; these have a certain persistent significance. We may not know the meaning of a cave painting in Europe nor who the "artist" was, but the sheer existence of the painting establishes the truth that someone painted on the cavern wall. Can a claim of artifactual truth be falsified? Perhaps so, in cases where our perceptions of concrete reality are found to be mistaken ("it's not a painting, but a stain from water seepage" or "your eyes are fooling you").

2. *Propositional truth* applies to claims about reality that are more-or-less univocal and clear by intent, at least in the context of those who understand their purpose. Newspapers, scientific reports, and logical analyses are intended primarily as propositional truth claims that correspond exactly to the matter in question, at least insofar as their context is concerned. Such was Alexander Campbell's point in his discussion of truth. These claims may be falsified by showing contrary evidence, by refuting their reasoning and logic, or by showing that their context no longer applies.

3. *Truth as disclosure* applies to complex expressions that, taken as a totality, project particular historical and cultural understandings (which may well have changed) as well as more universal possibilities for comprehending reality.[14] Many kinds of expressions are valued primarily for the truthfulness that emerges in their concreteness and universality. Myths and symbols, works of art and literature, philosophical and theological systems, and broadly encompassing scientific theories all disclose meanings that go beyond the propositions they contain. The claim that there is truth in scriptural statements that should not be taken literally, as in "God created man in his own image," is a claim about the power of symbolic or figurative expressions to illuminate reality truthfully. The statement expresses the relationship between God and humanity, not the physical appearance of God or God's gender or preference for masculinity. Such disclosures

may be verified by their power to illuminate various aspects of reality, or they may be falsified by showing their irrelevance or failure to illuminate that which they would understand.

4. *Truth as transformation* applies to claims that are authenticated by the practical understanding and engagement of the people who express them; these expressions inherently demand that those who hear them change or act responsively.[15] The message and work of people like Martin Luther King, Jr., and Mother Theresa—persons who "speak the truth by doing the truth"—exemplify the social and moral character of many transformative truth claims, as do ethical imperatives or "performative" utterances, which by their nature demand response. Transformative truth claims can be falsified by showing that the speaker is not authentically engaged in matters spoken about, and by demonstrating the inappropriateness or injustice of the claim with respect to the people and communities these transformative demands would touch.

Clearly, all these models of truth may be present simultaneously. The point is that different kinds of truth claims must be interpreted and assessed in different ways, according to different criteria. All four models play some role in contemporary foundational theologies, including this one.

A Disciples View of Foundational Theology

Foundational theology is not the same as systematic theology. While systematic theology is primarily concerned with interpreting the symbols and doctrines of Christianity for a given time and situation, foundational theology is concerned with what makes the Christian experience of faith and hence Christian thought a possibility at all.

A distinctly Disciples theology is not simply the same as Christian theology written by Disciples of Christ. We do not or should not claim, as a community, to have a distinctive body of doctrinal interpretation. As Christians, Disciples are indeed concerned with the teachings and symbols of the whole "Church universal." As Christians, we are committed to interpret God's relationship to the world, the person and work of Jesus Christ, sin and grace, sanctification and the Christian's task in the world. But such doctrinal concerns identify us as Christians, not as Disciples. As Disciples we are especially concerned with the foundations of Christianity's experience of faith—that is, with the norms and limits of Christian experience, however diverse its forms. To us, these foundations support any Christian's right and responsibility to interpret doctrine freely, guided by church communities but not bound by their censure. We affirm this freedom not because we denigrate doctrine, but precisely so that the teachings of the churches, with their plurality of implications, can be interpreted urgently and openly. But because we have valued freedom of interpretation so highly, we can use no single source of doctrinal interpretation to define the center of our community as we make claims on behalf of the whole of Christianity. Without lapsing into sentimentalities, we do wish to describe Christianity's experience of faith as something singular. But Disciples also wish to show that Christian experience not only tolerates doctrinal pluralism, but actually generates it.

By calling Disciples theology foundational, I mean that unlike most other confessing communities, we are defined less by doctrine per se than by certain affirmations we make about the Church's shared experience. Among the traditional and contemporary divisions of theological studies, foundational or "fundamental" theology has been regarded as inquiry into the possibilities of doing theology at all. Foundational theologies analyze religious language and experience, consider the criteria by which religious claims may be evaluated, and develop methods by which other theological tasks, such as the systematic or practical, can be reasonably pursued.[16] While confessing communities are most often distinguished from each other at the level of systematic theology (the interpretation of doctrines and symbols), the Disciples community is defined by foundational concerns. Disciples, as Christians, confess Jesus Christ, not a foundational theology, but when we express who we are as a community among Christians, we manifest commitments that can best be described as foundational. We generally do not define ourselves by any systematic interpretation of doctrine, and our practical theologies will usually be consistent with our foundational inclinations.

To be sure, Disciples have produced systematic theologies in the past, such as those of Alexander Campbell and Robert Milligan. But the movement is more readily characterized by its restorationist and ecumenical motives and by its insistence on reasonable interpretation. Disciples are mainly trinitarian and have visible Calvinist roots; the theologies of our founders were typically theologies of sanctification.[17] But these facts do not define us so much as suggest our historical-religious color. Certainly Disciples biblicism and ecumenism have had doctrinal implications, for better or worse. Our debates over baptism by immersion and closed communion have been doctrinal debates of the worst sort; our attention to the multifaceted importance of baptism and our views on communion as a festival of remembrance represent doctrinal interpretation of a better sort. Both become part of the ongoing Christian conversation about the meaning of Christ and his Church.

On the other hand, it is gravely unfortunate that Disciples as Christians have neglected systematic theology, relegating it to the status of nonessential "opinion." Doctrine is essential to the self-understanding and world-understanding of all Christians, for it is through doctrinal interpretation that distinctly Christian claims are made. Doctrine is the way that Christ's Church interprets reality. But doctrine is not what makes Disciples Disciples or the Christian Church the Christian Church. Thus, the foundational theology I am speaking of is not claimed by Disciples to represent another "brand" of Christianity. All the Disciples claim is to have a distinctive account of the possibilities, limits, and norms of Christian experience—a claim they propose to all Christians. All the Disciples claim for their community is a distinctly realistic interpretation of what makes all Christians Christian.

The foundations of a religious tradition include symbols and stories that disclose ultimate values and meanings. These meanings are overdetermined, superabundant, and subject to many interpretations. A religious tradition also includes principles which guide the understanding of those symbols and which properly order life around them, and these principles also are given to multiple interpretations. In traditional Judaism, for example, God's will for Israel is revealed and remembered in the Exodus event, and the implications of that symbol for liberation and freedom are ordered in the principles of the Covenant Code (including the Ten Commandments). When communities within Judaism—such as modern Orthodoxy—set out to interpret their tradition, their self-interpretation must account for both the foundational symbols and the normative principles (*Halacha*) by which Jewish life as a free people is prescribed. The legal principles especially cause controversy, for they concern proper limits, responsibilities, and self-definition. Christian communities and their controversies follow similar patterns. For Luther, meaning is manifest in the Word of God, which reveals God's mercy through the event of Christ; this meaning is ordered by such principles as *sola scriptura* (scripture alone) and *sola gratia* (justification by grace alone through faith).

When a community within a religious tradition interprets itself, it is both descriptive and selective. It chooses and describes certain symbols within its tradition that give basic definition to the others, and it chooses certain ordering principles that seem to that community most fundamental for understanding the implications of the symbols. The first may be called symbolic norms, the second cognitive norms, and both are constantly redefined in light of the community's changing situation and understanding. Thus, when the Disciples of Christ interpret what makes all Christians Christian, they choose and describe certain symbolic and cognitive norms as the essential basis of Christian community. Disciples claim to be founded on symbolic and cognitive norms that disclose the inclusiveness of all Christians within a broad framework; they have intended *not* to select norms that would establish themselves as the only authentic Christians.

Most recent interpretations of Disciples of Christ foundations have taken the form of historical studies or of historical theology.[18] But there have been exceptions to this approach. I have already mentioned Frank Gardner's interpretation of the Confession of Faith. In viewing the Confession as performative speech that establishes a relationship, Gardner is interpreting an important symbolic norm for Disciples foundational theology. Another exception is W. B. Blakemore's justly famous essay in which he says that all Disciples thought—conservative, liberal, or middle-of-the-road—can be characterized as "Reasonable, Empirical, Pragmatic."[19] He argues that our controversies have always assumed a common method and disputed over how broadly or narrowly to define the data to be interpreted by that method. Conservatives limit the data to scriptures alone; liberals often tend toward natural theology. But for both groups, the demand to be reasonable, empirical, and pragmatic exemplifies a common cognitive norm for all Disciples, the interpretation principle. The Campbells used the resources of Lockean empiricism to interpret their faith, and Blakemore used American pragmatic and empirical philosophies. I propose to use the insights of recent interpretation theories and perspectives on religious experience to again redefine the interpretation principle.

One element that might seem missing in this attempt at foundational theology is an explicit metaphysics or ontology. The Disciples as Disciples have only the most general metaphysical commitments, namely to the concreteness of actual experience and the relationships that constitute it. We also are generally committed to the notion that reasonable thought can really—if not completely—comprehend reality in a reasonable way. Beyond that, all the Disciples insist on is that reason be used to interpret our religious texts. Our vague metaphysical commitments demand that we stick to the concretely actual, and the Confession of Faith and the Bible are the pivotal, concrete expressions and experiences that all Christians interpret. The following foundational norms and symbols do not characterize Disciples only, but describe what Disciples consider characteristic of all Christian thought. Together they make up a Disciples foundational theology:

Cognitive Norms

1. *The ecumenical principle,* or the unity of the Church based on a shared confession of faith in Christ. This principle functions as a limit that defines Christian life and thought in terms of the community, the Church universal, and gives thought its context.

2. *The restoration principle,* or the ongoing reorientation of the Church's life and thought toward the biblical witness of Christ's messiahship. This principle defines and limits Christian witness by centering it on the community's choices of biblical texts (the canons) that proclaim Christ's relationship to God and humanity. This principle defines the center but not the periphery of Christian interpretation; it can acknowledge other objects of Christian interpretation (such as tradition or nature) and is not refuted by historic Christian disagreements about the canon itself.

3. *The interpretation principle,* or the imperative to interpret the meaning of Christ and the scriptures according to a free, reasonable, and responsible conscience in the context of community. This principle defines Christian thought as a part of religious life, an act of piety that examines what the Church confesses on the basis of biblical and traditional witnesses.

Symbolic Norms

1. *The confessional norm,* or the confession that Jesus is the Christ, the son of the living God, and Savior of the individual and the community that so confesses. It is often proclaimed in the slogan, "no creed but Christ."

2. *The biblical norm,* or the Holy Scriptures as the place where one finds the central reference for that confession. The confession has reference not only to the confessor and to the contemporary community of Christians, but also to the original witnessing communities that made the confession and interpreted it.

When these cognitive and symbolic norms are brought together, they illuminate how Disciples understand themselves with respect to the authority of their symbols, their participation in a biblical and interpretive tradition, and their distinctively ecumenical approach to Christian theology and practice.

The authority of the symbolic norms is evident when Christians in community interpret the truthfulness of their disclosures. The Confession of Faith and the Bible function not so much propositionally as symbolically, mythically, and organically—as a whole complex of meanings. Their power to illuminate reality and transform life emerges only in active, interpretive encounter; they do not entail univocal propositions that affect a passive mind like self-evident bits of data. As performative speech, the Good Confession is not a proposition but an action that situates the actor in the mysterious relationship between Christ and his Church. The relationship is mysterious because it is irreducible. It is simply given in the act of confession, underived from anything else—just as love is mysteriously present in the confession of love, or commitment in the speaking of promises, or personal presence in speech itself or in the making of signs. No specified interpretation of this action is prescribed, but the act itself places the person under the religious imperative to interpret the confession throughout his or her life. The Confession of Faith gives rise to interpretation and to propositional claims, not vice versa.

So it is with the authority of biblical texts. Every biblical proposition is interpretive: each is so historically and culturally conditioned by changed contexts that with intellectual honesty none can be claimed authoritative at a propositional level. Even where statements seem propositionally unambiguous (as in Lev 19:18 or 1 Cor 13), careful consideration shows them to be both context-bound and exceedingly multidimensional, and hence they disclose universal truth only in the historical and contemporary processes of Jewish and Christian interpretation and common life. The import of the biblical norm is not that the Bible is the only source of truth Christians are to interpret, but that it is the only source of truth we *must* interpret. The Bible functions as the Church's hierophany, the manifestation of the sacred Word that is the revelatory center of the religious community. Although we may and should look to other sources of truth and other elements of the Christian tradition besides the Bible, we *must* interpret the scriptures, for such activity is essential to the Christian's self-definition. The Bible is the objective, artifactual center of the community's experience of faith, and only in the interpretive encounter do its texts speak.

When we enter this interpretive activity, we become part of an ongoing interpretive process that finally includes the texts themselves. There is nothing in the New Testament that is not part of the Church's own early interpretation. The early strands we uncover—such as Jesus' teaching of the Kingdom of God through sayings and parables—themselves interpret Jewish experiences of faith. They point back to the Hebrew Scriptures, and again we find ourselves in layer upon layer of interpretation reaching into the dim antiquity of the Fertile Crescent. The Bible demands interpretation because it *is* interpretation. No strand stands by itself in the community; no one witness is singularly authoritative for all Christians. Even canonization—an arbitrary, historically conditioned process that resulted in several different constitutions of the Christian canon—is no detraction from the Bible's being the hierophany of the Word. Canonization is itself a performative, confessing activity that is part of the Church's ongoing interpretive process. If the canon's boundaries are ragged, no less so are the scriptural texts themselves. Their raggedness and historicity do not diminish their being the pivotal symbol and artifact, the center of Christian interpretation. Perhaps systematic theology should say at this point that God does not act before interpretation but in its midst. The meandering history of biblical sources might well be seen, then, as a history of interpretive activity in which communities have come to hear God speaking with special authority.

When Disciples envision themselves ecumenically in relation to other Christian communities and to other faiths, their theology and practice is challenged to be both distinctive and pluralistic. This is true in different ways in respect to the foundational, systematic, and practical tasks of Christian theology.

At the foundational level, what most distinguishes the Disciples of Christ is the effect of combining the principle of free and reasoned interpretation with the principles of restoration and ecumenism. The interpretation principle focuses on the symbolic event to be interpreted, while recognizing that the scriptures themselves are part of the same interpretive event we ourselves are participating in. To be a biblical people is to be an interpreting people. Interpretation is our piety, our religious obligation. No reasonable methods of interpretation or conclusions are arbitrarily foreclosed, so long as they seriously confront the scriptural witnesses as a matter of ultimate concern.

We claim to interpret Christian doctrine only as Christians, not as Disciples, so there can be no distinctively Disciples systematic theology. While our foundational theology may be inevitably Christocentric, our systematic reflections as Christians might be directed toward creation and providence, justification and sanctification, or the tragic and sinful condition of humanity before God's penultimate judgment and ultimate love. The pluralistic global village will not be comprehended by any one religious style or theological tradition. Christianity is called to interpret not only what is written in the scriptural center of its community, but also the world which is its setting, its "fateful hour." To be true to both tasks, the Church must generate theologies that critically and self-critically press their own limits, if dialogue or conversation is to be achieved among the crossfires of competing ideologies and interpretations.

Perhaps the most distinctive feature of Disciples thought at the practical level is that interpretation is our praxis and practice, our most visible form of piety.[20] We realize this in our local, regional, and general gatherings. Disciples generate practical theologies whenever their congregations, agencies, institutions, and people are at work in the world and are transformed by the needs of the world. Education can be considered as an example. The interpretation principle implies that the resources for Disciples practice and thought must come from the whole of the Christian tradition. Our ecumenical explorations have made us realize that the time for theological illiteracy is over and that Disciples must learn their faith from the entire Church universal. Likewise, if our foundational insights are truly valuable, then Disciples must also realize that the time for illiteracy about our own tradition is over. We have brought something significant to the conversation among Christians; we bring it expecting to judge and be judged in mutual support and criticism. Similarly, the time for illiteracy about the distinctive disclosures of truth in non-Christian religious traditions is over. We will understand our own religious nature and human nature only in mutually critical exploration of distinctly different religious ways of looking at things. In such discussion and inquiry, there will be no necessary boundaries to what we may interpret, only a necessary center. To fail to be transformed by the encounter with others in a pluralistic world is, perhaps, to betray the truth disclosed in the Christ we confess. Christ on the cross, betrayed by those who claimed him, should tell us that Christians, like all peoples, will never corner the market on truth.

Disciples do claim that all Christians are normatively united in the activity of confession and in the thoughtful and practical interpretation of the scriptural witness. We claim that this confession and interpretive task are what distinguish and limit Christian experience at the center, and all who live in this confession and continuing interpretation live in the institutional and religious life of the Church. Any other test of faith, according to the Disciples, is unwarranted and unjust.

That is not the only thing Disciples have to say, nor is it all Christians must say about what it means to be a Christian. But it is something distinctly worthwhile that Disciples have said in the past and should say in the future, amid the ongoing conversation and service of love shared by Christians everywhere.

Notes

[1] See Langdon Gilkey, *Reaping the Whirlwind: A Christian Interpretation of History* (New York: Seabury Press, 1976).

[2] See David Tracy, *Blessed Rage for Order: The New Pluralism in Theology* (New York: Seabury Press, 1975).

[3] See Wayne C. Booth, *Critical Understanding: The Powers and Limits of Pluralism* (Chicago: University of Chicago Press, 1979). Booth discusses what could be termed the "ethics" of pluralism in the context of literary criticism; many of his observations are applicable to theology and other critical disciplines.

[4] See Dwight E. Stevenson, "Faith Versus Theology in the Thought of the Disciple Fathers," in *The Reformation of Tradition*, ed. Ronald E. Osborn, Vol. 1 of *The Renewal of Church: The Panel of Scholars Reports*, ed. W. B. Blakemore (St. Louis: Bethany Press, 1963), pp. 33–60.

[5] Thomas Campbell, *Declaration and Address*, Centennial Edition (Corapolis, Pennsylvania: Record Publishing Co., 1909), pp. 16–17.

[6] See Alfred T. DeGroot, *The Restoration Principle* (St. Louis: Bethany Press, 1960), pp. 134–85.

[7] Royal Humbert, ed., *A Compend of Alexander Campbell's Theology* (St. Louis: Bethany Press, 1961), p. 266, n. 3.

[8] The Panel of Scholars, which worked from 1956 to the publication of their three volumes in 1963, represents the fullest sampling of Disciples reinterpretation. The Panel may be said to have written in a time of crisis. Ahead of them was the uncertain promise of restructuring the "brotherhood" into a "denomination." Behind them was a fruitful half-century of liberal Disciples thought based on modern biblical criticism, historical consciousness, and irenic ecumenism. The Panel was trying to inventory and consolidate the implications of this process. However, the timing of their writing was not propitious in terms of contemporary history and theology. Considerable historical, cultural, and theological upheaval began just about the time their work was finished. George G. Beazeley, Jr., points out in *The Christian Church (Disciples of Christ): An Interpretive Examination in the Cultural Context* (St. Louis: Bethany Press, 1973), pp. 54–55, that liberal Disciples were rather late in appropriating any benefits from neo-orthodoxy. In addition, the Panel was in no position to account for Vatican II, radical theology, liberation theology, or the contemporary focus on hermeneutics. And process theology (as interpreted through students of Charles Hartshorne, like John Cobb or Eugene H. Peters) did not begin to have its recent impact until just after 1963. The panel may have represented the culmination of an era rather than the beginning of a new one, and new directions for interpretation were immediately needed. Both Vatican II and radical

INTERPRETING DISCIPLES

theology motivated much of the hermeneutical reflection on interpretation that makes a retrieval of the restoration principle possible.

[9] Ralph G. Wilburn, "A Critique of the Restoration Principle: Its Place In Contemporary Life Thought," in *The Reformation of Tradition*, pp. 215–53.

[10] Humbert, *Compend*, p. 30, quoting from *Christian Baptist* 6 (no. 1, 1828), pp. 461–62.

[11] Frank N. Gardner, "The Revelation of God in Jesus Christ: With Reference to the Phrase, 'No Creed but Christ,'" in *The Reformation of Tradition*, pp. 98–110.

[12] See J. L. Austin, *Philosophical Papers* (London: Oxford University Press, 1961), pp. 220–39. It must be understood that performative speech *looks like* denotative speech, that is, speech that denotes something or makes a proposition that can be verified or falsified. But under certain conditions speech does not denote something so much as it *creates* something, *does* something, or *engenders* a situation. This is what is meant by a "performative utterance." When one says, "I promise," a promise is created, a situation of commitment has arisen. "I apologize" is another example, and—in the religious sense—"I confess." In each case, the performative character of the utterance is tied to the context in which it is made. See also Austin's *How to Do Things with Words* (New York: Oxford University Press, 1962). In the context of Christian worship, performative speech is also ritual speech, that is, a ritual action. As ritual, the utterance can also be considered as symbol—which is another aspect of the Confession's way of disclosing truth by establishing a true relationship.

[13] See Paul Ricoeur, *Interpretation Theory: Discourse and the Surplus of Meaning* (Fort Worth, Texas: Texas Christian University Press, 1976).

[14] See Tracy, *Blessed Rage for Order*, p. 23.

[15] See David Tracy, *The Analogical Imagination: Christian Theology and the Cultural Pluralism* (New York: Crossroad, 1981), pp. 58, 69ff.

[16] David Tracy discusses the three "disciplines" of theology—fundamental, systematic, practical—in *The Analogical Imagination*, pp. 54–79. Some will know what Tracy calls fundamental theology by the term "philosophy of religion," when pursued in a nonconfessional context. My use of the idea of foundations differs from Tracy's or from philosophy of religion insofar as I claim that in the case of the Disciples, it does distinguish the thought of a confessing community.

[17] On Disciples Calvinism, see Royal Humbert's Introduction in *Compend*; on sanctification, see Clark Williamson, "Theology and Forms of Confession in the Disciples of Christ," *Encounter* 41 (Winter 1980), pp. 53–71.

[18] In addition to *The Renewal of Church: The Panel of Scholars Reports*, see

George G. Beazeley, ed., *The Christian Church in Cultural Context*, and William Tucker and Lester G. McAllister, *Journey in Faith: A History of the Christian Church (Disciples of Christ)* (St. Louis: Bethany Press, 1975).

[19] W. B. Blakemore, "Reasonable, Empirical, Pragmatic: The Mind of Disciples of Christ," in *The Reformation of Tradition*, pp. 161–83.

[20] This suggestion that Disciples "piety" is especially identified by the activity of interpretation is not meant to contradict the four types of Disciples piety as understood by D. Newell Williams: theistic, legalistic, moralistic, and personalistic; see Williams, "Disciples Piety: A Historical Review with Implications for Spiritual Formation," *Disciples Divinity House Discussion Papers on Disciples History and Contemporary Issues*, series no. 2 (Chicago: Disciples Divinity House, 1983). Williams notes that any individual's piety typically involves interpreting two or more of the types, and that theistic piety is in fact the most pervasive and theologically appropriate. Theistic piety is particularly relevant to a community that finds its commonality in the interpretation of scripture.

Ambivalence by Design:
Disciples Structures of Church

DENNIS L. LANDON

It [approval of the Provisional Design for the Christian Church (Disciples of Christ) in 1968] was a move of great significance for the heirs of the Stone-Campbell movement. The enthusiasm for this action was such that the assembled delegates spontaneously broke into the Doxology after the vote approving the motion. The approved design was the result of eight years of effort led by a hard-working Commission on Restructure and participated in by thousands of Disciples. The actions shifted the Disciples into a new concept of what it meant to be the church. The Christian Church (Disciples of Christ) would spend many years implementing this action.[1]

ALMOST TWENTY YEARS after that Kansas City Doxology, the Provisional Design has become simply the Design. The heirs of the Stone-Campbell movement have welcomed another generation, one which has come of age in a restructured church. While the implementation of the Provisional Design is sometimes accompanied by imprecation and petition as well as by doxology, there are few within the Christian Church (Disciples of Christ) now who would deny the appropriateness of Restructure or argue that the church is the worse for it. Nevertheless, the assertion that approval of the Provisional Design "shifted the Disciples into a new concept of what it meant to be the church" provokes a number of questions. Indeed, the statement is itself ironic, for, as few external observers missed, the new concept the Disciples embraced in Restructure was one they had known about, and righteously rejected, for 160 years—the concept of denomination. We became (or, rather, admitted having become) one among many churches. No more a religious movement standing aloof from the divisions of Christianity in order to offer a vision of unity, the Disciples became the one thing they had most eloquently decried.

That irony does not detract from the achievement of Restructure, nor deny its necessity, but it does suggest that powerful forces at work in Restructure were not always recognized or acknowledged by the participants, and that the issues addressed directly may not have been the only issues at stake. The reflections here attempt to analyze one subtext in the Disciples story—the conflict between autonomy and authority—and to reflect on how that conflict was addressed, but not resolved, by Restructure. To do this we shall have to look at the history and development of the Disciples organizational structure, the antecedents of Disciples thought in the Enlightenment of the eighteenth century, and the insights of social theory regarding both the development of social organizations and types of authority and leadership before we can return to the question of what happened and didn't happen in our Restructure.

In the midst of the religious ferment of nineteenth-century America, the movement led by Thomas and Alexander Campbell and Barton W. Stone offered a vision of Christian community in which, they believed, differences of doctrine, polity, and practice could be superceded and made irrelevant by a universal, common submission to the one Lord of the Church. These reformers held that this unity was already present, waiting only on the decisions and actions of believers, who—once they had been shown the vision—would abandon their divisive habits and align themselves with the universal fellowship of all who confessed Jesus Christ as Lord. The reformers believed with equal confidence that the New Testament contained not only the revelation of God's salvation but also, in its description of the first, the blueprint of church order. These two themes—the oneness of all believers in Christ and the restoration of New Testament Christianity via the apostolic template—would be the two main elements of the movement's self-definition well into the twentieth century.

Freedom—In the Service of Certainty

In its beginning the movement was anti-creedal, anti-clerical, and anti-institutional. The Church was one, but the Church was also many, composed of individual believers who valued their individual freedom at least as much as they affirmed their essential unity. The reformers appealed to the minds and hearts of individuals, and their congregations were associations of individuals. Individuals were freed from priests, and congregations from hierarchies, by scripture itself. Of Alexander Campbell's statement that "an individual church or congregation of Christ's disciples is the only ecclesiastical body recognized in the New Testament," D. Ray Lindley remarks that Campbell's "campaign against creeds was at once an attempt to free the living church from a dead church, to liberate the local church from an ecclesiastical hierarchy, and to emancipate the individual believer from priestly presumption."[2] The rejection of institutional authority over the Christian and over the congregation is an abiding theme—and the source of an abiding dilemma—for Disciples. The reformers sidestepped the question of institutional authority by extending the authority of scripture to matters of organization and practice no less than to matters of faith. They believed they could bring about the God-given unity of the Church by fully restoring New Testament Christianity. They would return the Church to a purity inseparable from their vision of unity. Restoration and unity were, for them, intertwined, providing both the destination and the route, the end and the means.

If unity was their goal and restoration their program, a certain variety of rationalism was their method. Rationalism and its seedbed, the Enlightenment of the eighteenth century, contain at their centers not so much a system of thought as a thorough-going and fervent affirmation of the autonomy, intellectual power, and basic freedom of the human individual. With that affirmation rides the assumption that all truth, including religious truth, lies open to those who would see. The power of the unfettered mind and the autonomy of the individual were the twin beacons of the intellectual world from which the Stone-Campbell movement emerged. But along with such convictions about the power and freedom of the individual also existed a strong desire for certainty and authority—for objective truth, individually apprehended. Present-day Disciples make much of the rough-and-ready independence of our frontier ancestors, of their pragmatism and their love of freedom. But we forget that these traits developed as they pursued absolute certainty and a vision of unity much more conformist than our own experience of cultural pluralism would lead us to expect.

Disciples participated in a paradox that was part of the Enlightenment as a whole: human minds were free to search experience, examine the world, and draw conclusions about truth, but it was assumed there were objectively correct conclusions that would eventually be drawn and with which all people of good will would agree. For modern liberals, tolerance is a value in itself; for the early Disciples, tolerance was of instrumental value, useful in opening the door to truth. Thus, first-generation Disciples considered the Bible alone the appropriate object of newfound light of human reason, and they expected an eventual religious consensus among those of good will.

The Enlightenment rejection of dogma, with which the Disciples concurred, issued also from a negative view of history. The reformers saw human events through time, until the reformation of the nineteenth century, as the progressive imprisonment of the human mind and spirit by dogma and institution; now, through reason guided by the Holy Spirit, humanity would be released into a new age of freedom. Restorationism was a leap backward into the future, passing over eighteen centuries of history to a community not humanly constructed, but divinely ordained and now recreatable—the Apostolic Church. Thus, we find Alexander Campbell arguing in the same debate, first:

> Weak minds are the slaves of old times, and of old customs. They need the crutches of antiquity, and human authority. But men of vigorous minds ask, *what is truth?* not *who* says it.

and later:

> I am opposed to all innovations. Innovations, with me, are not the creations of last year, last century, nor of the last millennium. Innovations are customs, usages, rites, doctrines that commenced one year after John wrote the word amen at the end of the Apocalypse.[3]

Truth, divinely ordained and humanly appropriated through reason and assent to the witness of the New Testament, was the only legitimate authority for individual faith and for the practices of the Church. The reformers read the Bible not only as a theological document, but as a lawbook and a constitution as well.

Thus we have a movement which espoused freedom of thought in the service of absolute certainty. David Harrell is correct when he says that "the religious personality of the Disciples of Christ had decided schizophrenic tendencies. They were fanatics with a compulsive sense of mission; and yet they were nineteenth century rationalists with an almost psychotic aversion to fanaticism. Most Disciples were a perplexing mixture of these two elements. They could be tolerant or intolerant; they could be dogmatic or broad-minded; they could be sectarian or denominational—and it was never quite obvious which course they would follow."[4]

In fact they went both directions to varying degrees. Our concern here, however, is with those who, knowingly or not, took the course toward becoming a denomination. Members and leaders of the Christian Church (Disciples of Christ) tend to see the departure of the Churches of Christ and the Non-Denominational Fellowship of Christian Churches and Churches of Christ ("Inde-

pendents") as the resolution, in two stages, of the conflict between the pursuit of Christian unity and the pursuit of restorationism as the only acceptable road to that unity. Conventional
wisdom holds that liberals rejected restorationism because it was
an unrealistic program—particularly in the face of historical-
critical biblical research—and that conservatives rejected a developing definition of unity because it had neither love for the
ancient order of things nor commitment to the absolute authority
of scripture as lawbook and constitution as well as gospel. While
correct, the popularity of this analysis obscures a more basic conflict with which our part of the Stone-Campbell movement continues to struggle—the question of legitimate authority within the
church beyond the local congregation. The Gordian knot of our
ambivalence about authority has been neither untied nor severed.

Power and Authority

Disciples ecclesiology has always been both high and low.
Thomas Campbell, in the *Declaration and Address* of 1809, declared
in his first proposition "that the church of Christ upon earth is
essentially, intentionally, and constitutionally one; consisting of
all those in every place that profess their faith in Christ and obedience to him in all things according to the scriptures" and in his
second proposition that "the church of Christ upon earth must
necessarily exist in particular and distinct societies, locally separate from one another."[5] A Church exists which is one and universal, and there are societies—congregations—through which
the one Church exists. The relation between the two was not of
great concern while the Campbells and Stone were calling Christians out of the existing denominations and into societies that
made up one church "free from all mixture of human opinions
and inventions of men."[6] Nor should we expect much postulating
of extra-congregational organizations from men who had suffered
rejection and abuse precisely because of those organizations. The
high ecclesiology of the universal Church has never been reflected
in Disciples polity; indeed, the affirmation of one Christian

Church to which all believers belong but which human organizations corrupt has left Disciples with individualism and congregationalism—not *ecclesia*—as the mythic center of their corporate life. Just as autonomy and authority remain in conflict in the realm of ideas, ecclesiology and polity have always been at war within the organizational life of Disciples and other free church Protestants.

This is not to say that Disciples who are conscious of their heritage have not kept that high ecclesiology alive. Many bear witness to the Church that is one in essence, intention, and constitution and whose unity may yet be shown forth in the world of churches and denominations. Many remain adamant that the confessions and commitments that Christians share still have the power to overcome the differences that divide us. Yet we remain ourselves primarily members of "particular and distinct societies." Like most American Protestants, we will define church—if asked to do so quickly—as the place where and the people with whom we regularly worship the God revealed in Jesus Christ. Disciples did not find it appropriate to attempt to relate the oneness of the Church to the organization until compelled to do so by forces in the larger world of the denominations. We remain congregationalists in matters of polity, and our own history illuminates the inherent conflict between organization (which is the institutionalization of authority) and the principle of congregational autonomy (which is an organizational projection of individualism).

To create an organization is to establish channels of power, lines of authority, and conventions of leadership. Without these there is, in fact, no organization. Religious organizations are not exempt from this rule; whatever their theological or doctrinal convictions, they will develop ways for decisions to be made, for policy to be created, for programs to be carried out. But an organization, religious or not, will create a polity particular to its history and informed by that history's strengths and contradictions. In fact, writes Paul Harrison in *Authority and Power in the Free Church Traditions*, "one of the most effective ways of discovering internal contradictions within a doctrinal system is to study the dilemmas experienced by the church when its people attempt to express their beliefs through their polity."[7]

Some definitions are in order at this point. By "power" I mean the ability of a person or group of persons to determine the actions of another person or group without regard for the latter's desires or needs. "Authority" is the right to exercise power within a specific context. The people within that context recognize as a leader the one who holds authority. They expect him or her to exercise it; indeed they will think irresponsible or incompetent the leader who does not. The test for the presence of power in an organization is the likelihood that particular commands will be obeyed or that particular intentions will come to pass. The test for authority is assent by those commanded to the legitimacy of the commands and the appropriateness of the intentions which those commands represent. Max Weber defined three ways that authority is legitimated. *Traditional authority* is based on traditions that extend beyond the memories of the people currently in the group. *Rational-legal authority* is based on the technical qualifications of the leader and on the fact that he or she holds a particular office in the organization. *Charismatic authority* is based on the personal, nonrational powers of the leader; people experience the charismatic leader as an exceptional person, whom they follow and obey because he or she makes them want to follow and obey.

In the Church we experience all three sorts of authority. Any parish minister or layperson knows the power of "the way things have always been done here" and the power of people or families who have always defined how things have always been done. We also know that a broader sense of past—the Stone-Campbell movement, for instance, and ultimately the Bible—can be invoked to legitimate what people want to do. We know or know of those among us who can influence opinions and actions through the power and winsomeness of their personalities. These two sorts of authority—traditional and charismatic—will always be important, even necessary, in any organization. In the case of the Church they are to be tolerated and even cultivated. But it is the establishment of rational-legal authority that both points to

INTERPRETING DISCIPLES

and is enmeshed with the contradictions of an extracongregational organization based on the principles of personal and congregational autonomy. Neither before nor after Restructure have
Disciples been willing to define the legitimate authority of those
who become their leaders, and this unwillingness, it seems, is a
result of the basic incompatibility between the goal of being one
church and the tradition of congregational autonomy.

Authority versus Autonomy

The first century of Disciples history shows a consistent
pattern of creating associations and societies—local, regional,
and national—to organize and promote certain goals. The history also shows a simultaneous aversion to making these associations representative of, or accountable to, the churches. Associations were established as societies of individuals who sponsored
particular tasks and appealed to other individuals for support. Arguments for the necessity and efficiency of extracongregational
organizations were opposed out of the convictions that the local
church must be the supreme authority in the movement, that
conventions and societies—no matter how constituted—could
not legitimately speak for nor exercise authority over the congregations, and that the New Testament blueprint for the Church
did not include entities beyond the local congregation. In spite of
organizations established, covenants made, and structures developed, this congregationalism has held sway even after the creation of the Christian Church (Disciples of Christ), and it remains
the starting point for all discussions of Disciples polity. We believe that the Church is one and we want our church to be one,
but we mistrust those who might hold authority, claim influence,
or exercise power within that corporate body. We cherish and defend our personal and congregational autonomy, but we are still
drawn to each other by history and inclination, and we value
what we represent to each other and what we do together. This
ambivalence about the necessities of institutional life permeates
our history.

Only seventeen years after the Campbell and Stone movements came together in 1832, the Disciples held their first national convention. Impetus for such a gathering came from the rapid growth of the movement and the accompanying vision of programs of evangelism and ministry to which individual congregations alone could never aspire. State conventions and missionary societies had begun to form, and Alexander Campbell had begun to give his support to cooperation among the churches. The creation of colleges, Bible societies, and tract societies, all appealing for financial support, also made a national gathering desirable. The personal commitment of D. S. Burnet, an Ohio preacher who was one of the founders of the American Christian Bible Society, was also instrumental in bringing together in Cincinnati the General Convention of the Christian Churches of the United States of America in October 1849.[8] Directors of the Bible Society and the Tract Society met in the same setting prior to the convention.

While those gathered in Cincinnati agreed about the benefits of cooperation to spread the gospel, they held contradictory assumptions about the nature of the meeting itself. Campbell seemed to favor a representative gathering composed of messengers chosen by the churches and state societies, and some participants had been selected in that manner. Burnet preferred an enlargement of the society pattern—a gathering of those giving spiritual and financial support to the cooperative efforts proposed—and an even greater number of participants arrived on that basis. The first action of the convention was to recognize all those present as legitimate delegates rather than risk censure by rejecting any person's credentials. Constituting itself as the American Christian Missionary Society, the gathering agreed to sell annual and life memberships and directorships and called for the election of twenty-five managers to conduct the society's business in concert with the elected officers and directors.[9]

Those who had created a national convention after only seventeen years as a movement could hardly be faulted for their reported enthusiasm. Nevertheless, the conflict between the need for organization and the commitment to congregational autonomy is apparent in the compromise so quickly agreed to in Cincinnati and in the adjustments made in the Society twenty years later.

By 1869 the American Christian Missionary Society was alive and active but underfinanced and under attack. Its detractors argued that there could be no missionary society except the local church, that the local church must be the supreme authority in the movement, that general conventions—even those composed of delegates selected by the churches themselves—could not speak for the churches, that the New Testament order for the Church did not include conventions or societies, that raising funds for the convention and societies was wasteful and costly, and that the national and state organizations would eventually lead to ecclesiastical tyranny.[10] Financial support for the Society's work had been fitful at best, and competing institutions closer to the people—colleges and district and state organizations—were emerging rapidly. The May 1869 meeting of the Society proposed that a committee review the problem and make proposals for the future. This they did at Louisville that October.

The Louisville Plan called for a General Convention made up of messengers from the state conventions, whose members were messengers from the congregations and the district conventions (which were also to be composed of congregational messengers). The plan also called for the formation of general, state, and district boards, each headed by a corresponding secretary. In the General Convention each state would have two delegates plus one additional delegate for every five thousand members in the state. Churches were urged to pledge a specific dollar amount each year; the district secretary would keep half for the district and forward the rest to the state secretary, who would keep half of that and send the remaining 25 percent to the treasurer of the general board. The Louisville Plan was adopted with only two dissenting votes, and the General Christian Missionary Convention, reclaiming the name of the first national gathering, succeeded the American Christian Missionary Society.

Disciple Benjamin Franklin (1812–1878), one of the foremost opponents of the Society, helped frame the Louisville Plan. He proclaimed it "simple, natural and wise" and said, "Let us hear no more of societies and plans, but work."[11] Yet only ten years later he opposed the Convention: "But we do not now go against it merely because it is not a good human scheme, or because it did not succeed; but because it is a *human scheme*, with the intention to go against all schemes of the kind. We put it and all the conventions and human creeds on the same footing, and go against them because they are *human*; organized in *human wisdom* and not in the *wisdom of God*."[12] Indeed, the Louisville Plan did not succeed, in large part because of an amendment introduced by J. W. McGarvey at the time of the plan's acceptance, which made the percentage division of the churches' funds optional at the pleasure of the churches.

By 1874 the Disciples had experimented with both Burnet's society of committed individuals and Campbell's convention of church representatives and rejected both in turn. Loren Lair quotes an observer of those years: "They opposed the old plan because it was not a cooperation of the churches and they opposed the new because it was a cooperation of churches."[13] Nevertheless, the society model is the one that prevailed for the next hundred years. Its hallmark was the refusal to give legitimacy to any institutional authority except the local church.

By the middle of the twentieth century, Disciples had created numerous variations and elaborations on the society theme: a home missions society, a foreign missions society, the Christian Woman's Board of Missions, the National Benevolent Association, the Board of Church Extension, and the Board of Ministerial Relief. These were united in 1920 into the United Christian Missionary Society, with the same voluntary relationship, and the society held its annual meeting at the time of the General Convention—by then called the International Convention. The various state and district organizations had continued to elaborate their functions, in some cases moving more toward being associations of churches than societies of individuals. Attempts to recreate a delegate convention during 1910–1917 failed, but a

INTERPRETING DISCIPLES

new constitution adopted in 1917 continued the mass assembly and established a Committee on Recommendations to organize and clear business items for convention action. Significantly, members of the Committee on Recommendations were originally elected as delegates from the state societies.

The creation of the United Christian Missionary Society could not be described as a change in polity. It was a bureaucratic adjustment, necessary and laudable in the face of the many financial appeals to individuals and churches from the many societies and because mission suffered from the overlapping efforts. The birth of Unified Promotion in 1935 was also more bureaucratic than political. This promotion and fund-raising instrument was controlled by the societies that chose to use it, and it was accountable to them rather than to churches. The Disciples' antiecclesiasticism and aversion to authority remained, even as the range of operations expanded, budgets grew, and arenas of power proliferated.

Even these moderate organizational developments were accompanied by dissonance and dissent. Critics denounced the creation of every society and agency as a betrayal of scriptural mandate and of congregational autonomy, and these criticisms affected profoundly the instrumentalities created. The Disciples' convictions about liberty in nonessential matters led to a willingness always to compromise on polity when opponents phrased their objections in the language of biblical essentials. Consequently, at least in hindsight, the structures that were created always seemed a few steps short of what the situation required.

We were caught from the beginning in the Enlightenment conflict between spiritual autonomy and institutional authority, between individualism and pragmatism. We have seen, often better than others, the need for Christians to work together for the sake of God's kingdom, but we have been unwilling to acknowledge that working together requires an appropriate measure of authority—that is, of acknowledged and legitimated power—among their constituent parts.

Seen in the light of previous organizational development,

the 1968 Restructure and its elaborations seem another stage in an ongoing process rather than a shift to "a new concept of what it [means] to be the church." The creation of the Christian Church (Disciples of Christ) represents the most sophisticated attempt so far to make a workable accommodation between authority and autonomy. The Design's vision of one church in three manifestations—congregational, regional, and general, each with its own autonomy and each fully the church—seems to allow a measure of effective denominational structure without openly rejecting congregational autonomy.

The Institutionalization of Ambivalence

In one of his articles for *The Panel of Scholars Reports* (1963), W. B. Blakemore wrote of "The Issue of Polity for Disciples Today." With rare and admirable candor he demonstrated that the term congregational polity could no longer represent a viable and valid conception and that, whatever more adequate conception of church organization Disciples might come to, it would not be adequately designated by congregational polity.[14]

Using both Disciples tradition and the experiences of the Congregational Christian Churches as they approached their merger with the Evangelical and Reformed Church, Blakemore identified five different concepts of congregational polity that existed, "mixed and unclarified," within the Disciples of Christ. The first concept restates the principle of congregational autonomy: nothing other than a local congregation can be called a church, and local congregations therefore may not enter into any associations for any purpose. The second and third concepts accommodate practical need, admitting first that associations of individuals may be allowed for legitimate purposes, although these associations are in no way churches, and then that supralocal organizations are necessary and inevitable and may even be called church, but must remain under the control of local congregations. The fourth concept makes a larger jump: local congregations are autonomous in their operations, and associations and the like are *also* congregations which have their own authority and autonomy. In the fifth concept an association has rights and powers not derived from the congregations but originating with the associations; an association operates as "the highest authority with respect to those churchly functions which it is peculiarly able to carry out." Thus,

> with respect to churchly functions which it cannot fulfill, [the congregation] must place itself at the service of those associations which can fulfill those functions, though never at the expense of destroying its ability to fulfill its own appropriate functions. In other words, with respect to the religious life there are areas in which a local congregation is 'autonomous' and other areas where it is not. The same thing is, in the formal sense, true of a state convention, or a benevolent association, or any other association established to carry out a function that belongs to the church.[15]

The first two of these five concepts represent the antipodal views of the first century of Disciples organizational practice. The third is the traditional position of the Congregational Christian churches and of the American Baptist Churches; it was a view that was only becoming somewhat acceptable among Disciples during the fifties and sixties. The fourth, attributed to the Congregational scholar Douglas Horton, attempts to reconcile concepts one and two. The fifth view of congregational polity, and the one Dean Blakemore urged the church to consider, is the concept that seems to have informed the Disciples' creation of one church in three manifestations.

The most significant organizational aspect of the restructured church was its successful creation of a delegate assembly at the general level. It was, in fact, this achievement that finally qualified the Disciples as a denomination in the eyes of the church world. Decisions could now be made, on behalf of the general manifestation of the church, that would be legitimate and credible to our fellow denominations. Disciples could decide to join the Consultation on Church Union or other ecumenical projects *as a church,* they could speak to the nation and the world through the actions of a representative body.

At the same time, however, we must note that the composition of the General Assembly's voting delegation creates a body so large as to beg the questions of its representativeness as well as its practicality. A minimum estimate of potential voting delegates exceeds fifteen thousand persons; in practice about one-half that number actually attend. The General Assembly includes two or more persons from each congregation, three or more delegates elected from each region, chief executives of all educational institutions and administrative units, all recognized clergy, and all members of the General Board. Actually, since few congregations provide financial support for their delegates (though many do so for their ministers), the assembly consists of those who have the leisure and the wherewithal to be present—not so great a change from 1950, or from 1849. Congregations which do not, or cannot, provide delegates are not in fact represented, though some pastors do consider themselves to be representing their churches.

Nevertheless, the General Assembly does possess authority to make policy decisions for the general church and to supervise the structures by which congregations allocate financial support of denominational ministries and report upon those ministries. It does not possess authority to compel any action by a congregation, nor do the officers and general ministerial staff which it nominally elects. The vast majority of any General Assembly's business docket involves reports of administrative units and resolutions, informative and advisory in nature, regarding social, political, and religious issues. Much time is also spent reassuring those present and those remaining at home that the Assembly's actions are not binding on the congregation.

In place of the International Convention's Committee on Recommendations, the Design provides for the General Board—one-half elected by the General Assembly from the voting membership of the previous assembly and one-half elected by the regions. One-third to one-half of the General Board's membership must be clergy. The General Board examines and prepares reports and resolutions for General Assembly action but also has administrative authority between General Assemblies. It may not itself make policy. In addition, the Administrative Committee of the General Board has responsibilities for coordination, supervision, implementation, and planning. It also has the authority to fill, between assemblies, vacancies in offices elected by the General Assembly. Other general units of the church—such as the Divisions of Homeland and Overseas Ministries, Board of Church Extension, Division of Higher Education—elect their own governing boards and choose their own executives with the advice and consent of the general officers and executives and the General Assembly or General Board.

The General Assembly convenes every other year, while the General Board meets yearly and the Administrative Committee of the General Board meets twice each year. Only the General Assembly has the authority to make policy for the church, and then only within the purview of the general manifestation. Actions of the General Board and Administrative Committee must be consistent with—or later affirmed by—General Assembly action. The Design says nothing about the authority of officers of the General Assembly (who are volunteers) or the general officers of the church (who are employees). The assembly officers are to preside over the appropriate meetings. The general officers' described duties are broad but shallow. The General Minister and President, for example, is to "be concerned for the pastoral care and nurture of the Christian Church (Disciples of Christ)," be the church's chief executive officer, and "represent the Christian Church (Disciples of Christ) in interchurch relations and in ecumenical circles."[16] This description, considering the size and infrequent meetings of the representative bodies and the volunteer status of the Assembly officers, suggests enormous responsibilities for the general officers but says little about how the whole church expects these responsibilities to be carried out.

In one sense the whole church need have no expectations of the general level leaders, because by the Design their actions have no impact upon the regions or congregations beyond what has been mandated by the policy-making and representative General Assembly. In another sense, of course, many of their actions affect the content and style of resources (educational, promotional, supportive) that will be available to the other manifestations. Further, to the outside world of churches and nations, the general manifestation is the whole church, and the general officers represent 1.2 million members, not just the denominational bureaucracy. It is a slippery path that the general-level leaders must tread; they must find or fashion enough power to run the church itself without appearing to wield power or seek authority.

Leadership—A Balancing Act

Paul Harrison has modified Weber's rational-legal type of authority and calls it *rational-pragmatic* or *rational-expediential* authority. In this case the power that leaders come to possess is not grounded in the authority of their offices but in how well they are able to make things work, what personal loyalties they are able to command, and what sanctions they control. Their power is informal, rising from their ability to assign and demote associates, their control over procurement and allocation of monies, and the perceived voting strength of their respective constituencies within the representative bodies. Formal authority is generally reserved for the settlement of disputes and is usually related to appointing, disciplining, and dismissing personnel.[17] In our current structures the one point at which formal authority comes into play and conflict is recognized and can be attributed is in the allocation of basic mission monies, a process overseen by the Commission on Budget Evaluation.

Harrison attributes the development of informal authority in the American Baptist Convention to the Baptists' refusal to grant formal authority to any association other than the local church. It is not at all clear that the Disciples' creation of a kind of legal authority moving within three concentric circles is significantly different in effect. Formally, the leaders of the general church are ultimately accountable to the representatives of the congregations, the regions, and the clergy (the General Assembly), though these three groups are not accountable to them. Informally, it is not possible for general level leaders to obtain policy definitions and action authorizations from the General Assembly or the General Board between their meetings, nor are these bodies really able to supervise the leaders or devise policy *ex nihilo*. Rather, the general church executives quite properly must define the issues, prepare the timelines, interpret the financial implications of proposed actions, and work to shape the perceptions and judgments of those to whom they are formally accountable. The executive will function as a gatekeeper in relation to the representative bodies, collecting information and communicating or withholding it as he or she thinks best. In our system authority flows upward from the congregations, but policy and planning flow downward from the leader-executives. Denied authority by the structure, leaders must cultivate the right balance of power, influence, prestige, and winsomeness to do what they have been called to do.

On the regional level this problem is intensified. With some variation, the regional structures are analogous to the general level: alternate-year assemblies that set policy, a regional board elected from districts, and a professional staff. Within established policy the regional boards and their program units plan programs of education, nurture, witness, and outreach for and on behalf of the congregations. Regional ministerial staff (usually a Regional Minister and President and one or more Associate Regional Ministers) organize resources and supervise the implementation of programs, provide pastoral services to congregations and clergy and represent the region denominationally and ecumenically. But like the general-level executives, these leaders have little formal authority with which to accomplish these tasks. They must construct pragmatic and expediential authority from the raw materials at hand, including personal constituencies, control over information, influence in policy making, program planning, the nominating process, and whatever informal sanctions are from time to time available. A widely recognized but rarely discussed informal power of the regional ministerial staff is its ability to influence or even determine ministerial placements through the control of personal files and through personal evaluations. Since Disciples clergy cannot see their complete placement files, the latter is a formidable sanction whether or not it is ever used.

Regional executives require *authority* as well as power in order to fulfill their very broadly defined responsibilities, but a typical regional structure gives them little or no authority. Therefore, they also must seek *power* to complete the tasks they are expected to perform. The possibility of abuse of power is a direct result of the failure to define, and thus circumscribe, authority. Where authority is undefined, illegitimate authority is hard to detect and misuse of power can be neither adjudicated nor prevented without resort to the sort of informal power that only the executives themselves are practiced at using. In addition, where authority is undefined, the failure of a leader to fulfill his or her responsibilities is easily excused by pointing to his or her lack of authority.

Ambivalence about authority permeates the history of our church structures. The first generation's fear of ecclesiastical tyranny has persisted for a century and a half, affecting every effort to create an acceptable organization for mission and witness and making discussion of the issue difficult. The continuing ideal of congregational autonomy has kept denominational leaders and agencies at arm's length from those they serve, even as the constituency claims control over them. The structural compromises made in order to achieve some measure of concerted effort have resulted in more rather than less power being placed in the hands of the church's leaders. That by and large they seem to use that power responsibly in the midst of broad and undefined expectations and shallow authority is more a tribute to their commitment and to God's care for the Church than to the genius of the structures.

To the extent that there are no direct challenges to the current structures and few criticisms of the structures per se, we should say that the accommodation is a successful one; the creation of a constitution which includes some points of authority and a process for amendment should insure general stability for some time to come. How long the current structures will remain effective may depend on whether the systems of informal authority and acquired power necessary for their functioning will reach and maintain equilibrium or will become so volatile as to threaten the structures themselves.

All this is to say that the restructured Christian Church (Disciples of Christ) is not a radical break with the history of Disciples organization, any more than the General Christian Missionary Convention was a radical change from the American Christian Missionary Society, or the United Christian Missionary Society more than an elaboration and consolidation of previous patterns. In every generation Disciples have had to devise church organizations for a people whose zeal for getting things done was equaled only by their mistrust of organizations. Our organizations and structures have become more efficient, more elaborate, and more stable, but our basic assumptions about the dangers of defining and designating authority have only rarely been addressed. Seen in the light of our organizational history, Restructure is only the most recent accommodation to, and not a resolution of, an old and ongoing conflict.

Notes

[1] William E. Tucker and Lester G. McAllister, *Journey in Faith: A History of the Christian Church (Disciples of Christ)* (St. Louis: Bethany Press, 1975), p. 443.

[2] Alexander Campbell, quoted by D. Ray Lindley in "The Structure of the Church: Freedom and Authority in Matters of Policy," in *The Reformation of Tradition*, ed. Ronald E. Osborn, Vol. 1 of *The Renewal of Church: Panel of Scholars Reports*, ed. W. B. Blakemore (St. Louis: Bethany Press, 1963), p. 191.

[3] Ibid.

[4] David E. Harrell, Jr., *Quest for a Christian America: The Disciples of Christ and American Society to 1866* (Nashville: The Disciples of Christ Historical Society, 1966), p. 39.

[5] Thomas Campbell, *Declaration and Address of the Christian Association of Washington* (Washington, Pa.: Brown and Sample, 1909), p. 16.

[6] Ibid., p. 4.

[7] Paul M. Harrison, *Authority and Power in the Free Church Tradition* (Carbondale and Edwardsville, Ill.: Southern Illinois University Press, 1959), p. 6.

[8] Loren E. Lair, *The Christian Churches and their Work* (St. Louis: Bethany Press, 1963), pp. 8f.; Winfred Ernest Garrison and Alfred T. DeGroot, *The Disciples of Christ: A History* (St. Louis: Bethany Press, 1948), pp. 242–47.

[9] Garrison and DeGroot, *Disciples History*, p. 247.

[10] Lair, *Christian Churches*, pp. 104–105.

[11] Garrison and DeGroot, *Disciples History*, p. 355.

[12] Ibid.

[13] Lair, *Christian Churches*, p. 107.

[14] W. B. Blakemore, "The Issue of Polity for Disciples Today," in *The Revival of the Churches*, ed. W. B. Blakemore, Vol. 3 of *The Renewal of Church: Panel of Scholars Reports*, ed. W. B. Blakemore (St. Louis: Bethany Press, 1963), pp. 52f.

[15] Blakemore, "Polity for Disciples Today," pp. 75–76.

[16] *The Design for the Christian Church (Disciples of Christ)*, July 1978, paragraph 40.

[17] Harrison, *Authority and Power*, pp. 67–73, 83.

INTERPRETING DISCIPLES

CHAPTER THREE: WORSHIP

Style and Substance in Christian Worship

FRANK BURCH BROWN

STYLE, AS EVERYONE KNOWS, has to do with the *way* something is done or communicated; substance has to do with *what* is done or communicated. Thus we can say that worship is the substance of much Christian corporate activity, and the substance of the act of worship itself is the praise and service of God. Yet Christians of different kinds clearly worship in different ways; they use different styles in praising God.

The fact that styles of Christian worship differ has come to seem, in the eyes of many of us, something that is inevitable and perhaps not terribly consequential. Today the majority of the Christian Church (Disciples of Christ) would still endorse a worship style that we feel is basically true to the patterns of the New Testament church. But, like a good many other Christians who see or seek unity in the conspicuous diversity of Christendom, we are inclined to view the various ways Christians worship as mostly superficial aspects of a common Christian faith and practice. With certain other "free church" Protestants, we tend to be relatively indifferent to such "nonessentials" as the way a worship service is ordered,[1] the sort of music that is used, the structure of the space surrounding us, or even the manner in which the communion elements are distributed. Taking a degree of pride in our reasonableness, we say that what really counts is simply that we gather, that we sing, that we commune, that we preach and hear the Word, and that in all this we acknowledge Christ as Lord.

The kind of liturgical freedom found in the Disciples of Christ has an important place in Christian unity-in-diversity. But just as style and substance are intimately related in art, so they are in worship. The medium invariably affects the message. Consequently, the relation between style and substance in worship deserves closer scrutiny than it is often given. Indeed, an adequate understanding of this matter is crucial to any reflection on what Disciples can and should be in the coming years. As a first step toward such understanding, it may be helpful to consider worship—even Protestant worship—in terms of ritual. This will provide a basis for evaluating the ways in which Word and Sacrament are combined in the ritual structure of Christian, and especially Disciples, worship and for identifying those features that give our worship identity and continuity without excluding cultural diversity and historical change.

Worship and Ritual

In some sense all Christian life is an act of worship. "And whatever you do, in word or deed, do everything in the name of the Lord Jesus, giving thanks to God the Father through him" (Col 3:17). Our Calvinist forebears acknowledged this in their unique fashion when they declared that the chief aim of human existence in all circumstances is to "glorify God and enjoy him forever."

Yet worship is also something special within life. It is marked by sacred places and times, by specific acts and attitudes. In this sense it is an intentional activity wherein God's preeminent honor (worth-ship) is confessed and expressed. Christian worship is not simply eating, talking, and socializing. It involves special acts of prayer and praise, sermon and sacrament, so fashioned as to give glory to God and so ordered as to nurture a right relationship between oneself, others, and the divine Other. In short, worship can be seen as an especially focused and enlivened response of the human creature to the Creator's graceful self-giving.

That human beings need to set aside special times and places for such a response has sometimes been interpreted as a sign of our sinfulness, since neither Eden nor the New Jerusalem is described in scriptures as requiring temple or altar. At the least, this need for sacred space and time is an indication of our finitude. But even the secularity of the modern world cannot long obscure this need, and it requires no more apology than the fact that, in our secular existence, even though everyday experience includes a measure of aesthetic delight, we nonetheless need to have works of art—of song, dance, poetry, and story. However, the form of activity most fully responsive to the human need and divine imperative for worship is not art per se, but ritual. In specifically Christian terms we could say that vital discipleship requires vital worship; vital worship entails vital ritual.[2]

The mere mention of ritual may, of course, make our Protestant souls uneasy. We immediately think of hocus-pocus, vain repetitions, empty ceremony, the smoke and smell of incense. But even the Reformers realized that what God ordains for worship does not stand in complete opposition to the universal need to which ritual testifies. Calvin quotes with approval Augustine's observation that human beings "cannot be welded together in any name of religion, whether true or false, unless they are bound in some partnership of signs or visible sacraments." Calvin merely supplements this by observing: "Since our most merciful Father foresaw this need, at the outset he instituted definite exercises of piety for his servants."[3] As anthropologists and historians of religion have commonly used the word "ritual," and as I will be using it here, the term designates just such "exercises of piety."

About ritual in general several significant things can be said. For one thing ritual is a matter of enactment rather than of attitude or feeling only. Religious ritual, moreover, normally involves acts that are based on traditional patterns and that sanctify events or processes felt to be central to the life of the people and their community. Rituals attend various stages of life, for example, or different seasons of the year. Frequently they constitute a stylized or symbolic reenactment and remembrance of events recounted in sacred stories, usually involving gods or exemplary mortals. Thus ritual is in certain respects like art. Not only does it incor-

Style and Substance in Worship

porate arts like story-telling, dance, song, and visually orna-
mented objects, but it also entails "performance," whether by a
leader or by participants; it employs sensory media that are essential to its message; and it is to be experienced as a unified
whole with a certain dramatic contour or aesthetic rhythm. This
means that one cannot radically alter the form of a ritual without
radically altering its content. The style is part of the substance.
Finally, however, the aim of ritual is not purely artistic. Serving a
complex social and religious function, it engenders, restores, and
maintains what is regarded as a right relationship among members of a human community and between that community and
higher realities generally thought of as divine. In short, it is both
informative and transformative of human life and possibility.

Anyone who has partaken of Christian communion or attended a Christian wedding or funeral should recognize these
events as instances of ritual in the sense just explained. It is true
that the Protestant Reformers intentionally simplified nearly all
the forms of Christian ritual and that the restoration movement
simplified these forms still further. But a simple ritual remains a
ritual. Certainly this could be said of the comparatively simple
worship services of present-day Disciples of Christ churches. In
all these services we use largely traditional patterns of speech and
symbol to recall and proclaim the mighty acts of God, and specifically of God in Christ. We prepare for and anticipate the
transformation of self and society in relation to God. We experience an aesthetic and psychological progression in which word,
music, color, gesture are all significant, partly because of the way
they are ordered and combined. Through these media we as a
community become attuned to what we perceive to be both the
primordial and the ever-creative power of the Spirit. Our very
words bear witness to this: "As it was in the beginning, is now,
and ever shall be"; "This do in remembrance of me"; "Thy kingdom come on earth as it is in heaven." If, in our acts, we repeatedly emphasize remembrance (*anamnesis*) and expectation (*prolep-
sis*), we do so in order to realize anew the significance of life here
and now. This is the overall intent of our songs and prayers, our

confessions and sermons, our offerings, ordinances, benedictions, banners, buildings, and perhaps even business. And this is why a Disciples worship service can be seen as fundamentally a ritual, not entirely different in its form and intent from rituals found in all parts of the world.

But to say that our worship takes the form of ritual is not to suggest, of course, that it is automatically authentic and edifying. One is reminded of the scathing condemnations of Roman Catholic ceremony penned by Luther, Zwingli, and Calvin. Although these Reformers strike us as uncharitable at times, and sometimes unfair, they leave no doubt as to their conviction that the devil is prepared to make use of supposedly "holy" acts. Thus, in Calvin's view, humans will always worship something, but that something may not be God. In point of fact, Calvin claims, the human mind is a factory for the perpetual production of idols.[4]

If we grant that this warning against idolatry, however harsh, enunciates an important scriptural insight, we cannot from our perspective help but marvel at Calvin's own confidence that the forms of worship he himself prescribes are thoroughly and permanently in accordance with God's will. It is disconcerting to discover Calvin resisting any variation in his approved liturgy and forever railing against those "who introduce newly invented methods of worshipping God."[5] In any case, it should be plain that no particular style of worship or ritual is immune from the danger of idolatry. Hence, no form of ritual—including that of the Calvinists and their Disciples of Christ descendants—can for all time go unquestioned.

With respect to the Disciples of Christ, such questioning has naturally taken place whenever thoughts of division or of union with other Christians have been in the air, as they almost always are. And it seems particularly in order now, at a time when modern scholarship has increasingly undercut the ideals of the restoration movement and when the implications of that fact have begun to sink in. Confronted with the evident diversity of early church practice and belief, the problematic nature of biblical interpretation, and the cultural biases of the restoration movement itself, we Disciples continue to face crucial questions as to our identity and mission.

For certain other groups in parallel circumstances, the questions raised and the answers sought have largely been issues of belief. These concerns we also share, but because the Disciples of Christ have traditionally—and not always profitably—eschewed theology, our questions are more characteristically framed either in terms of moral practice or of worship. Obviously, this essay cannot examine every facet of our worship life; however, two issues seem central not only to an understanding of Christian ritual as a whole, but also to an understanding of the actualities and possibilities of Disciples of Christ worship in the present moment. In examining each of these issues—the relation of Sacrament to Word and of Christian unity to diversity—we will see how questions of style and substance are interconnected. Two questions in particular apply to the evaluation of Disciples worship: first, is a given aspect of our worship true to the scriptural principles commonly acknowledged to be fundamental to Christian faith? (Here I naturally give special consideration to Protestant and restoration themes and interpretations.) Second, in the light of what we know about meaningful ritual in general and of the historical practices of particular worshiping communities, can a given aspect of our worship be said to constitute a vital and effective component of ritual in the present moment? These two questions exist in creative dialogue. Their answers, when taken together, should meet the criteria of appropriateness and adequacy which certain philosophical theologians have drawn for testing the validity of basic theological truth claims: they should be both appropriate to the Christian tradition and reflect an adequate understanding of human experience.[6]

Word and Sacrament

The ritual events central to Christian worship from its beginnings have almost always included both the spoken word and sacramental act. But the relation between the two has been different in different times and places, and understanding their historical development clarifies the Disciples ritual traditions.

In the primitive church, the services emphasizing scripture and verbal interpretation, which were often modeled on worship in the Jewish synagogue, generally took place at a separate time from the services of the Lord's Supper, though both kinds of service were held frequently and usually weekly.[7] The ritual of baptism, while eventually giving rise to full-fledged creedal statements, did not at first entail an elaborate liturgy.

By the middle of the second century, both the service of the Word and the service of the Lord's Supper had become a common feature of Sunday morning worship. The first was a "public" service called the *Synaxis*, or "meeting," which included a greeting, scripture readings, psalm singing, more readings, a sermon, the dismissal of all who had not been baptized or confirmed, and prayers. The second service was the *Eucharist*, or "thanksgiving," in which gestures like the kiss of peace and the breaking of the bread were prominent and in which the ritual meal itself was obviously the focus. Although words were still an essential part of the sacrament—the words of institution being especially important—the focal media of the Eucharist were sensory and bodily rather than verbal.

Between the fourth and the ninth centuries, most people in the areas ministered to by the Church were at least nominal Christians. Confirmation as well as baptism took place in infancy. It is no surprise, therefore, that the service of the Word and the service of the Supper became one. At the same time, however, the focus of the whole liturgy shifted toward the Eucharist, for which the scripture readings, sermon, and prayers were essentially preparatory. And because now those in attendance rarely partook of the sacred meal, partly out of awe and partly for fear of being unworthy, the rite became more and more a matter of sight.[8] This was especially true in succeeding centuries, as the altar was moved further from the people and the celebrant stood with his back to them, uttering Latin words in a low tone which few could comprehend. Not surprisingly, the high point of the

Mass in the high medieval period became the elevation of the Host and chalice following the consecration, punctuated by the triple ringing of a bell. The faithful thus attended something like a sacred drama. But for them it was a drama of signs more than of words—visible signs augmented, at High Mass, by the extensive use of music. Having heard, at most, a sermon of moral exhortation containing very little instruction or theological interpretation, the laity were left to participate in the rest of the service primarily through private meditation, distant observation, and sometimes fervent imagining accompanied by minimal intellectual understanding. Word had been overshadowed by ritual deed. And the meaning of the ritual itself had been altered.

Needless to say, the Protestants of the sixteenth century sought to rectify what the Catholics themselves would eventually admit was an imbalance. But, as is so often the case, the reaction itself was extreme. To be sure, Luther, Calvin, Cranmer, and possibly even Zwingli, all at first envisioned that Holy Communion would be a regular part of worship on Sunday, especially since they assumed (perhaps incorrectly) that this was true of the earliest Christian worship. But the laity, unaccustomed to partaking of communion every week, rejected the idea. And because the Reformers opposed any form of Holy Communion that involved no communicants, the normal Sunday morning service became, whatever its title, essentially a service of the Word.

This development was tolerable, of course, only because the Word itself, in the form of scripture, prayer, and preaching, had now been consciously elevated to a level of preeminence alien to medieval worship and perhaps to all previous forms of Christian worship. And while the extensive role accorded to music in Reformation worship may have granted this art a quasi-sacramental function, music would never crowd out the Word. Luther and Calvin both contended that the sermon was essential to every occasion of worship. In Luther's words, "Everything shall be done so that the Word prevails. . . . We can spare everything except the Word. We profit by nothing so much as by the Word."[9] While Calvin insisted that there is "nothing more useful" in the church than the Lord's Supper, he too viewed the reading and preaching of the gospel as the "incomparable treasure of the church."[10] Indeed, Calvin argued that "the right administering of the Sacrament cannot stand apart from the Word. For whatever benefit may come to us from the Supper requires the Word: whether we are to be confirmed in faith, or exercised in confession, or aroused to duty, there is need of preaching. Therefore nothing more preposterous could happen in the Supper than for it to be turned into a silent action, as has happened under the pope's tyranny."[11]

The Catholic celebration of the Eucharist had not, of course, been literally silent. The words of consecration, however inaudible, were deemed necessary in order for the elements to become sacramental. Calvin's concern, to which we will return, was that the visible sign should always be accompanied by, as he put it, "the true explanation of the mystery." By this he meant not that words would explain the mystery away but that words would locate for the congregation the nature of the mystery and of the divine promises it signified and sealed. Without such audible, intelligible interpretation there could be no real sacrament but only "a lifeless and bare phantom."[12] The same, according to Calvin, was true of baptism no less than of the Lord's Supper, since the proclamation of the Word is what begets the faith required for the spiritual efficacy of the ritual cleansing.[13] In keeping with this view, Calvin explicitly stated that justification and sanctification, while requiring the preaching of the gospel, do not absolutely require the visible sign and seal of either of the two sacraments.[14] Clearly, with the Reformation, the Word had taken precedence over all else.

At this point some of us identified with the Disciples of Christ might be forgiven for anticipating that the proper balance between Word and Sacrament, having eluded both medieval Catholicism and Reformation Protestantism, could surely be said to have been achieved in the restoration movement of the early nineteenth century. We whose worship patterns derive from that movement (itself partially a derivative of Calvinist, Baptist, and

Congregationalist piety) normally observe the ordinance of the Lord's Supper each Sunday, and on these occasions we also sing, pray, preach, and read scripture. Hence there is reason to believe that the Disciples of Christ have the possibility of fulfilling, in our style of worship, Calvin's frustrated desire to bring Word and sacrament together in such a way that the deeper meanings of each would be manifest. I would hold that this is indeed our potential and that it is consonant with the spirit of primitive Christian worship, in which the services of the Word and the Supper were regularly held and soon conjoined. But I also believe that for us to fulfill the potential inherent to our form of worship, we must become more attentive to both Word and sacrament and to the way in which they are combined in our ritual. This becomes clear when we reflect on the place of the Lord's Supper in our worship.

Those who have pondered the worship patterns of Disciples of Christ declare that the Lord's Supper is the heart of what we are about as a worshiping community. Moreover, this claim can be supported by a good deal of evidence, including the fact that Alexander Campbell's *The Christian System* includes a lengthy description of a service he found especially meaningful and worthy of imitation—a service in which there was no sermon (due to the absence of a qualified preacher) and in which a simple communion ceremony was central.[15] As regards the spiritual benefit of partaking of the Lord's Supper, the substance of restoration ideals is clear. With reference to the weekly act of communion, Alexander Campbell remarks, "Ties that spring from eternal love, revealed in blood and addressed to [our] senses, draw forth all that is within [us] of a grace of eternal life."[16] It is true that the terminology preferred by Disciples—"remembrance" and "ordinance"—can lend itself to a comparatively impoverished conception of the ritual act. "Remembrance" does not adequately convey the connotations of the Greek and scriptural word *anamnesis*, which suggests "calling back" or "making present again." And the word "ordinance" indicates only that what we do is ordained—implicitly by Christ—without saying anything about the *meaning* of what we do, which is far more than dutifully remembering historical facts pertaining to a meal eaten two thousand years ago. But Alexander Campbell himself defines the term "ordinance" in a nonreductive way, specifically stating what the word itself does not, namely, that an ordinance is not simply a prescribed practice but is also a particular "mode in which the grace of God acts on human nature."[17] He also says, quite forcefully, "This institution [of the Lord's Supper] commemorates the love which reconciled us to God, and always furnishes us with a new argument to live for him who died for us. [The person] who feels not the eloquence and power of this argument, all other arguments assail in vain."[18]

Peculiar as the word "argument" may sound in this connection, it serves at least implicitly to suggest that the sacrament itself interprets the Word of scripture, sermon, prayer, and song. The ritual of the Lord's Supper moves us to a new realization of our unity in Christ and argues in a tangible, experiential, and distinctive way for the claims of the gospel. We could reasonably conclude that sacrament and Word are mutually interpretive, existing in complementary relation. If the Lord's Supper is the heart of our worship, then the Word is its mind; it is the union of heart and mind that comprises the soul of the worshiping community of Disciples.

This, at least, is the potential. And theoretically there is much to commend the modes of worship by which the restoration leaders hoped to see that potential realized. In our tradition we uphold the value of liturgical freedom and flexibility, which provides for enormous adaptability to varying circumstances. We encourage lay participation, thereby enhancing a sense of community and equality before God. Our kind of ritual is unpretentious, and our usual practice secures a place for both sacrament and Word in our worship.

But what *kind* of place? Are we sufficiently aware of how easily freedom and simplicity in ritual can degenerate into carelessness and insensitivity? If one looks at the way in which Disciples actually practice communion, one senses a certain tension between the importance we verbally ascribe to the ritual act and the style with which we typically carry it out. In two-thirds of the Disciples churches that observe weekly communion, the communion precedes the sermon,[19] which an ordained minister preaches and which occupies by far the greatest amount of time and attention in the service. As a result, the Lord's Supper stands, in relation to the sermon, in the structural position of preamble or preparation. Even when it follows the sermon, moreover, it tends to occupy a subordinate and indeed an anticlimactic position, due to its brevity and informality—"informality" meaning not simplicity per se but inattention to form.

To verify this one need only look honestly at what happens during communion. Consider the relatively perfunctory character of most of our communion prayers, the efficiency and speed with which we like to see the bread and wine distributed, the scarcity of ritual gestures, especially in the absence of any loaf to break or any vessel from which to pour. Consider how very little tactile and substantive quality there is to the mass-produced bits of cracker or bread so popular now. One can hardly imagine their ever having been part of one loaf, though we are asked to see them as symbolic of the one body of Christ broken for us. Consider, too, how the dominant visible sign on the table itself is seldom the bread or the wine (or juice) but a shining, metallic container that, layer by layer, will break down into the trays holding the bread and tiny cups of liquid. The elements of the Supper emerge not from anything associated with the fruit of God's earth or with human flesh but from a cool and impassive object. Think, finally, of the utterly passive role usually played by most of the congregation. Although these believers are all declared to be priests before God, here they frequently play the part of inactive recipients, neither speaking, standing, nor kneeling. As they partake, they sit facing forward, row on row, unable to see their co-communicants or to respond directly to those who hand them the food that supposedly celebrates their oneness in the Lord. And the food itself? There is precious little to taste or see. "Take, eat" seems more like "Take, nibble." The apostle Paul himself, who warned against gluttony and drunkenness at the

Lord's Supper, would surely have been amazed to see such caution. No wonder God, whose signs of bounteous grace these elements are and whose sacrificial love they represent, can seem at such a time more absent than present, more merely remembered than fully recognized.

Word and sacrament: juxtaposed, too often the one speaks at length and commands attention while the other silently and briefly testifies with ambiguous acts and almost invisible signs. To claim that God cannot make use of this manner of worship, or of any other for that matter, would be presumptuous. To declare that none of us find it meaningful is patently untrue. But to say that the Lord's Supper is at the heart of our worship is to ignore the relation between substance and style.

Although this account of our ordinary communion practices is intentionally exaggerated, it suggests some ways in which this aspect of our worship life can be made more meaningful. In this connection, two additional observations may stimulate reflection. First, we need not abandon our heritage of relative simplicity in worship, nor need we be highly formal. But whatever order of worship we adopt, and in whatever manner we choose to partake of the Supper, we need to be aware that any ritual act that is to be of significance to those involved must be given time, space, and attention of body and mind. However often a ritual is observed, the signs and gestures, the sights and sounds, must accord with the intended significance of the act. I would apply Paul's admonition that everything be done "decently and in order" (1 Cor 14:40).

My second observation, oddly enough, recalls Calvin's insight concerning the importance of Word to sacrament. His view, I will grant, may be extreme. But the sacrament will take on greater significance when we are careful to establish some recognizable connection between the Word proclaimed in the sermon and the meaning of our central ritual act. After all, a ritual—and especially a simple ritual—is meaningful only when those who practice the ritual have come to share some sense of the religious and communal significance of what they are doing. But today such understandings are severely threatened, within the church and without, partly because many of us find quite strange and incredible the very idea of significant community and of God's real presence and liberating power, without which the Lord's Supper is little more than a social custom. We may still remember and speak of a Jesus who died that we might live. But the hope of a genuinely redemptive purpose for countless lives suffering from hunger, injustice, oppression, or sheer monotony often seems illusory. In such a context it is imperative not only to perform ritual acts but to interpret them anew and to see more clearly how the world as a whole is potentially sacramental, as Augustine, Calvin, and Alexander Campbell each recognized in his own way.

This is not a call for longer sermons, and certainly not for a new dogmatism. The Disciples' characteristic distaste for theological dogmas has preserved us from endless and bitter controversies over whether Christ is present at (or in) the sacrament by virtue of transubstantiation, consubstantiation, transsignification, or some other process. But we need theological reflection, and conversation nonetheless, for it seems that in their laudable effort to promote unity and simplicity, the leaders of the restoration movement employed a language of word and ritual that was not inherently as rich as their faith. If that faith is to remain alive in our day, it will depend in part on renewed reflection on the meaning of the sacraments, of which the Lord's Supper is the most prominent. In this way we can perhaps rediscover how to let both Word and sacrament have their say.

Unity and Diversity

Among students of theology and liturgy there is a growing conviction that what we believe and practice as Christians is profoundly shaped by how we worship, while worship in turn is shaped by our beliefs and practical commitments. To affirm this is but to extend the twofold meaning discernible in the ancient Latin expression, *lex orandi, lex credendi* ("the law of praying [is] the law of believing").[20]

But if it is true that even the *way* we worship is a matter of consequence to religious belief and life, this could be discomfiting to ecumenically minded groups such as the Disciples of Christ. Worship patterns are undeniably very different among the many groups calling themselves Christians and even among groups that claim to share many of the same beliefs. If you baptize by sprinkling infants and we by immersing believers, if you emphasize the sacraments and we emphasize preaching and healing, if you use an organ and sometimes trumpets in church while we use guitars or sing unaccompanied or simply keep quiet, how can we be certain that your people are really our people and your God our God? Or should we simply forget about differences, trusting that somehow all roads lead in the end to the same place?

In dealing with vexing questions of this kind, Disciples have been fond of two maxims. The first is, "In essentials, unity; in nonessentials, liberty; in all things, charity." This sounds good, but, except for the part about charity, it is of limited practical use because the problem is to decide what is essential and what is not. Besides, there is the possibility that what is essential to your worship life is not essential to mine. The second maxim, which sounds more promising, is the all-but-creedal statement: "Where the scriptures speak, we speak; where the scriptures are silent, we are silent." Ideally, this could be an unambiguous guide to what is essential. But difficulties arise because the scriptures themselves speak from different perspectives, with different emphases, from historical and cultural settings very different from our own. Although we can hardly afford not to listen devoutly to what the scriptures have to say, the very act of listening involves engaging them in a dialogue. Similarly, trying to speak where the scriptures speak entails trying to make sense of what they say, which means using some thoughts and words of our own. Furthermore, our idea of the way the scriptures actually speak has changed greatly since the early decades of the last century. Whereas Alexander Campbell believed that God guaranteed the scriptures to have meanings that are "fair, stipulated, and well-established,"[21] virtually all modern students of the Bible are struck by the fact that the basic teachings of Jesus, for instance, are largely expressed in parables and in preaching full of perplexing metaphors and paradoxes.

Lastly, various modern thinkers have questioned the whole system of philosophical standards that Disciples have invoked for well over a century to show the reasonable and empirical basis of our faith and worship. These modern philosophers and theologians argue persuasively that experience and reason are far more complex and subtle than the religious (or philosophical) inheritors of the Enlightenment ever assumed.[22] What reason and experience seem to tell us now is that there is no short route to unity, to essentials, and to conclusions as to when diversity either clearly does or does not matter.

So what are we to do? Is there any way to conceive how our different approaches to worship can somehow serve the same goal of glorifying God? Is there any hope of supporting Thomas Campbell's conviction that "the church of Christ on earth is essentially, intentionally, and constitutionally one"?[23] On the other hand, is there any way to affirm unity-in-diversity without totally surrendering the idea that some practices are preferable to others? To help us move toward some answers, two analogies apply to the concern Disciples have for promoting unity while retaining the integrity of our worship style in the midst of change:

Analogy 1. We have repeatedly been reminded in recent years that each of us passes through different stages of life and of faith. Most of us are aware that, as we go through such stages, we ourselves change. The person about to retire is not exactly the same person as the one who nervously tackled the job for the first time many years before. The parent celebrating the first birthday of the first child is not exactly the same person as the one who contemplated pregnancy and saw the child enter the world. On the other hand, most of us have an unshakable intuition that, despite such changes, we are not totally different selves from one moment to the next or from one stage of life to another. In some inexplicable way, we transcend the sheer passing of things by informing our moments with memories, desires, and purposes that no single moment of existence could manifest.

In the Church, as in human experience, there can be unity and identity within historical change, if we take seriously the scriptural claim that the Church as a whole is the body of Christ imbued with the Spirit. Just as our own bodies change, so must the body of Christ which is the Church—remembering that the Church in this sense is not the local congregation alone but the community of all who belong to Christ and have their identity in that belonging. In short, the living Church cannot remain completely the same. Even when it uses ancient words and rituals, the meanings are to some extent different because the experiences of the members are inevitably different.

This thought may be offensive if one thinks that God dislikes history and difference and change. But, as I see it, the moment God decided to make two people instead of one—and to make them male and female at that—God let it be known that difference is not to be despised. The moment a tree in Eden produced fruit, it produced the seeds of change. The Fall, therefore, is not the introduction of change itself but of negative change that destroys the relationships that make change meaningful and good. That which meaningfully guides and unites the Church from age to age corresponds to that which gives continuity to a person from stage to stage. It is a source of purpose that both dwells in and transcends the body as such. In the case of human beings, we call this the self, the spirit. In the case of the Church, we call this the Spirit of God in Christ.

The natural conclusion is that what matters most is the mutually responsive and responsible relationship among all members of the body and between us and God "in whose will is our peace." Ultimately, a belief or mode of worship is to be judged by whether it promotes right relationships—justice, harmony, and love of God and neighbor. This rules out dogmatism, because to some extent any belief or practice that allows a given community insight into its relationship to others and to God might be less ade-

Style and Substance in Worship

quate or effective in another historical situation. But it also rules out total relativism, because a right relationship cannot be based on perceptions that are completely false. The very process of discerning what constitutes a true and right relationship between self, others, and God involves a dialogue with scripture, the continual reinterpretation of which decisively shapes and reshapes the identity of the worshiping community. In any case, however, the power that binds worshipers together and to God is ultimately from God; therefore, the final judgment as to whether this or that form of worship is faithful likewise belongs to God. Our own judgments—even those of congregations and denominations— must be recognized as provisional, though necessary.

For Disciples of Christ, one practical implication of what I have said is that, since identity within change is both natural and possible, we can hope to be true to the spiritual and scriptural impetus of the restoration movement without being bound to its desire to replicate New Testament practices and to literalize New Testament beliefs. Since a right relationship to God and others is what is essential, we can be open to incorporating into ritual, song, and sermon new images of right relationship, such as those provided by process, liberation, and feminist theologies. But just as one cannot disown one's past without losing oneself, so we must not neglect the burden and joy of continually reappropriating our past and of letting it challenge and enrich both the style and substance of what we do in the present.

Analogy 2. A second analogy, taken from music, suggests a somewhat different cluster of observations about how there can be unity-in-diversity when modes of expression coexist at the same moment in history. Human beings the world over sing songs, including love songs, but styles differ. *Porgy and Bess* speaks a different love language from *Tristan and Isolde*. Porgy, in fact, speaks of love differently from Bess, Tristan from Isolde. No song within any one style duplicates exactly what another song in the same style expresses, and certainly no style duplicates the expressive resources and meanings of another. But one recognizes that somehow love can be authentically expressed in different songs and in different styles. At the same time, one knows that certain expressions of love are more limited and superficial and that musical styles are not equally suited to expressing all kinds of love. Although value judgments can best be made by those immersed in the styles in question, or at least well acquainted with them, questions of excellence can be raised from both within and outside a given tradition of making music.

The expression of love within a given style of music is rather like the enactment of worship within the ritual vocabulary of a particular religious tradition such as the Roman Catholic, reformed, or free church. The relation between different musical styles of expressing love is like the relation between different styles of worship. Theoretically, therefore, the substance of worship can be shared to a significant extent, even though each worshiper's individual experience and each tradition's communal experience can never be precisely the same as any other. By the same token, the relative adequacy and breadth of expression possible within a given worship tradition may not match the standards of another tradition and may not be realized in various instances of worship within that very tradition.

If this second analogy is acceptable, clearly the first priority of any religious group is the integrity and excellence of its own native style of worship. Someone might object that such talk of "excellence in worship" makes it sound as though we can somehow force God to become powerfully present if only we set things up right. But it should be noted that we seldom express such reservations about urging excellence in preaching. The persistence and patience of God does not excuse us from taking care when we shape the substance of worship through ritual forms. Though the language of worship should be one we can understand, it also should constitute a deepening and transfiguring of the everyday, in keeping with the transformation that religion requires of the mundane self and reality. With respect to the practices of Disciples churches, this would mean attending to the possibilities of relatively restrained and simple worship. It would not mean emulating in every service the impressive formality and elaborate ritual of "high" Episcopal services or the emotional abandon of Pentecostal groups. Nonetheless, we should be conscious that, where religious styles differ, our religious experiences and perceptions will in some measure also be different.

Even if such differences matter, they do not necessarily prevent right worship for any of us. The differences need not be absolutely decisive, and most Disciples wish these differences might not be deeply *divisive*. Keeping in mind that some divisions may be warranted, we can at least minimize divisiveness and enrich our own tradition if we become acquainted with other styles and include aspects of those styles that most naturally broaden and enhance our own worship. The inherent flexibility of Disciples worship lends itself to this very possibility. This, I believe, is a great asset in our pluralistic society. The only way in which people of different ethnic, racial, economic, and cultural backgrounds can long sustain a worship life together is for aspects of their corporate worship to reflect and respect the stylistic vocabularies of those present at worship. This inevitably means becoming "multilingual" in one's music and ritual even as one tries to avoid sheer eclecticism. For Disciples it might mean that our typically sober and pragmatic spirits would learn from others a way to respond more fully to such things as new forms of music, visual design, and liturgical drama or dance. This development might seem inconsistent with our reputation of emphasizing head over heart,[24] but perhaps that reputation was never fully deserved. Alexander Campbell insisted that transformation in Christ is not merely practical or intellectual but total, involving "a change of views; a change of affections; a change of state; and a change of life."[25] "Once for all," he wrote, "let it be distinctly noted, that we appreciate nothing in religion which tends not directly and immediately, proximately and remotely, to the purification and perfection of the heart."[26] If this falls short of Methodist warmth, it nonetheless reminds us that any medium that speaks to the whole person, heart as well as mind, has a unique potential in worship. The arts are just such media.

In the end, however, it is not enough to learn only from

INTERPRETING DISCIPLES

other Christians, nor is it enough to reach out only to them. The agenda that history sets for us now is very much larger and still more challenging. As citizens of the world, we must begin to find ways to acknowledge in worship and ritual, as in theology and ethics, that God's purpose surely must encompass more than the sphere of Christianity alone—just as music expressive of love encompasses more than any one style or even one family of styles.

As Christians, we can fully affirm the constancy of God's dynamic relation to human beings precisely because God's unchanging will is to relate lovingly and creatively to all peoples and to all things. As students of ritual and religion, we can affirm that, for their part, human beings in all their diversity are constant in their underlying will to find purpose within the whole of life and to act out meaningful patterns related to an ultimately significant whole, whether or not it is conceived of as divine. Therefore, it is neither unreasonable nor unchristian to suggest that the various world religions may, in their diverse ways, be responsive to the reality and will of God. Even non-Christian religions seek to illumine our relation to the created order and to what transcends and gives meaning to life. They do not shine a single light down a single path; the paths themselves often seem to diverge as well as to converge. But Disciples and other Christians, guided by the light they themselves have seen, must not close their eyes to other lights or fail to scrutinize both critically and appreciatively whatever those lights reveal. However exclusive a symbol the Christian cross may appear to be, it indicates that the grace of God is wonderfully and even shockingly adaptive to the human situation. This being the case, Disciples may be able to see more fully the global meaning of God-in-Christ and to confront, perhaps for the first time, both the problems and the possibilities of true ecumenicity. In this way both the style and substance of our worship might give greater glory to the God of all peoples and things.

Notes

[1] Many students of worship, especially outside the "free church" tradition, would insist that the order of worship itself makes a very important theological statement. Clearly this is the position of James F. White, whose many books on worship have shaped the thinking in the present essay to a considerable extent. I am grateful to Professor White for making comments on an earlier version of this chapter.

[2] For theories of ritual and worship, see Ninian Smart, *The Concept of Worship* (London: Macmillan, 1972); Victor Turner, *The Ritual Process* (Chicago: Aldine Co., 1969); Clifford Geertz, *The Interpretation of Cultures* (New York: Basic Books, 1973). A recent, detailed bibliography of ritual studies is provided by Ronald L. Grimes, "Sources for the Study of Ritual," *Religious Studies Review* 10 (April 1984): 134–45.

[3] John Calvin, *Institutes of the Christian Religion*, Book IV, xiv, 19.

[4] Ibid., Book I, xi, 8.

[5] Bard Thompson, ed., *Liturgies of the Western Church* (Cleveland: Collins, 1962), p. 195.

[6] See, for example, David Tracy, *Blessed Rage for Order: The New Pluralism in Theology* (New York: Seabury, Crossroad Book, 1975), pp. 32–63.

[7] See Ferdinand Hahn, *The Worship of the Early Church*, trans. David E. Green (Philadelphia: Fortress Press, 1973), p. 72. See also Theodor Klauser, *A Short History of the Western Liturgy* (London: Oxford University Press, 1969), pp. 7–8.

[8] Even sight was minimized in the Eastern rite, with its use of a veil or screen. See Dom Gregory Dix, *The Shape of the Liturgy* (London: A. & C. Black, 1945), pp. 483–84.

[9] Quoted in Thompson, *Liturgies*, p. 98.

[10] Ibid., p. 191.

[11] Calvin, *Institutes*, Book IV, xvii, 39.

[12] Quoted in Thompson, *Liturgies*, p. 192.

[13] Calvin, *Institutes*, Book VI, xiv, 4.

[14] Ibid., 14.

[15] Alexander Campbell, *The Christian System* (Cincinnati: Standard Publishing Company, 1839), pp. 290–92.

[16] Ibid., p. 273.

[17] Quoted in Paul A. Crow, Jr., "Ministry and the Sacraments in the Christian Church (Disciples of Christ)," *Encounter* 41 (1980): 75.

[18] Campbell, *Christian System*, p. 274.

[19] W. B. Blakemore, "Worship and the Lord's Supper," in *The Revival of the Churches*, ed. W. B. Blakemore, Vol. 3 of *The Renewal of Church: Panel of Scholars Reports*, ed. W. B. Blakemore (St. Louis: Bethany Press, 1963), p. 232.

[20] See Geoffrey Wainwright, *Doxology: The Praise of God in Worship, Doctrine and Life* (New York: Oxford University Press, 1980), pp. 218, 221, 517.

[21] Alexander Campbell, *The Christian System* (Reprint, Nashville: Gospel Advocate, 1874), p. 3.

[22] I am thinking particularly of arguments of process philosophers like Whitehead and of European phenomenologists like Heidegger and Ricoeur.

[23] Quoted in Lester G. McAllister and William E. Tucker, *Journey In Faith: A History of the Christian Church (Disciples of Christ)* (St. Louis: Bethany Press, 1975), p. 44.

[24] See W. B. Blakemore, "Reasonable, Empirical, Pragmatic: The Mind of Disciples of Christ," in *The Reformation of Tradition*, ed. Ronald E. Osborn, Vol. 1 of *The Renewal of Church: Panel of Scholars Reports*, ed. W. B. Blakemore (St. Louis: Bethany Press, 1963), p. 165.

[25] Campbell, *Christian System* (1964), p. 44.

[26] Ibid., p. 215.

Where the Scriptures Speak, We Quarrel: Biblical Approaches in the Disciples Founders

LOWELL K. HANDY

IN THE FIRST TWO DECADES of the nineteenth century, several new religious movements which arose in the United States shared the notion that sectarian divisions of the Church had developed when ideas, expressed in various creeds, superseded the scriptures. The leaders of these movements broke from their original denominations when they found it impossible to subscribe to beliefs they could not substantiate from biblical texts. They assumed that if the Church could rid itself of "man-made" additions and return to the early Christianity presented in the New Testament, there would be a united Church, a united body of Christ. The pattern for this united Church, they argued, could be found in New Testament writings; thus the Bible was the central concern of the movement.

The Christian Church was the largest denomination to arise from these attempts at restoration. The denomination was founded, for the most part, on the work of four men: Barton W. Stone, Thomas Campbell, Alexander Campbell, and Walter Scott. From their personal experiences in the sectarian infighting of Presbyterian factions and, later, of the Baptists, each of these men came independently to the conclusion that the Bible was the only legitimate authority for the Church. Each of the founding figures states this opinion in strong terms. Stone, in coproducing

the "Last Will and Testament of the Springfield Presbytery,"
wrote:

> We *will* that the people henceforth take the Bible as the
> only sure guide to heaven; and as many as are offended
> with other books, which stand in competition with it,
> may cast them into the fire if they choose; for it is
> better to enter into life having one book, than having
> many to be cast into hell.[1]

Thomas Campbell, in his "Declaration and Address," observed
that

> nothing ought to be inculcated upon christians as ar-
> ticles of faith; nor required of them as terms of com-
> munion; but what is expressly taught and enjoined
> upon them, in the word of God. Nor ought any thing
> be admitted, as of divine obligation, in their church
> constitution and managements, but what is expressly
> enjoined by the authority of our Lord Jesus Christ and
> his Apostles upon the New Testament church; either in
> expressed terms, or by approved precedent.[2]

Alexander Campbell declared in *The Christian System*:

> The Bible, or the Old and New Testament, in Hebrew
> and Greek, contains a full and perfect revelation of
> God and his will, adapted to man as he now is.[3]

And Walter Scott stated in his preface to *The Gospel Restored*:

> These churches, with few exceptions, adopted the
> holy scriptures as their exclusive guide in religion, and
> rejected the dangerous creeds and confessions of
> Christendom, which have operated so fatally on the
> unity of the church. This formed the first positive step
> towards that return to original ground, for which the
> present century is distinguished.[4]

Although these men agreed that the Bible is the sole basis for the belief and structure of the Church, they used it selectively, relying on the New Testament for guidance about the Church they sought to build. Thus the real scriptures of the movement were the books of the New Testament, especially those dealing with the structure and unity of the Church, and use of the Old Testament depended on the individual founder. Alexander Campbell created a controversy which split the Baptists and the Disciples when he separated the Testaments in his sermon on the law. He stated that the Old Testament was sufficient for the worshipers of the Old Testament but that the New Testament was sufficient, by itself, for New Testament worshipers. This distinction had also been made even earlier, when Thomas Campbell had proposed in his "Declaration and Address":

> That although the scriptures of the Old and New Testament are inseparably connected, making together but one perfect and entire revelation of the Divine will, for the edification and salvation of the church; and therefore in that respect cannot be separated; yet as to what directly and properly belongs to their immediate object, the New Testament is as perfect a constitution for the worship, discipline and government of the New Testament church, and as perfect a rule for the particular duties of its members; as the Old Testament was for the worship, discipline and government of the Old Testament church, and the particular duties of its members.[5]

In this view the Old Testament was useful to the Church only insofar as it was referred to in the New Testament. Walter Scott, taking a somewhat different stance, found the Old Testament a "figure" and "type" of the New:

> Restricting our researches to the Bible, we find it divided into two parts, namely, the Old Testament and the New—or the Jewish and the Christian Scrip-

tures—the former the shadow, the latter the substance—the first typical, the second antitypical.
These interact harmoniously with each other, and the
whole is perfectly consistent, with itself.[6]

Scott's view thus separated the Testaments but maintained them as
a compatible unit.

Although the Bible was central for the four leaders, the way
they interpreted it and used it differed. Some simply used the text
available and read it with the current understanding, but others
felt a need to explain the proper method for reading a biblical
text. In all cases there were discrepancies between theory and
practice. While Stone, the Campbells, and Scott all drew on the
Bible as the foundation for the Disciples, each approached the
material in his own way and should be taken separately.

Barton W. Stone (1772–1844)

Stone, the first of the four to be active in the restoration
movement, and the only one born in America, was the least complex in his handling of the Bible. He believed it was possible for
anyone to read the Bible and, taking the literal meaning, to
understand the text correctly, although the Holy Spirit needed
to be working in the individual to make that happen. Stone felt
that on this point Alexander Campbell's writings were not "sufficiently explicit on the influence of the Spirit," although in private
conversation the two men apparently agreed.[7] Stone, arguing for
careful reading of the scriptures with the aid of the Holy Spirit,
urged "that candidates for the Gospel ministry henceforth study
the Holy Scriptures with fervent prayer, and obtain license from
God to preach the simple Gospel, *with the Holy Ghost sent down from
heaven*, without any mixture of philosophy, vain deceit, traditions
of men, or the rudiments of the world."[8] He could not accept the
idea of needing help to understand the scriptures; beyond the
Holy Spirit's aid in reading the texts, nothing else was needed:
"We may take the Bible alone, and Bible facts, without note or
comment as the only standard of faith and practice, and of chris-

tian union; yet without the spirit, union can never be effected, nor continued."[9] All who read the scriptural texts would understand and would come to conclusions similar to Stone's: "Finally we *will*, that all our *sister bodies* read their Bibles carefully, that they may see their fate there determined, and prepare for death before it is too late."[10]

Yet Stone obviously did not always come to the same conclusions as the other "sister bodies" nor the other Disciples founders. He differed with the Presbyterians over the theological notion of the trinity. Not being able to substantiate it in the texts of the New Testament, he refused to take it as an article of faith, and on this point he diverged from Alexander Campbell as well. His position that the scriptures were the final word led Stone to disavow any creeds or confessions and to require only that what was in the text of the Bible be taken as truth. When he disagreed with the Presbyterians on the question of the atonement, Stone also found himself arguing against Thomas Campbell on the substitutionary doctrine. In this debate he stated that Campbell was interpreting the scriptures too literally, while Campbell felt Stone was not taking the Bible seriously enough.[11]

Although Stone argued that the common person could read and understand the Bible with the help of the Holy Spirit, he had a seminary education and could read Greek and later learned Hebrew. In dealing with words such as "atonement," he made use of the original languages. But his scholarship in the biblical texts was fairly standard for the time: he strung together long lists of Bible quotations and defined the points to be made by choosing, uncritically as to their contexts, passages useful for his argument.[12] Since this was the common method of the time and one he was comfortable with, Stone saw no need for the new methods of interpretation which would engage the attention of Alexander Campbell.

Stone's interest in the Gospel, as preached, lacked a sense of the Bible's historical grounding. This approach, also typical of the period, assumed that the Bible spoke to contemporary time:

Old Babylon was ultimately destroyed by the righteous judgment of God. The desolation of Old Babylon was so entire that its ruins cannot be found. The desolation of Mystery-Babylon shall be so complete, that its place shall not be found on earth forever. O! let us hear the warning voice of heaven. "*Come out of her my people,* that ye be not partakers of her sins, and that ye receive not her plagues!" (Rev. 18:4) Too long have our eyes been directed to Rome when we have read of Babylon. Thus have we deceived ourselves. As the spiritual Jerusalem is only known by the character she bears; so spiritual Babylon is to be known in the same way.[13]

This passage shows both pre-historical-critical interpretation (which is to be expected, since historical criticism was concurrently developing in Germany) and Stone's willingness to interpret scriptures in a manner not consistent with the rule of obvious meaning.

Stone's method for understanding scriptures, therefore, was fairly simple. The text was assumed to be clear in itself; it was intellegible to anyone with the aid of the Holy Spirit. His own methodology for scriptural study was basically that of the period, with more emphasis on the text of scripture than on Church dogma. His primary aim was to unite the factioned churches, and to that end Stone was willing to allow differences, as long as they were grounded in a reasonable interpretation of the Bible and not in creeds and confessions:

> We ourselves agree not on every point with brother Campbell, and he in the same points, differs from us. What then? Shall we not fraternize? Shall we not unite as Christians? Shall we quarrel about our difference of opinion like the world before us? Shall we love each other the less? No. We are determined that diversity of opinion shall not be a bar to Christian fellowship.

I stand on the old ground, the Bible, to acknowledge everyone to be my brother, sister, and mother, who does the will of my Father, who is in Heaven. To do otherwise is antiscriptural and sectarian; from which may the Lord preserve us all.[14]

Thomas Campbell (1763–1854)

Thomas Campbell had the most academic training of the founders, having studied at the University of Glasgow from 1783 to 1786 and at "Divinity Hall" from 1786 to 1791.[15] Through his involvement with the Anti-Burgher Seceders, Campbell came to the conclusion that there must be a way to unite the churches on common ground acceptable to all. The answer, it seemed to him, was not something new, but a return to the early church and the text of the Bible:

We have no nostrum, no peculiar discovery of our own to propose to fellow-christians, for the fancied importance of which, they should become followers of us. We propose to patronize nothing but the inculcation of the express word of God—either as to matter of faith or practice;—but every one that has a Bible and can read it, can read this for himself.—therefore we have nothing new.[16]

As I have noted, Thomas Campbell made a distinction between the importance of the Old Testament and that of the New. This distinction was one of value: "And all these were but Old Testament saints, whose scriptures were as far inferior to ours, as moon-light is to sun-shine."[17] For the purpose of the Church, the New Testament was self-sufficient. It was a possibility and, indeed, a duty for each person to read and understand these texts without the aid of "any human interpretation of it."[18] Unlike Stone, he acknowledged that even though the texts were "divinely revealed truths"[19] which the common people could read with correct understanding, there was no reason to believe that everyone would arrive at the same interpretation:

INTERPRETING DISCIPLES

Should it be farther objected, that even this strict literal uniformity would neither infer, nor secure unity of
sentiment.—It is granted that, in a certain degree, it
would not; nor, indeed, is there any thing, either in
scripture, or the nature of things, that should induce us
to expect an entire unity of sentiment, in the present
imperfect state.[20]

However, Thomas Campbell thought that there ought to
be some method for avoiding fallacious interpretations of the
Bible and for reading it properly. In an article for *The Millennial
Harbinger*, he set out a list of pertinent questions for studying any
section of the scriptures:

1. Who is the writer or speaker of the portion read, or
of any particular part of it?
2. To whom is it written or spoken?
3. What historical facts are contained in it?
4. What commands are contained in it?
5. What doctrinal declarations?
6. What invitations?
7. What promises?
8. What threatenings?
Lastly, the why, when, and where those things were
spoken or written, still remain to be considered, and
are circumstances sometimes worthy of particular attention, in order to [gain] a correct understanding of
particular passages.[21]

These questions are the rudiments of what would become literary
and historical criticism. That Campbell did not work them out
well is understandable, since this type of criticism was yet to
arise. While Thomas Campbell asked the usual questions of the
literal text (what is the doctrine, what are the promises, what are
the threats?), of major importance is his concern for context, a
significant difference from Stone's method of listing large numbers
of proof texts lifted out of context. Even in his sermons Thomas

Campbell insisted that nothing be stated that was not clearly intended by a passage's context and historical setting.[22] If his ability to determine the historical setting was hampered by lack of information, he was in no different position than any other biblical scholar of the time, since the great discoveries of the Ancient Near East were still in the future.

Thomas Campbell did not address the questions of writer and audience, whose implications have been of major concern to subsequent critical study of the Bible. While he usually stayed very close to the text and preferred to use the text as literally as possible, without expanding its meaning, he could make interpretations which were not clearly from the text; concerning Matt 28:16, 18, 20, and Mark 16:15, 16, he concludes:

> From this portion of the divine testimony it evidently appears 1st. That the apostolic commission is founded upon the official authority of Christ. 2nd. That it embraces every human creature, without exception. 3rd. That the subject matter of their preaching and teaching is *exclusively* intended for the salvation of the nations. 4th. The apostolic preaching was for a time entirely oral, being addressed only to the ear. Wherefore it was said that "faith comes by hearing." 5th. That when the Apostles had fulfilled their commission, had finished their work, by publishing the gospel and law of Christ to the nations, and had left it fully recorded in the possession of the churches, it necessarily follows, that, henceforth, oral dictation ceased to be authoritative; and, that both the church and the world must, thenceforth, depend exclusively upon what was written, for their instruction and salvation; and consequently, that preaching of proclaiming did, in its just and primary import, then for ever cease; and teaching alone remain.[23]

Thomas Campbell usually avoided this method of inferring meaning beyond the intent of the text, but on occasion he resorted to it. His inclination to favor infant baptism he acknowledged to be such an interpretation.[24]

A fine example of using the Bible as his authority on a given topic is his short article on slavery.[25] This work begins with citations of all biblical passages (Old and New Testaments) where the matter is mentioned. Campbell then reads all the passages, finds what they say about the institution of slavery, and lists these results with the citations noted. He then answers the person who had written concerning his views, first pointing out the possible good results of slavery, using incidents of the Old Testament, and finally condemning the institution as practiced in the United States because American slavery does not meet any biblical requirements of an acceptable form of slavery and because no Christian, on the basis of New Testament rules for what a Christian should be, could approve or practice it. He concludes that slavery will be totally destroyed. The article is untypical of Thomas Campbell insofar as it makes use of Old Testament texts, something he very seldom used in his writings. But it is interesting to notice that he senses the difference between the cultural context of the practice of slavery in the Old Testament and moral teachings inconsistent with slavery in the New. This, of course, reflects to a certain extent his division between the Testaments, but it also shows that he was willing to bend his reading of the scriptures to condemn an institution he felt needed condemning (a step not taken by Alexander Campbell). Throughout the article his points of argument are in his own words, using textual citations only to bolster the major points and not as a series of quotations.

Thomas Campbell's method for interpreting the scriptures was more complex than Barton Stone's. Like Stone, he insisted on reading the Bible for its literal meaning, but he also allowed room for inferential interpretations which could be shown to derive clearly from the texts. He worked almost entirely from the New Testament, which he believed to be sufficient, though he held the Old Testament "as of equal authority with the New."[26] He understood the need to know the historical context of the passage and was willing to negate part of scripture if that was required in order to live according to the New Testament traditions as he saw them. He could read his own views into the texts. Perhaps the most notable example of this, one that governed his life, was his belief that the New Testament showed

> 1. That there was a time when all Christians comprised but one sect. 2. That every one who believed the Gospel which the apostles preached, and was baptized upon a confession of this belief, was esteemed a Christian, and none else. . . . 4. That specimens of the Gospel preached by the apostles, the belief of which entitled to baptism, are recorded in the Acts of the Apostles; (see Acts ii, iii, x, and xiii;) so that we can be at no loss about the ancient apostolic Gospel, the belief and obedience of which had the promise of salvation.[27]

Alexander Campbell (1788–1866)

Alexander Campbell was the most prolific writer among the movement's founders, and the most critically astute. He published the *Christian Baptist* and the *Millennial Harbinger* to help Disciples understand the scriptures and to bring churches together. Though he was the son of Thomas Campbell, he arrived independently at the position of taking the Bible as sole authority for church unification. He had attended the University of Glasgow during the 1808–1809 academic year, and upon coming to the United States, found that his opinions, made while separated from his father, were substantially the same. He proceeded to work on the problem of the divided Church, but his main interest was in understanding the Bible.

Like the other leaders of the restoration movement, Alexander Campbell felt that the average person could understand the intent of the scriptures, but he differed with his father and Stone in seeing the need for extensive work to make the texts understandable. The literal meaning of the scriptural texts might not be the correct meaning; some were intended to be figurative. In

INTERPRETING DISCIPLES

addition, there could be several levels of figurative meaning. To make these matters understandable to the average reader, Alexander Campbell wrote much: in addition to his two journals, both of which had extensive works dealing with interpretation and the meaning of words, he wrote guides for reading the scriptures. In one work he included an eighty-five page section on biblical interpretation, which presented in short form his era's terms and methods of literary interpretation.[28] The second edition reduced this section to a reprint of his method, as explained at the end of the interpretation section in the first edition.[29] His translation of the New Testament included introductions and aids.[30]

Alexander Campbell realized that a proper reading of the Bible could not be accomplished if the text of the Bible before the reader had errors or was unintelligible. He perceived that changes in the English language since the time of the King James Version had made the wording archaic, and some words had been mistranslated altogether. He decided to produce a modern English translation of the New Testament, in which everything would be clear and correspond as nearly as possible to the Greek. The English text he chose to work with was one produced by the combined efforts of George Campbell, James MacKnight, and Philip Doddridge. He corrected their text with the aid of Greisbach's critically sophisticated Greek text, which meant that some passages were dropped or placed in italics to show their doubtful status. For each of these changes Campbell provided annotation to support his decision. In the translation itself Campbell used the method of one English word for one Greek word where this was possible, and he tried to use common English words instead of those which had taken on ecclesiastical meaning.[31]

His method for interpreting the scriptures was different from the other founders'. Campbell had been favorably impressed with the work of Professor Stuart[32] of Andover Theological School, who, like the German critical schools just forming, sought to have the biblical text read as one would any other text. Campbell agreed:

"Where the Scriptures Speak"   83

The words and sentences of the Bible are to be translated, interpreted, and understood according to the same code of laws and principles of interpretation by which other ancient writers are translated and understood; for, when God spoke to man in his own language, he spoke as one person converses with another—in the fair, stipulated, and well-established meaning of the terms. This is essential to its character as a revelation from God; otherwise it would be no revelation, but would always require a class of inspired men to unfold and reveal its true sense to mankind.[33]

Moreover, Campbell was aware that the Bible was written by several authors over a long period of time:

The *Oracles of God*, commonly called the Bible, or *The Book*, including the Old and New Testaments,—contemplated in a *literary* point of view, is the work of at least *thirty-five* independent authors. This volume was on hands for the long period of about fifteen hundred and fifty years; from the giving of the law by Moses, to the close of the vision and prophecy by John the Apostle. Some of its authors were shepherds, kings, priests, fishermen, and of other callings in society. They spoke and wrote in different languages; at least, in Hebrew, Chaldee, and Greek; and lived in countries considerably remote from each other.[34]

Even though he had made the distinction between the Old and New Testaments quite clear in his sermon on the law, Alexander Campbell held that the Old Testament must be understood in order to understand the New:

Remember that the authors of the New Testament were Jews, and well versed in the Jewish Scriptures; and that an intimate acquaintance with the Jewish Scriptures, is indispensable to your knowledge not only of the ancient communications, but to an acquaintance with the style and phraseology of the New Testament authors.[35]

So, more than his father, he used the Old Testament in his works, though his references tended to be restricted to New Testament allusions. He interpreted the Old Testament texts literally and symbolically, as "types" of the New Testament. Thus Campbell could see in Isaac the prefiguration of Christ:

> Observe too, there is no one now to carry the wood but his son, Isaac. It was a strange spectacle—the offering, carrying the wood that was to consume himself. Do you recollect any thing in the New Testament, that is typified in this solemn transaction? It is a picture of our Savior carrying the cross upon which he was to be crucified up the hill of Calvary.[36]

He recognized three levels of Old Testament symbols, depending on the closeness with which they correspond to New Testament narratives.[37] Even with this interpretive method he thought some things in the scriptures were too solemn or mysterious to be made common, and there was a danger of skeptics making fun of "types" by reading them as realities.[38]

Alexander Campbell proposed seven rules for interpreting the scriptures. These were the basis of an "understanding distance":

> Rule I. On opening any book in the sacred scriptures, consider first the historical circumstances of the book. These are the order, the title, the author, the date, the place, and the occasion of it.

> II. In examining the contents of any book, as respects precepts, promises, exhortation, &c. observe who it is that speaks and under what dispensation he officiates. Is he a Patriarch, a Jew, or a Christian? Consider also the persons addressed—their prejudices, characters, and religious relations. Are they Jews or Christians—

believers or unbelievers—approved or disapproved? This rule is essential to the proper application of every command, promise, threatening, admonition, or exhortation, in the Old Testament or New.

III. To understand the meaning of what is commanded, promised, taught, &c., the same philological principles, deduced from the nature of language, or the same laws of interpretation which are applied to the language of other books, are to be applied to the language of the Bible.

IV. Common usage, which can only be ascertained by testimony, must always decide the meaning of any word which has but one signification; but when words have according to testimony—(i.e. the Dictionary)—more meanings than one, whether literal or figurative, the scope, the context, or parallel passages must decide the meaning; for if common usage, the design of the writer, the context, and parallel passages fail, there can be no certainty in the interpretation of language.

V. In all topical language ascertain the point of resemblance, and judge of the nature of the trope, and its kind, from the point of resemblance.

VI. In the interpretation of symbols, types, allegories, and parables, this rule is supreme. Ascertain the point to be illustrated; for comparison is never to be extended beyond that point—to all the attributes, qualities, or circumstances of the symbol, type, allegory, or parable.

VII. For the salutary and sanctifying intelligence of the oracles of God, the following rule is indispensable:— *We must come within the understanding distance.*[39]

The first two of Alexander Campbell's rules essentially repeat the content of Thomas Campbell's. Rule one requires knowing the cultural setting of the passage, since its context has a bearing on its meaning.[40] For the most part, Alexander Campbell attempted to use the rule, but his method tended to be restricted to the data contained in the Bible. This is not because information was lacking on the New Testament period or that of the early Church; indeed, in one work Alexander showed he could treat the classical material on early Church history with careful and balanced reason when he disavowed Josephus's witness for Jesus on the grounds that it was a suspect passage.[41] He knew and used the non-Christian materials from both Roman and Jewish sources of the period. But he usually did not use these materials in his studies of the texts, since he took the Bible to be self-sufficient: "The writings of the prophets and apostles contain all the divine and supernatural knowledge in the world."[42] Even so, he recognized that the various authors wrote in their own words and had their own purposes in writing; thus he was able to list the reasons for the four evangelists' gospels and their differences in intent.[43] Already Campbell had realized that these works were different in nature and purpose, though he did not carry this train of thought out to any degree.

The second rule presupposes his division of history into three ages:

> It must always be remembered by him who would be a scribe, well instructed in the kingdom of Heaven, that the whole Bible comprehends *three* distinct dispensations of religion; or three different administrations of mercy to the human race. These are the Patriarchal, Jewish, and Christian ages of the world.
>
> There are three high priesthoods, viz: that of Melchizedek, that of Aaron, and that of Jesus the Messiah; and under each of these, there will be found a different economy of things. A knowledge of the leading peculiarities of each is essential to an accurate knowledge of any one of them, and the right interpretation of the Bible.[44]

Campbell argued that the ages were separate, and a person living in one could not be acceptable to God in the same way as someone from another. Therefore, passages created in one age would not necessarily be binding in the next. He also noted that everything which is said is not of equal value, since different people have different authority and live in different ages. His views lead to the practical notion that different passages can be interpreted differently.

The third rule restates the idea that the scriptures should be read as though they were intelligible in common speech. This rule allowed Campbell to use the methods of literary study as aids to the reading of scripture and to publish them for others in *A Connected View.* He, of course, made much of this type of interpretation but dealt with the scriptures as sacred texts, never quite viewing them as "other books."

The fourth rule continues the third into the manner of determining meanings of words. Alexander Campbell used not only the occurrences in the Bible but also his education in classical Greek to determine meanings. His work on Greek vocabulary was outstanding.[45] On the other hand, his attempts to use Hebrew were not as successful. He advocated two rules for translating. First, he translated into common words terms which were usually left in anglicized Greek and had acquired ecclesiastical meanings:

> Lastly, we have on the one side avoided the scrupulositie of the Puritanes, who leave the old ecclesiastical words, and betake them to others; as when they put *washing* for *baptisme,* and *congregation* instead of *church:* as also on the other side, we have shunned the obscuritie of the Papists in the *azymes, tunike, rationall, holocausts, pasche,* and a number of such like. . . .[46]

The most notable of these changes was his use of "immerse" for "baptize."[47] Although this was a very successful method in his translation of the New Testament, Campbell strangely does not

INTERPRETING DISCIPLES

use it when dealing with Hebrew; he translated Deut 6:4 as "Hear, O Israel, Jehovah our Aleim is one Jehovah" and "the Lord our God is one Lord."[48] The translation poorly anglicizes the Hebrew word for "god" ("Jehovah" also being a poor, but accepted, anglicization of the divine name); the second translation uses the standard "Lord" for the personal name of God in the Hebrew text. Campbell's translations also appeal to "the Dictionary" as final authority. While he had been educated in the classics, it is clear from his word studies in the Appendix to *The Sacred Writings* that his dictionary is the New Testament.[49] Again, while he did well with the Greek, his Hebrew was very poor: "Of this rib God made the being called woman, which means in the Hebrew tongue, taken out of man."[50]

Campbell's fifth and sixth rules for scriptural understanding deal with the interpretation of "types" and allegories—those passages which Campbell saw as prefigurations of the New Testament and those narratives with multiple intended meanings. His basic concern was not to carry comparisons beyond the author's intentions in the original passage: allowing the acceptance of intentional allegory in the scriptures in certain places does not allow free reign on interpretations. Alexander Campbell believed that finding the central idea of the allegory would clarify its simple (and complete) meaning. Concerning 1 Cor 5: 6–8, he wrote:

> Here it ought to be observed, that the proper or literal meaning of the primary or leading term in an allegory, when ascertained, explains the whole allegory. *Leaven* is here the metaphor of a corrupting principle. One person in Corinth of corrupt principles, might be injurious to the whole church, if retained in it, on the same principle that a little leaven leavens the whole mass. This metaphor being understood, the allegory is easily apprehended.[51]

The argument for the simple interpretation of these narrative forms and for meanings taken in context reflects his critical judgment. Even here, however, he was capable of stretching his own rules, as in the aforementioned interpretation of Isaac.

The seventh rule states the intent of the interpreter to understand the text.

> There is a distance which is properly called the *speaking distance,* or the *hearing distance;* beyond which the voice reaches not, and the ear hears not. To hear another, we must come within that circle which the voice audibly fills.
>
> Now we may with propriety say, that as it respects God, there is an understanding distance. All beyond that distance cannot understand God; all within it can easily understand him in all matters of piety and morality. God himself is the centre of that circle, and humility is its circumference.[52]

Since the scriptures were written in a language to be understood by human beings, the reader's goal is to understand them fully:

> Every one, then, who opens the Book of God, with *one aim,* with one ardent desire—intent only to know the will of God,—to such a person the knowledge of God is easy; for the Bible is framed to illuminate such, and only such, with the salutary knowledge of things celestial and divine.[53]

Alexander Campbell's method, as he set it out, was an extraordinary critical methodology for its time, and later Disciples have pointed to it to show the early critical work of the denomination. Campbell was more critically exact and careful in his work than the other founders, and certainly his method was the most nearly like the work beginning to be done then in Germany. However, it must be pointed out that he never worked out the full importance of his method. Indeed, his interpretations were often governed as much by custom and the methods of the day as by his system. Although he understood the methods of the academic study of texts and wished to incorporate them into his work, he remained always a believer reading "The Book":

> The Bible is a book of facts, not of opinions, theories, abstract generalities, nor of verbal definitions. It is a book of awful facts, grand and sublime beyond description. These facts reveal God and man, and contain within them the reasons of all piety and righteousness, or what is commonly called religion and morality.[54]

Walter Scott (1796–1861)

Scott was foremost a preacher in the movement. Born in Scotland, he entered the University of Edinburgh in 1810 and completed a five-year course of study before moving to the United States. As a schoolmaster in Pittsburgh, he became convinced of the danger of creeds and the need for the Church to ground itself in the Bible.[55] His method of interpreting the scriptures differs considerably from that of the other three founders in several respects.

The most noticeable is his fondness for citing famous authorities, a characteristic of scholarly tomes of the period. He tends to include as much of his accumulated knowledge as he can fit into a given work. He begins his tract on the death of Christ:

> The Scriptures are the sacred literature of the world. On their mysterious pages all the problems of the ancients—Hesiod, Epicurus, Lucretius, and Plato— touching the origin of matter and nature, of things and man, of life, death, and immortality, find an authentic and felicitous solution.[56]

These lists of names occur often; but, in addition, he likes to quote extensively from the famous, including:

> One whose gigantic intellect pierced through all past ages and institutions, and who himself was the most extraordinary hero and emperor the world ever be-

held—the great Napoleon—compared with whose judgment, that of atheists, deists, dualists, tritheists, polytheists, and pantheists is but that of children or madmen.[57]

As this example might suggest, his choice of authorities is not that of a careful exegete. Indeed, his is the least sensible and most complicated of the founders' methods. Behind his method is Sir Isaac Newton's work on prophecy, which influenced several scholars for a time. Scott's reliance is only slightly acknowledged,[58] yet a great portion of his book *The Messiahship* considers the question of the world's ages, using general and often detailed restatements of Sir Isaac Newton's work.[59] While Newton put as much history into his work as he could, Scott added further and more modern examples. This method makes for very difficult reading, and the extraneous material confuses his arguments. However, it should be remembered that Newton was seen as the epitome of the rational, reasonable scholar, so Scott was attempting to bring what he saw as the best of critical scholarship to his work on the Bible.

The center of the Bible for Scott was the Messiah: "the fall of man, and his recovery by Jesus Christ our Lord form a great drama, of which God is the author. The chief personage is the Messiah, and his mighty and subtle antagonist is an archangel in arms."[60] The idea of the Messiah, he contended, was what held the Bible together: the New Testament deals with the Messiah historically, while the Old Testament foretells him.

Therefore, the Old Testament was as useful to Scott as the New, and he interpreted it at great length. Some of it he took literally, but he was much less likely to take the literal meaning, or to be constrained by it, than were the other three founders. He had no qualms about assuming time and creation long before Adam; though the influence of geology is evident, Scott takes even this to be supported by the Bible:

Years ago, we thought the beginning of this world was when Adam came upon it: but we have discovered that thousands of years before that God was forming chaotic matter to make it a fit abode for man, and putting races of creatures upon it, that they might die and leave traces of his handiwork and marvelous skill, before he tried his hand on man. But this was not the beginning, for revelation points us to a period long ere this world was fashioned, to the days when the morning stars were begotten.[61]

Scott's usual method for dealing with the Old Testament was to view it as a source of "types" of the New Testament; this he saw as being in scripture itself:

> Having drawn the line of demarkation between the typical and the antitypical hemispheres of Revelation, that is between the Old Testament and the New, I sought within the limits of the former, for types— points of elevation from which I could trace out with greatest profit to the reader both the philosophy and the logic of Types and Symbols.
>
> I determined to assume no responsibility in my choice either of he [sic] one or the other, but to be guided in this by Scripture, and to reat [sic] as types and symbols only persons and things which the Holy Scriptures pointed out as such.[62]

He presents the standard type/antitype of Melchizedek and Christ.[63] However, he also expands to some strange comparisons, such as his parallel of the line from Abraham to Christ with that from Nimrod to Christians.[64] Yet, because of the importance of history and "types" in the Old Testament, Scott's works, even those on subjects solely of the New Testament, deal with the Old.[65]

If his tracts and books are large, inclusive, and unwieldly, his articles cover the same span of material and remain compact and readable. For example, his article on "True Holiness" begins with reference to the greatness of God and Christ followed by New Testament witnesses (the trinity). Then he defines the term, not by the passages but by the definition of a "great scripturean," and admonishes the reader with a page of examples collected from the Old Testament. Finally, he mentions the resurrection of the end time as the reward for living in holiness.[66] What is significant in the article is that the scriptural passages are not the basis of his definition; that he has gotten elsewhere, from one of his quotations. There is also a list of people cited for holiness; here several scriptural citations form a list unconnected to the argument.

In some of his works Scott takes a series of passages and sets them out so that they can be considered together. On the incarnation, for example, he lists reports by Zachariah, Jeremiah, Isaiah, David, Mary, Paul, John, and the Lord Jesus; he then shows how they are all consistent.[67] He also uses this listing method to present in short fashion a given idea or section of the Bible, such as Adam's sin set out in twenty-four numbered points with their scriptural citations.[68] Even when defining a term he sets forth all the possibilities and then works back to the one he thought correct.[69] This method, if somewhat verbose, at least has the advantage of laying all his evidence before the reader.

Scott had a sense of the historical setting of some passages. Like Alexander Campbell, he worked with a tripartite history of the world, though a different one:

> The Scriptures describe man as having existed in three stages, a natural, a preternatural state, and a state of respite. The first is described as good, the second as evil, and the third as partaking of both good and evil. The good is that in which man existed before the fall; the evil, that into which he was plunged by the fall; and the state of respite is that in which he now exists.[70]

Scott portrayed each of these periods as quite different from the others. Even beyond these broad periods, he made some attempt to set the Bible in context:

INTERPRETING DISCIPLES

If we look at the world at the time God's Son appeared to take our place in law, and consider the political condition of men under the governments which they had framed and adopted, then it was a scene of unmixed tyranny [sic], iron, Roman, imperial tyranny on the side of the rulers; and on the side of the people, base submission and prostitution of all political equality and manly right.[71]

Moreover, he used extrabiblical sources to substantiate his positions and quoted them at length in his texts.[72]

Scott's method, in summation, was not original, nor was it critically chosen. He was impressed by famous names more than by exacting scholarship. His interpretations of the texts were heavily influenced by his ideas on salvation, which he held to be those of the New Testament. More than the other founders he used the Old Testament, but in so doing he made it a preface to the New rather than an individual work. His method of collecting and presenting all the evidence and providing some sort of historical setting prefigured later critical methods, but his actual implementation lacked critical substance. His theory was fairly simple: the New Testament is literal history and the Old Testament is to be read as a prophecy of the future and as "types" of the New. He was seriously attempting to use the biblical text reasonably by employing the methods of and quotations from those acknowledged to be great. Thus, his method—or collection of methods—is somewhat tortured. But for Scott, the sole reason for reading the Bible was for the religious life; he was a preacher.

Reader, obey the gospel; enter, by faith and immersion, his kingdom on earth and you shall receive the Holy Spirit; and, when you do so, walk in the Spirit; cherish and reverence his blessed presence in the soul, by a life and behavior becoming the gospel, and all your better hopes and better wishes will be realized, at the appearing of our Lord Jesus Christ.[73]

Thus the four principal founders of the Stone-Campbell movement used several methods to arrive at a similar result. Interestingly, the "liberal" and "conservative" divisions which have since occurred in the movement have been defined not so much by method of scriptural interpretation as by result. This suggests that plurality of method has been more widely accepted than plurality of interpretation. In short, the factions take to the biblical texts the answers they intend to find in them, which was not the founders' intent.

The founders of the Christian Church revealed both unity and diversity in their biblical interpretation. All held that people not only can but must read the texts for themselves. Yet no two founders used the same method of interpretation. Some of their approaches were highly fanciful, while others were very literal. Yet all agreed that one should aim to understand the texts as they stand. They all created interpretive methods to cover the variables, although none of them held fast to his own rules for interpretation.

These men began by seeking to reconcile Christian churches through the basis of Christian faith, the Bible. They turned from creeds and confessions which they could not affirm themselves and instead would affirm only what was in biblical texts. Each man sought in different fashion to discover what exactly was in the texts. For the most part all were willing to use new ideas and different methods if these helped them understand—at least until they had established their own methods—and each quite differently sought to induce a reasonable and responsible reading of the texts through his particular approach.

Thus, for the Christian Church, the Bible is the sole authority of the believing community. It is clearly wrong, by the church's own tradition, to accept the particular biblical interpretations of its four founders as doctrine; this is exactly what they were against. Moreover, their methods of biblical interpretation allow of no authoritative approach to the texts. Instead, each Christian must individually discover a serious, reasonable, and responsible interpretation from direct confrontation with the

Bible. Each founder tried to develop an interpretive method to aid readers in Bible study, yet no two methods were alike. There, perhaps, may be the overriding principle that the founders established—that a plurality of interpretations need not be divisive but instead could strengthen the Church.

Notes

[1] Barton W. Stone, "The Last Will and Testament of the Springfield Presbytery," quoted in John Rogers, *The Biography of Eld. Barton Warren Stone, written by himself: With Additions and Reflections* (Cincinnati: J. A. and U. P. James, 1847), p. 52.

[2] Thomas Campbell, *Declaration and Address* (Pittsburgh: Record Publishing Company, Centennial Edition, 1909), p. 16.

[3] Alexander Campbell, *The Christian System in Reference to the Union of Christians, and a Restoration of Primitive Christianity as Plead in the Current Reformation* (Cincinnati: Bosworth, Chase, & Hall Publishers, 1839), p. 15.

[4] Walter Scott, *The Gospel Restored. A Discourse of the True Gospel of Jesus Christ, in which the facts, principles, duties, and privileges of Christianity are arranged, defined, and discussed, and the gospel in its various parts shewn to be adapted to the nature and necessities of man in his present condition* (Cincinnati: O. H. DeNough, 1836), p. 1.

[5] T. Campbell, *Declaration and Address*, p. 16.

[6] Walter Scott, *The Messiahship or Great Demonstration, written for the union of Christians, on Christian principles as plead for in the current Reformation* (Cincinnati: Bosworth, Chase, & Hall Publishers, n.d.), p. 10.

[7] Rogers, *Biography*, p. 77. The quote is from the section of Stone's autobiography.

[8] Stone, "Last Will," p. 52.

[9] *Christian Messenger* 10 (1836): 30, quoted in William Garrett West, *Barton Warren Stone: Early Advocate of Christian Unity* (Nashville: Disciples of Christ Historical Society, 1954), p. 126.

[10] Stone, "Last Will," in Rogers, *Biography*, p. 53.

[11] The exchange between Stone and Thomas Campbell is summarized in West, *Barton Stone*, p. 160, and in Lester G. McAllister, *Thomas Campbell: The Man of the Book* (St. Louis: Bethany Press, 1954), pp. 221–25.

[12] Barton W. Stone, "A Compendious View of the Gospel," second section of *The Apology of the Springfield Presbytery*, in Rogers, *Biography*,

pp. 191–221. His method is clearest in the section where he answers objections by reciting quotations, some of which are quite dubious (such as that on faith concerning Cushi and David, p. 210).

[13] *Christian Messenger* 2 (1827): 27, quoted in West, *Barton Stone*, p. 210.

[14] *Christian Messenger* 9 (1835): 108f, quoted in West, *Barton Stone*, p. 193.

[15] McAllister, *Thomas Campbell*, pp. 24–30. This section deals with the higher education of Thomas Campbell and the major influences at the schools during the period he was attending.

[16] T. Campbell, *Declaration and Address*, p. 24 (Campbell's appendix).

[17] Thomas Campbell, "On Personal and Family Devotion," *Millennial Harbinger*, n.s., 3 (1839): 394.

[18] T. Campbell, *Declaration and Address*, p. 3.

[19] Ibid., p. 41 (Campbell's appendix).

[20] Ibid., p. 37 (Campbell's appendix).

[21] T. Campbell, "On Personal and Family Devotion," p. 394.

[22] McAllister, *Thomas Campbell*, p. 146. Thomas and Alexander regularly critiqued each other's sermons concerning the correctness of context.

[23] Thomas Campbell, "The Divine Order for Evangelizing the World," *Millennial Harbinger*, n.s., 3 (1839): 25–26.

[24] This was an admission made by Thomas to Alexander Campbell, recorded in Alexander Campbell, *Memoirs of Elder Thomas Campbell, together with a brief memoir of Mrs. Jane Campbell* (Cincinnati: Bosworth, Hall, & Chase Publishers, 1871), p. 24.

[25] Thomas Campbell, "Elder Thomas Campbell's Views of Slavery," *Millennial Harbinger*, 3d ser., 2 (1845): 3–8.

[26] Thomas Campbell, "Letter to the Editor of *The Gospel Advocate*," in A. Campbell, *Memoirs of Elder Thomas Campbell*, p. 185.

[27] Ibid., pp. 185–86.

[28] Alexander Campbell, *A Connected View of the Principles and Rules by which the living oracles may be intelligibly and certainly interpreted: of the foundation on which all Christians may form one communion: and of the capital positions sustained in the attempt to restore the original Gospel and order of things* (Bethany, Va.: McVay and Ewing, 1835), pp. 15–99.

[29] A. Campbell, *The Christian System* (1839), pp. 15–18. Essentially the content of pp. 96–97 of *A Connected View*, it was reprinted as a tract and was printed in the *Millennial Harbinger*, 3d ser., 3 (1846): 23. It will be discussed below.

[30] This translation went through several editions, beginning in 1826 and with minor adjustments continuing through the editions.

[31] Cecil K. Thomas, *Alexander Campbell and his New Translation* (St. Louis: Bethany Press, 1958), is a study of the origins, method, and reac-

tions to this translation. Much information has been collected in this book, including Alexander Campbell's intentions and methods for translating.

[32] Campbell reprinted an article of Stuart's in the *Millennial Harbinger* 3 (1832): 64–70, 106–11.

[33] A. Campbell, *The Christian System*, pp. 15–16.

[34] A. Campbell, *A Connected View*, pp. 17–18.

[35] Ibid., p. 65.

[36] Alexander Campbell, *Familiar Lectures on the Pentateuch, delivered before the morning class of Bethany College, during the session of 1859–60,* ed. W. T. Moore (Cincinnati: H. S. Bosworth, Publisher, 1867), p. 151.

[37] A. Campbell, *A Connected View*, pp. 72–73.

[38] A. Campbell, Pentateuch, p. 154.

[39] *Millennial Harbinger*, 3d ser., 3 (1846): 23.

[40] He accepted unquestioningly the traditional explanations for the books of the Bible. Thus, for Campbell, Moses wrote the books of the Pentateuch (*Pentateuch*, p. 69), and the apostles Matthew and John were the authors of the Gospels bearing their names (*The Sacred Writings of the Apostles and Evangelists of Jesus Christ, commonly styled the New Testament. Translated from the Original Greek. By Doctors George Campbell, James MacKnight and Philip Doddridge. With Prefaces, various emendations, and an appendix,* 6th ed. [Cincinnati: Franklin and Rice, 1874], p. xxi).

[41] Alexander Campbell, *The Christian Preacher's Companion or the Gospel facts sustained by the testimony of unbelieving Jews and pagans* (Centreville: R. E. Neal, 1836), reprinted 1891, pp. 10–11.

[42] A. Campbell, *A Connected View*, p. 15.

[43] A. Campbell, *Sacred Writings*, p. xv.

[44] A. Campbell, *A Connected View*, p. 94.

[45] An interesting list of the parallels of translated words by Campbell and the Revised Standard Version appears in Thomas, *Alexander Campbell Translation*, pp. 41–42.

[46] A. Campbell, *Sacred Writings*, p. lv.

[47] Ibid., p. 76.

[48] A. Campbell, *The Christian System*, p. 19; mistakenly cited as Deut 5:4.

[49] Campbell argues that for Hebrew there is only the Old Testament and for the Greek of the New Testament there is only the Septuagint beyond the New Testament (*Sacred Writings*, p. viii).

[50] A. Campbell, *Pentateuch*, p. 78.

[51] A. Campbell, *A Connected View*, p. 36.

[52] *Millennial Harbinger*, 3d ser., 3 (1846): 23.

[53] Ibid., p. 24.

[54] A. Campbell, *The Christian System*, p. 18.

[55] William Baxter, *Life of Elder Walter Scott: with sketches of his fellow-laborers, William Hayden, Adamson Bentley, John Henry, and others* (Cincinnati: Bosworth, Chase, & Hall, Publisher, 1874), pp. 37–38.

[56] Walter Scott, *HE NEKROSIS, or the Death of Christ, written for the recovery of the Church from sects* (Cincinnati: Walter Scott, Publisher, 1853), p. 3.

[57] Scott, *The Messiahship*, pp. 152–53.

[58] Ibid., p. 49.

[59] Especially evident is the material on the Latin Kingdom, its breakup, and the Church of Rome. Sir Isaac Newton, *Observations upon the Prophecies of Daniel and the Apocalypse of St. John: in two parts* (London: J. Darvey and T. Browne, 1733), pp. 30, 47, and 75.

[60] Scott, *The Gospel Restored*, p. 9.

[61] Scott, *The Messiahship*, pp. 224–25. The "morning stars" are referred to in Job 38:7.

[62] Ibid., p. 11.

[63] Ibid., p. 72.

[64] Ibid., p. 67.

[65] For example, his work *HE NEKROSIS, The Death of Christ* begins with a long section on Adam.

[66] *The Millennial Harbinger* 1 (1830): 325–28. He wrote articles for Alexander Campbell's journals under the name "Philip."

[67] Scott, *The Messiahship*, pp. 222–26.

[68] Scott, *HE NEKROSIS, The Death of Christ*, pp. 16–18.

[69] For example, in *The Messiahship*, pp. 284–85, he gives twelve translations for *baptizo*.

[70] Scott, *The Gospel Restored*, pp. 9–10.

[71] Ibid., p. 275.

[72] So, for example, he includes as background the correspondence of Pliny and Trajan in *The Gospel Restored*, pp. 393–95.

[73] Ibid., p. 571.

INTERPRETING DISCIPLES

Understanding "The Understanding Distance" Today: The Love Command of Jesus

MARY W. PATRICK

SOPHISTICATED CHRISTIANS have for some decades harbored the suspicion that the Disciples founders sought to restore a golden age of early Christian purity and unity that existed primarily in the minds of New Testament authors. The historical truth of the matter appears to be that early Christians were a contentious lot, disagreeing from the very beginning about Jesus, the Christian life, the organization of churches, the conduct of worship, the role of women, and almost everything else. What we read in the New Testament is part recollection, part nostalgia, and part polemical portraiture designed to persuade the reader to see things the author's way.

An equally sophisticated and no less committed reading of the founding of the Disciples movement might well argue that the founders invite their followers not to a mythical golden age but to what each can read for herself in the Bible. In other words, the restorationism of the founders is based not on historical reconstruction but on biblical literature. For the Disciples founders, to be a Christian is to take the gospel literature as gospel truth.

According to this reading, modern historical skepticism is but the current episode in a long and varied history of faithful Christians carefully reading Scripture. Such careful reading need not be avoided like some dread disease, for it will not of itself turn Christian believers into unbelieving cynics or anti-Christian despisers. Indeed, the historical vision of contentious Christians may be a bracing tonic that makes clear what the founders knew: the Bible is literature.

The literary approach of this essay serves the agenda the Disciples founders proposed. The essay will use modern literary methods to interpret a single passage of Scripture—"You shall love the Lord your God . . . and . . . You shall love your neighbor as yourself" (Matt 22:37, 39)—within a context set by Alexander Campbell and will suggest specific implications of literary method for today's church.

In his essay on biblical interpretation, Lowell Handy quotes Alexander Campbell's seven rules for interpreting Scripture. The last of these states the general contextual principle into which the others fit. The "indispensible" rule, says Campbell, is to "come within the Understanding Distance." To explain this concept, Campbell asks us to imagine a circle; at its center, God speaks, and beyond the circumference of the circle we can't make out what God is saying. Inside the circle we can understand the word of God; outside the circle there is no understanding. The radius of the circle defines the limits of what Campbell calls "the understanding distance."

In Campbell's diagram the circumference of understanding is called "humility." Humility, thus, serves as the criterion for knowing whether an interpreter is within the understanding distance. For purposes of this essay, humility becomes the criterion for selecting methods of biblical study that give promise of bringing hearers within understanding distance. But "humility" is a quaint, old-fashioned word. What on earth makes a method humble? How would you recognize a humble method or a humble interpreter if you met one? Let me propose an answer. Several decades ago the adage was: "to understand a text you must first stand under the text." That principle seems to correspond to Campbell's criterion of humility. Humility, or standing under a text, means listening to the text, being attentive to nuances, structures, tensions.

It is clear that when Campbell used "humility" as a criterion for judging methods of interpretation, he did not recommend stupidity or anti-intellectualism. Quite the contrary; the first six of Campbell's principles represent the best critical methods of his day. Interpretation which stands under the text will take account of all philological, historical, and textual knowledge available.

In biblical studies, the new approaches which seem most likely to bring hearers within "the understanding distance" and to meet the criterion of humility are "literary methods." The term is an umbrella for a number of interpretive methods: rhetorical criticism, redaction criticism, genre criticism, canonical criticism, composition analysis, form criticism, and the source criticism at one time called literary criticism.[1] Use of the term "literary" need not abandon the gains of the last two centuries of historical criticism. Rather, this approach maintains the importance of the text as text. All "literary" approaches agree that meaning is to be found *in* texts, not behind them in events that the texts narrate, nor above them in ideas that the texts embody, nor even in front of them in social settings in which the texts function. The proper function of the historical critical tools of the professional biblical scholar is to interpret texts, and literary approaches focus attention on the communication of the text as a complex whole.

Literary criticism presupposes that texts "mean" more than one thing and that there is more than one doorway leading into a text. The plurality of meanings is not a contribution from the interpreter but is a characteristic of the text. This means that when the reader finds some passage meaningful in a new way, it is probable that that aspect or connection of the text is actually present in the text. There is no text in the whole Bible that has been exhausted of meaning.

Another presupposition of literary criticism is that meaning "spills over" from one passage to another. The meaning is not the private property of the text, nor is it a contribution of the interpreter. Rather, the meaning belongs to the conjunction of texts. Juxtaposing two passages may reveal something unseen before, something which "spills over" from the one to the other. We might even say that meaning accumulates and that the cumulative meaning is greater than the sum of the parts.

To tell someone "what the Bible says" is no simple matter. Because texts have a plurality of meanings that are cumulative, spilling over from one text to another, understanding a text involves interpretation of an interpretation of an interpretation. The process of finding several meanings in one text may be illustrated in the New Testament example of Jesus' command to love God and neighbor. The command to love is found in all four gospels and in Paul. Each of the New Testament writers finds the command full of meaning, yet each finds a somewhat different meaning and applies it to a different kind of situation. As we inspect the plurality of meanings for this commandment we will also observe spill-over from one text to the other and will see the meanings accumulate.[2]

Jesus' Sources of the Love Command in the Old Testament

> Hear, O Israel: The Lord our God is one Lord; and you shall love the Lord your God with all your heart, and with all your soul, and with all your might.—Deut 6:4–5

> You shall not take vengeance or bear any grudge against the sons of your own people, but you shall love your neighbor as yourself: I am the Lord.—Lev 19:18

The command which Jesus gave is composed of these two quotations from the Old Testament. The first is part of an early interpretation of the First Commandment: "I am the Lord your God, who brought you out of the land of Egypt, out of the house of bondage. You shall have no other gods before me" (Exod 20:2–3, repeated in Deut 5:6–7). The behavior which is commanded corresponds to the nature and activity of God. In the Ten Commandments the command to worship God and God alone comes from God's activity on behalf of his people. In

INTERPRETING DISCIPLES

Deuteronomy the command to love God totally, with all of one's faculties, comes from the unity and exclusive deity that is God's nature.[3]

"You shall love your neighbor as yourself" occurs part way through Lev 19, a chapter dominated by the recurring theme, "You shall be holy; for I the LORD your God am Holy" (Lev 19:2). The holiness of God's own nature is the basis for the command, and to "love your neighbor as yourself" partly explains what being holy is like.

Jesus' contribution is to place the two quotations from the Old Testament in the closest possible proximity, by this juxtaposition generating new meanings. When the command to "love your neighbor as yourself" is taken out of its place in Leviticus, it ceases to be one small detail buried in a chapter on being holy and acquires an elevated significance as part of the commandment which is "first of all" (Mark 12:28). Losing its basis in the holiness of God, the quotation acquires a new basis in the unity and exclusive deity of God. It is because God is one— centered, unified, singular, alone—that we are to love our neighbor as ourselves. To love God and to love one's neighbor are not two things but, in some sense, one.

Jesus' juxtaposition of the quotations from the Old Testament has created new meanings, as we have seen. Indeed much of Christian thinking through the centuries has been an effort to understand how the two parts of the command to love God and one's neighbor work together. Some thinkers have emphasized the one at the expense of the other:[4] some have interpreted love of God through love for neighbor; others the opposite. To decide that it was Jesus who put together two Old Testament passages and made them "first of all," as I have just done, is to make a historical judgment. To observe that several New Testament authors have repeated and interpreted Jesus' quotations in a different way is to make a literary judgment. Early Christian authors, like modern Christians, found the command to love meaningful, but each found a different meaning in it. What each has found is, in fact, present in the text.

And one of the scribes came up and heard them dis-
puting with one another, and seeing that he answered
them well, asked him, "Which commandment is the
first of all?" Jesus answered, "The first is, 'Hear, O
Israel: The Lord our God, the Lord is one; and you
shall love the Lord your God with all you heart, and
with all your soul, and with all your mind, and with all
your strength.' The second is this, 'You shall love your
neighbor as yourself.' There is no other commandment
greater than these." And the scribe said to him, "You
are right, Teacher; you have truly said that he is one,
and there is no other but he; and to love him with all
the heart, and with all the understanding, and with
all the strength, and to love one's neighbor as oneself,
is much more than all whole burnt offerings and sacrifices." And when Jesus saw that he answered wisely, he
said to him, "You are not far from the kingdom of
God." And after that no one dared to ask him any
question.—Mark 12:28–34

Scholars customarily say that the Gospel of Mark was the
first gospel written, a historical judgment I agree with both in
general terms and with respect to this passage. Mark 12:28–34
stands at the end of a series of controversy stories that begins at
11:27. In this series several high-ranking questioners confront
Jesus in the temple and attempt to trap him into saying something
for which he can be arrested. At the end of the series we meet a
questioner of equally high rank, a lawyer who is not hostile and
who sees that Jesus "answered them well" (Mark 12:28). Apparently, the lawyer perceives that Jesus is a skilled debater who
shares the lawyer's own convictions about the law. The question
"Which commandment is first of all?" is a simple one designed to
double-check his perception. Jesus responds to the lawyer's question by quoting two passages from a Greek translation of the Old
Testament: Deut 6:4–5 and Lev 19:18b. He concludes by put-

INTERPRETING DISCIPLES

ting the two in a class by themselves, "There is no other commandment greater than these" (Mark 12:31).

The lawyer's reply (Mark 12:32–33) approves of Jesus' identification of the commandments which are "first of all" and of his
surprising and audacious application of them. He begins, "You
are right, Teacher; you have truly said," then paraphrases the two
Old Testament passages. Finally, he applies the commandment by
saying that to love God and one's neighbor "is more than all
whole burnt offerings and sacrifices" (Mark 12:33). Surprisingly,
the lawyer's application assumes that Jesus intends to say something about worship, something against the sacrificial worship of
the temple in which he stands. There is nothing in the quotations
to demand that their meaning be limited in just this way. Indeed,
to set the quotations apart as "first of all" suggests a meaning
which is rather general and can be applied to various situations.
Equally surprising to the reader of New Testament passages, the
lawyer assumes his equality with Jesus. It never occurs to him that
Jesus is the Christ. Rather, he identifies Jesus as a member of a
group to which he himself belongs, a group which shares a conviction that the first of the Ten Commandments stands in opposition to the sacrificial worship conducted in the temple.

Jesus does not repudiate either the application to matters of
worship or the audacity of the lawyer in assuming equality. Quite
the contrary, Jesus observes that "he answered wisely" and commends him with the enigmatic expression, "You are not far from
the kingdom of God" (Mark 12:34). A reader of the rest of the
New Testament will suspect that the lawyer is in for some sur-
prises in the kingdom of God! Nevertheless, this much is clear:
Jesus aligned himself with sophisticated contemporaries, Jewish
and non-Jewish, Palestinian and non-Palestinian, who sought a
God who "does not live in shrines made by man" (Acts 17:24)
and who intended to worship such a God "in spirit and in truth"
(John 4:23).

This close reading of Mark 12:28–34 reveals several curi-
ous and disquieting matters. First, it was not Jesus by himself who
first quoted Deut 6:4–5 and Lev 19:18b as the commandment

which is "first of all." Rather, Jesus is part of a conversation going on around him, concerning the proper interpretation of the Old Testament and its implications for the situation at hand. Here, where we least suspect it, we find again that the Bible is an interpretation of an interpretation of an interpretation.

Second, the command to love one's neighbor as oneself is overshadowed, perhaps even eclipsed, by the command to love God. Only when you think of loving God is it reasonable to interpret the verb "to love" as if it were "to worship." The words in Deut 6:5 which prompt the lawyer to apply the verse to spiritual worship are the words "with all your heart, and with all your soul, and with all your mind," words which point to the inner self. The corresponding words in Lev 19:18b which refer to the self "as yourself" have no part in this interpretation. The joining of the two texts from the Old Testament reveals the partialness of the lawyer's interpretation in Mark 12:28–34. Surely, there is more meaning in the conjunction of the texts than he has found, some meaning which spills over from the one text to the other.

The Love Command in Matthew

> But when the Pharisees heard that he had silenced the Sadducees, they came together. And one of them, a lawyer, asked him a question, to test him. "Teacher, which is the great commandment in the law?" And he said to him, "You shall love the Lord your God with all your heart, and with all your soul, and with all your mind. This is the great and first commandment. And a second is like it. You shall love your neighbor as yourself. On these two commandments depend all the law and the prophets."—Matt 22:34–40

The Gospel of Matthew also contains Jesus' command to love God and one's neighbor but tells the story somewhat differently than Mark. Matt 22:34–40 is a controversy story: the questioner asks his question "to test him" (Matt 22:35). The question sounds innocent enough: "Teacher, which is the great commandment in the law?" (Matt 22:36). But the innocent bait conceals a barbed fishhook; if Jesus answers the question at all he will have said that some commandments are more important than others. It is very important to Jesus' hostile questioner and to the many others of his persuasion that each commandment be just as important as every other.

Jesus understands the hidden agenda of the questioner and places himself squarely against it. He quotes both Deut 6:5 and Lev 19:18b, and between them he inserts two sentences which place these commandments in a category separate from and higher than all the rest: "This is the first and great commandment; And a second is like it" (Matt 22:38–39a).

Jesus' hostile questioner is anxious to preserve the equal importance of each law because he and many others are sure that saying one law is more important denies God's authority behind the rest. Jesus replies specifically to their assumptions. When he places Deut 6:5 and Lev 19:18b in a separate category, he does not deny the importance of the rest. Rather, he places the command to love God and one's neighbor as the key to interpreting the others: "On these two commandments depend all the law and the prophets" (Matt 22:40).

It will be noted that Matthew has remedied several literary flaws in Mark's narrative. First, he makes Jesus, not the lawyer, the focus of the story, the only real actor in the drama and the sole source for revaluing the two Old Testament quotations. Second, he doesn't limit the command to love God and one's neighbor to any single situation, such as worship or sacrifices, but makes it the key to interpreting all Scripture applied to many situations.

It will also be noted that Matthew makes Jesus a literary critic. He specifically ascribes to Jesus three characteristics of literary criticism. First, Jesus takes the position that meaning resides in the text, in this case "the law and the prophets." Second, Jesus allows for a plurality of meanings to the text when he promotes the use of the great command as an interpretive key to unlock Scripture. Third, he encourages the accumulation of meanings around the command to love God and one's neighbor.

Understanding the Love Command

The Sermon on the Mount in Matt 5–7 shows how Matthew sees the love command operating in Jesus' mind. I am proposing that parts of Matt 5 show how the command "You shall love your neighbor as yourself" interprets all the laws that deal with social relations, and further, that parts of Matt 6 show how the command "You shall love the Lord your God with all your heart and with all your soul and with all your mind" interprets all the laws which regulate worship.

Matt 5 contains a series of antitheses: "You have heard that it was said. . . . But I say to you . . ." The first and last of the series should be the most important. The first prohibits anger: "You have heard that it was said to the men of old, 'You shall not kill.' . . . But I say to you that everyone who is angry with his brother shall be liable to judgment" (Matt 5:21–22). The last enjoins loving enemies: "You have heard that it was said 'You shall love your neighbor and hate your enemy.' But I say to you, Love your enemies . . ." (Matt 5:43–44). The verses which follow are careful to deny, in a series of questions, that mutual love is the kind of love required: "If you love those who love you, what reward have you? . . . You, therefore, must be perfect, as your heavenly Father is perfect" (Matt 5:46a, 48).

Several things seem clear about these antitheses. First, Jesus is interpreting the law, shifting from external, legally enforceable criteria in the law to criteria that are internal and spiritual. It is much easier, to cite the example in Matt 5:21–23, to catch someone who breaks the law by murdering than it is to catch someone who breaks the law by being angry. Jesus' interpretation makes it much harder to keep the law and much, much harder to measure how well someone is doing. Second, the key to Jesus' interpretation is "You shall love your neighbor as yourself." Love appears as a principle for making inner attitudes match exemplary behavior, for linking the avoidance of murder in Matt 5:21–22 with a corresponding avoidance of anger and, in Matt 5:27–28, an avoidance of adultery with an avoidance of lust. Third, the goal of Jesus' interpretation of the law is not mutual, reciprocal love.

Rather, Jesus interprets the law to encourage behavior and attitudes which imitate the perfection of God.

When Jesus summarizes his interpretation of the law as "You, therefore, must be perfect as your heavenly Father is perfect" (Matt 5:48), he enjoins behavior corresponding to the nature of God. This is the same correspondence we saw in Deut 6:4–5, where the command to love God is based on the nature of God; here the command to love one's neighbor has the same basis. Thus the meanings of Deut 6:5 and Lev 19:18b converge in Matt 5:40. The basis of Deut 6:5 spills over into the basis for Lev 19:18b. There is some sense in which the two laws have become one.

Matt 6 contains a series of injunctions for private religious practice, under the title "Beware of practicing your piety before men in order to be seen by them; for then you will have no reward from your Father who is in heaven" (Matt 6:1). The injunctions systematically cover the three major categories of private religious discipline—alms-giving, prayer, and fasting—and specify that these acts of piety be done so that the public is not aware of the doer. "When you give alms, do not let your left hand know what your right hand is doing. . . . When you fast anoint your head and wash your face" (Matt 6:3, 6, 17). The section concludes with general injunctions that make the same point, "Do not lay up for yourselves treasures on earth . . . but lay up for yourselves treasures in heaven" (Matt 6:19–20); "No one can serve two masters. . . . You cannot serve God and mammon" (Matt 6:24).

In Matt 6 Jesus interprets laws governing private practice of piety just as in Matt 5 he interpreted laws governing social relations. In Matt 5 the criterion was inner attitude; in Matt 6 the criterion is secrecy. Agreeing with his questioner in Mark, who thought loving God with all one's heart meant a kind of spiritual worship which made public sacrifices and temple worship inappropriate, Jesus is more specific in Matt 6: loving God with all one's inner powers means doing acts of piety in secret, where only God knows what an individual is doing. Piety for public display is service of mammon; only acts of piety done in secret constitute serving God.

These parts of the Sermon on the Mount illustrate the use of the command to love God and one's neighbor proposed in Matt 22:40, where Jesus claimed "On these two commands depend all the laws and the prophets." In Matt 5 and 6 he uses those two commandments as the key for interpreting Old Testament law governing social relations and acts of personal piety. In these chapters the meaning of Deut 6:5 and Lev 19:18b spills over onto other bodies of law, and the meanings in those other bodies of law accumulate around the command to love God and one's neighbor. The phrase "with all your heart and with all your mind and with all your strength" from Deut 6:5 is clarified by "in secret" in Matt 6 and by an emphasis on inner attitudes in Matt 5. The notion that the basis of obligation is the nature of God, a notion which comes from Deut 6:4, is quoted by Mark but not by Matthew; this idea appears in Matt 5 as God's perfection and in Matt 6 in "your father who sees in secret."

The Love Command in Luke

> And behold, a lawyer stood up to put him to the test, saying, "Teacher, what shall I do to inherit eternal life?" He said to him, "What is written in the law? How do you read?" And he answered, "You shall love the Lord your God with all your heart, and with all your soul, and with all your strength, and with all your mind; and your neighbor as yourself." And he said to him, "You have answered right; do this, and you will live."
>
> But he, desiring to justify himself, said to Jesus, "And who is my neighbor?" Jesus replied, "A man was going down from Jerusalem to Jericho, and he fell among robbers, who stripped him and beat him, and departed, leaving him half dead. Now by chance a priest was going down that road; and when he saw him

he passed by on the other side. So likewise a Levite, when he came to the place and saw him, passed by on the other side. But a Samaritan, as he journeyed, came to where he was; and when he saw him, he had compassion, and went to him and bound up his wounds, pouring on oil and wine; then he set him on his own beast and brought him to an inn, and took care of him. And the next day he took out two denarii and gave them to the innkeeper, saying, 'Take care of him; and whatever more you spend, I will repay you when I come back.' Which of these three, do you think, proved neighbor to the man who fell among the robbers?" He said, "The one who showed mercy on him," And Jesus said to him, "Go and do likewise."—Luke 10:25–37

The Gospel of Luke uses the command to love God and one's neighbor quite differently from either Mark or Matthew. In this passage the love command appears as the framework to the parable of the Good Samaritan.[5] The story is a controversy story; the question was asked "to put him to the test." The question, though hostile, is a matter of ultimate importance: "What shall I do to inherit eternal life?" (Luke 10:25).

Jesus' initial reply is to get his questioner to answer his own question, "What is written in the law?" (Luke 10:26). The questioner knows the law, of course: he makes a single sentence out of Deut 6:5 and Lev 19:18b. He takes the commonly accepted procedure of making a single verse represent all the rest and hopes to trick Jesus into saying that these laws are in a category by themselves. Jesus replies approvingly but enigmatically, "You are right; do this and you will live" (Luke 10:28), thereby avoiding the question as to whether he means "do *only* this" or "do this and all the rest which it represents." As a trick this is a failure; Jesus refuses to be cornered.

When the hostile questioner persists—"And who is my neighbor?"—Jesus replies with the story of the Good Samaritan.

Understanding the Love Command   113

The questioner expects an answer which draws limits on the concept of neighbor. Jesus can be accused of breaking the law if his answer is too inclusive. For example, it would be unacceptable for Jesus to include Gentiles in his circle of neighbors. In the story of Cornelius's conversion in Acts 10:1–11, 18, to cite just one example among many, Peter needed a vision and voice from heaven to persuade him that he should include Gentiles in his circle of neighbors: "You yourselves know how unlawful it is for a Jew to associate with or to visit any one of another nation; but God has shown me that I should not call any man common or unclean" (Acts 10:28). Unless the hostile questioner in Luke 10 heard the prohibiting voice of God himself, he would not permit Jesus to include Gentiles in his circle of neighbors.

By telling the story of the Good Samaritan, Jesus refuses to draw circles defining this or that group of people as neighbors. Once again, he refuses to be trapped by a trick question. What is it, then, that Jesus accomplishes by telling the story? Most commentators have said that Jesus refuses to take up the term "neighbor" in "You shall love your neighbor as yourself." Rather, they say, he takes up the term "love" and tells an example story in which the Good Samaritan is an example of loving one's neighbor. I propose that Jesus takes up neither "neighbor" nor "love" from the command; rather, he takes up the phrase "as yourself" and invites the hearer to experience mercy as the victim.

The story line is a familiar one. Someone was mugged, a couple of people who should have helped didn't, and someone who shouldn't have been involved helped a great deal. The story identifies the victim so vaguely that it could be anyone, "a certain somebody," and the mugging is described in sufficient detail for us to feel victimized. From our position as victim we see various passersby. Two are religious professionals who know that Lev 19:18b and other passages in the Old Testament mandate assistance. For reasons we can only imagine they pass on. Finally, someone stops, a disreputable someone from a disreputable group from whom no help is to be expected.

Both the motive and the activities of the Samaritan are described in some detail. "When he saw him, he had compassion, and went to him, and bound up his wounds, pouring on oil and wine; then he set him on his own beast and brought him to an inn, and took care of him" (Luke 10:33–34). As victim we are pleased someone stopped, yet we are also anxious or surprised or horrified that the one who stopped is a Samaritan. As victim we are overwhelmed by the generous care the Samaritan provides. Then, as if to insure among those who follow the fate of this victim that there isn't a dry eye in the house, Jesus makes the Samaritan pile generosity upon generosity: "The next day he took out two denarii and gave them to the innkeeper, saying 'Take care of him; and whatever more you spend, I will repay you when I come back'" (Luke 10:35).

When he finished the story, Luke tells us, Jesus rephrased the question about the definition of "neighbor" from the viewpoint of the victim. "Which . . . proved neighbor to the man who fell among the robbers?" (Luke 10:36). And, having heard the story, the hostile questioner knew the answer from the victim's point of view: my neighbor is the one who helps me in my need.

The final line in Luke's narrative about the command to love God and one's neighbor is "Go and do likewise" (Luke 10:37). Most Christians understand this injunction as an imperative to serve needy humanity, as if "do likewise" meant "Go, find a neighbor and be helpful." The reading I have proposed calls for a different reading of "Go and do likewise" as well. Since the parable begins with "as yourself" in Lev 19:18b and is designed to enable the hearer to experience mercy as a victim, "Do likewise" could then mean "Go, experience life as a victim" or "Go, imagine each event from the point of view of its victims." What Jesus has done is to make "as yourself" the key to interpreting social and political situations.

To imagine oneself as victim does not simply provide the key to appropriate social action, although that aspect exists. Rather, the issue in Luke 10:25–37 is inheriting eternal life. The claim Jesus makes in this passage is that to experience help from the victim's point of view is to be overwhelmed by a mercy that is God's own, a "sneak preview" of eternal life.

One difference between Matthew and Luke is subject matter. Matthew uses the command to love God and one's neighbor as the key to interpreting Scripture, while Luke uses it as the key to interpreting the human world which surrounds it. In both Matthew and Luke the command to love God and one's neighbor yields criteria of innerness, derived from the phrases "with all your heart and with all your soul and with all your mind and with all your strength" (Mark 12:30) and "as yourself" (Mark 12:31). In Matthew Jesus prohibits not only publicly verifiable murder but also private anger, and he promotes only those acts of piety done "in secret." In Luke, deeds of mercy are to be evaluated from the victim's point of view. The same criterion of innerness appears in Mark when the questioner applies the love command to spiritual worship without sacrifice.

Another difference between Matthew and Luke has to do with strategy. In Luke, Jesus could have answered the question "Who is my neighbor?" with an answer from Matthew, "You have heard that it was said 'You shall love your neighbor and hate your enemy.' But I say to you, 'Love your enemies'" (Matt 5:43–44). There are good strategic reasons for answering a trick question with a story that takes out the trick. Aside from strategy, however, the answer is the same: the story of the Good Samaritan can be thought of as a commentary on Matt 5:43–45, a story eliciting a response to the enemy who helps. Both Matthew and Luke understood Jesus to interpret "as yourself" in Lev 19:18b not in a reciprocal human way but in a unilateral way that does not calculate costs and that might well be called God's perfection.

The Love Command in John

> For God so loved the world that he gave his only Son, that whoever believes in him should not perish but have eternal life.—John 3:16

> If you love me, you will keep my commandments.

And I will pray the Father, and he will give you another Counselor, to be with you for ever, even the Spirit of truth, whom the world cannot receive, because it neither sees him nor knows him; you know him, for he dwells with you, and will be in you.

I will not leave you desolate; I will come to you. Yet a little while, and the world will see me no more, but you will see me; because I live, you will live also. In that day you will know that I am in my Father, and you in me, and I in you. He who has my commandments and keeps them, he it is who loves me; and he who loves me will be loved by my Father, and I will love him and manifest myself to him.—John 14:15–21

As the Father has loved me, so have I loved you; abide in my love. If you will keep my commandments, you will abide in my love, just as I have kept my Father's commandments and abide in his love. These things I have spoken to you, that my joy may be in you, and that your joy may be full.

This is my commandment, that you love one another as I have loved you.—John 15:9–12

Beloved, let us love one another; for love is God, and he who loves is born of God and knows God. He who does not love does not know God; for God is love. In this the love of God was made manifest among us, that God sent his only Son into the world, so that we might live through him. In this is love, not that we loved God but that he loved us and sent his Son to be the expiation of our sins.—1 John 4:7–10

The Gospel of John often shows Jesus mulling over topics on which he elsewhere makes statements that may be described as short and snappy.[6] If ever a text was written to be interpreted by what I have called "literary methods," the Gospel of John is that text. Here we have a work that weaves complex patterns of meanings, where words like "see" mean more than one thing and where meanings accumulate. It is not surprising to find that the two Old Testament quotations that form the command to love God and one's neighbor are not quoted directly in John; they are mulled over.

John 14 and 15, sometimes called Farewell Discourses, are meditations on the love command. The points they make are recognizable but, in many respects, quite different from those we have seen so far. In the first place, there is a reciprocal relation in these chapters between loving Jesus and keeping his commandments: "If you love me, you will keep my commandments" (John 14:15). The same reciprocity is also stated the other way around: "He who has my commandments and keeps them, he it is who loves me" (John 14:21).

When Jesus commands "love one another as I have loved you" (John 15:12), the reciprocal relation in the commandment is like that in the first of the Ten Commandments, "I am the Lord your God. . . . You shall have no other gods before me" (Exod 20:2–3). In the First Commandment, the imperative corresponds to the nature and activity of God; in Jesus' commandment, the imperative corresponds to the nature and activity of Jesus. In Deut 6:4–5, the nature and activity of God compel us to love God; in John 15:12, the nature and activity of Jesus compel us to love our neighbors. The meanings of Deut 6:4–5 and Lev 19:18b have converged so that the two laws have become one law, the only commandment Jesus offers in John. The words are quite different, but the point is not very far, I think, from that of Matt 5:48: "You, therefore, must be perfect as your heavenly Father is perfect." The little word "as" carries the weight of the correspondence for both Matthew and John.

A second set of passages in John also exhibits a distinctive understanding of the command to love God and one's neighbor. The relationship in these passages is anything but reciprocal: "As the Father has loved me, so I have loved you; abide in my love. If you keep my commandments you will abide in my love" (John 15:9–10). Here the little word "as" does not bear the weight of a correspondence between the nature of God and some behavior which is commanded. Instead, the word "as" indicates the priority of God's love and what we may call the environmental quality of love. The same set of points is made in John 3:16: "For God so loved the world that he gave his only son that whoever believes in him should not perish but have everlasting life." In both passages God takes the initiative; in both passages God's initiative is characterized as "love." That is what I mean by the priority of God's love. The phrases "abide in my love" (John 15:10) and "Have everlasting life" (John 3:16) indicate the environmental quality of love. John mulls over the command to love God and one's neighbor in the light of the first of the Ten Commandments and decides that God's love creates an environment in which we "abide," a churchly environment in which we are commanded to "love one another."

There are several ways in which John differs from Matthew, Mark, and Luke. The first, of course, is the stylistic habit of mulling things over. The style of John is very distinctive, but so are the interpretive moves. In the first place, John turns Deut 6:5, the command to love God, into the theological principle that God is love. The most direct statements are in the letter called 1 John: "God is love" (1 John 4:8) and "In this is love, not that we loved God but that he loved us" (1 John 4:10). In the second place, John shifts the scope of Lev 19:18b, turning the command to love one's neighbor into a command to engage in intensive reciprocal relations: "Love one another" (John 15:12).

How do the two distinctive emphases of the love command in John work together? How can divine initiative produce human mutuality? The answer lies in the role of Christ. There is a chain in John 15:9 of love imitating love, "As the father has loved me, so I have loved you." This chain of love creates the possibility of an environment of love in which Christians can "abide." Christ's love for Christians becomes a command that contains the environment-creating reciprocity between Christ and Christians: "This is my commandment, that you love one another as I have loved you" (John 15:12). The Christian response of obedience to Christ creates the environment in which Christians abide: Christians love one another with a mutual love in which Christ's love is present.

The Love Command in Paul

No one will deny that Paul thought a lot about love. He was the author, after all, of the beautiful speech in praise of love; his letter to the church at Corinth considers what sort of thing love is and inspects it from all sides. But 1 Cor 13 quotes no command, and certainly no double command. Paul knew the Old Testament, of course, but no one knows precisely how much he knew of what Jesus said. Paul knew both Deut 6:5 and Lev 19:18b, but did he know what the writers of all four gospels knew, that Jesus had put the two quotations together and set them in the forefront of his teaching?

In Rom 13:9 Paul exhibits acquaintance with Lev 19:18b and shows its function.

> The commandments, "You shall not commit adultery, You shall not kill, You shall not steal, You shall not covet," and any other commandment, are summed up in this sentence, "You shall love your neighbor as yourself."

It is clear that Paul thinks Lev 19:18b sums up the Ten Commandments and all Old Testament law. He has made Lev 19:18b the key to the interpretation of Scripture, much in the way that Jesus does at the end of the story in Matthew: "On these two commandments depend all the law and the prophets" (Matt 22:40). The only difference is that Paul knows only one commandment. He fails to quote Deut 6:5.[7]

In the very next verse, Rom 13:10, Paul shows another function of Lev 19:18b, "Love does no wrong to a neighbor; therefore love is the fulfilling of the law." It is clear in this verse that Paul thinks Lev 19:18b is also the criterion for ethical behavior. What is not clear is whether he knew how Jesus used the criterion of loving one's neighbor in the story of the Good Samaritan (Luke 10:25–37) or in connection with loving enemies (Matt 5:43–45).

To ask what Paul knew is to ask a historical question with an uncertain answer. Paul's discussions of love suggest that he knew that Jesus had issued a command to love God and neighbor, but the historical arguments for this hypothesis are weak. A literary approach to Rom 13:8–10 is more fruitful, since literary methods permit us to associate texts without knowing whether the authors were acquainted. A text in one of Paul's letters takes its meaning from the letter in which it occurs, from participation in the Pauline corpus, and from being part of the New Testament, a book which contains works by many authors.

I propose, as a literary exercise, to interpret Rom 12–13 as an application of Jesus' command to love God and neighbor. My initial perception is that Rom 13:8–10 is not isolated but is related to chapter 1, which uses the term "love" in verse 9. From this perception grows the outline of the whole passage, Rom 12:1–13:10, which relates to Jesus' double command to love God and one's neighbor:

> I appeal to you therefore, brethren, by the mercies of God, to present your bodies as a living sacrifice, holy and acceptable to God, which is your spiritual worship. Do not be conformed to this world, but be transformed by the renewal of your mind, that you may prove what is the will of God, what is good and acceptable and perfect.—Rom 12:1–2

This passage encourages "spiritual worship" which will result in transformation "by the renewal of your mind." One is reminded that the questioner in Mark proposed, and Jesus agreed, that the significance of the double command to love God and one's neighbor lay precisely in being "much more than all whole burnt offerings and sacrifices" (Mark 12:33), a phrase which is almost the definition of spiritual worship. If spiritual worship is what the double command of love in Mark and the command to love God in Deut 6:5 are about, then we are entitled to identify Rom 12:1–2 as another interpretation of Deut 6:5.

Just as Rom 12:1–2 interprets Deut 6:5, so Rom 12:3– 13:10 interprets Lev 19:18b, stating the major thesis of one of Paul's arguments at the beginning and again at the end. We have already seen that when Paul quotes Lev 19:18b directly at the end of the section in Romans 13:9, he gives it two functions, one as a key to interpreting Old Testament law and the other as a criterion for ethical behavior. At the beginning of the section, Rom 12:3, Paul writes:

> For by the grace given to me I bid every one among you not to think of himself more highly than he ought to think, but to think with sober judgment, each according to the measure of faith which God has assigned him.

Thinking with sober judgment indeed corresponds to the function Paul gives to loving one's neighbor in 13:9, the function of providing a key to interpretation. But "the measure of faith" is harder to interpret. I used to think of it as a measuring cup in which I could measure how much faith I had, yet that interpretation always made me uneasy because faith is not something you have more or less of. Those who translated the Revised Standard Version (from which I have quoted) may have had the same idea, because the Greek does not require all the sentences in this passage. Now, however, I understand "measure" as "criterion" rather than as "measuring cup." The "measure of faith" does not distinguish quantities of faith; rather it tells you whether your sober judgment is at all Christian or not. What is the criterion for marking a Christian sober judgment? Paul doesn't give the answer in 12:3 but waits until the end of the section in 13:9. The criterion for making a Christian sober judgment is "You shall love your neighbor as yourself."

> For as in one body we have many members and all the members do not have the same function, so we,

though many, are one body in Christ, and individually members one of another. Having gifts that differ according to the grace given to us, let us use them: if prophecy, in proportion to our faith; if service, in our serving; he who teaches in his teaching; he who exhorts, in his exhortation; he who contributes, in liberality; he who gives aid, with zeal; he who does acts of mercy, with cheerfulness.—Rom 12:4-8

When Paul defines sober judgment according to the criterion of love, he uses the image of the different functions of the various parts of the body. He had already used that image in 1 Cor 12, explaining how the image of the body was to be understood by associating it with 1 Cor 13, in praise of love. In Rom 12:4-8 he again associates the criterion of love with the image of a body and its parts,[8] to explain how his readers can apply the criterion of love to their own lives in the church.

Let love be genuine; hate what is evil, hold fast to what is good; love one another with brotherly affection; outdo one another in showing honor. Never flag in zeal, be aglow with the Spirit, serve the Lord. Rejoice in your hope, be patient in tribulation, be constant in prayer. Contribute to the needs of the saints, practice hospitality.

Bless those who persecute you; bless and do not curse them. Rejoice with those who rejoice, weep with those who weep. Live in harmony with one another; do not be haughty, but associate with the lowly; never be conceited. Repay no one evil for evil, but take thought for what is noble in the sight of all. If possible, so far as it depends upon you, live peaceably with all. Beloved, never avenge yourselves, but leave it to the wrath of God; for it is written "Vengeance is mine, I will repay, says the Lord." No, "If your enemy is hungry, feed him; if he is thirsty, give him drink; for by so doing you will heap burning coals upon his head." Do not be overcome by evil, but overcome evil with good.—Rom 12:9-21

The Greek of this passage requires more explanation than that of previous sections. The first phrase of verse 9 does not contain a verb in Greek and can, therefore, be translated properly as a description, "Love is genuine." Many of the verbs that follow are participles that need not be translated as independent imperatives in English but may be properly understood as adjectives which describe what "genuine" means. The beginning of the passage can be retranslated: "Love is genuine, hating what is evil, holding fast to what is good, loving one another with brotherly affection, outdoing one another in showing honor." In this retranslation, the passage describing love in Rom 12 strongly resembles the passage describing love in 1 Cor 13: "Love is patient and kind; love is not jealous or boastful; it is not arrogant or rude. Love does not insist on its own way; it is not irritable or resentful" (1 Cor 13:4-5).

The love described in Romans 12 is of two kinds: verses 9-13 describe love within the Christian community and 14-21 describe love toward outsiders. At the end of Rom 12, in verses 19-21, Paul commends the treatment of enemies, and his admonition corresponds to the commandment to love one's neighbor in Matthew 5 and in Luke. "Never avenge yourselves" corresponds to "love your enemies" (Matt 5:44), while "if your enemy is hungry, feed him" corresponds to what the Good Samaritan did.

> Let every person be subject to the governing authorities. For there is no authority except from God, and those that exist have been instituted by God. Therefore he who resists the authorities resists what God has appointed, and those who resist will incur judgment. For rulers are not a terror to good conduct, but to bad. Would you have no fear of him who is in authority? Then do what is good, and you will receive his ap-

INTERPRETING DISCIPLES

proval, for he is God's servant for your good. But if you do wrong, be afraid, for he does not bear the sword in vain; he is the servant of God to execute his wrath on the wrongdoer. Therefore one must be subject, not only to avoid God's wrath but also for the sake of conscience. For the same reason you also pay taxes, for the authorities are ministers of God, attending to this very thing. Pay all of them their due, taxes to whom taxes are due, respect to whom respect is due, honor to whom honor is due.—Rom 13:1–7

This passage discussing the proper relation of Christians to the state is a paragraph complete in itself, and many have wondered what it is doing here.[9] The fact that it is sandwiched between a description of love in Rom 12:9–21 and an explicit interpretation of Lev 19:18b in Rom 13:8–10 suggests that it may be an example or illustration of the law of love applied to relations with civil authorities.

> Owe no one anything, except to love one another; for he who loves his neighbor has fulfilled the law. The commandments, "You shall not commit adultery, You shall not kill, You shall not steal, You shall not covet," and any other commandment are summed up in this sentence, "You shall love your neighbor as yourself." Love does no wrong to a neighbor; therefore love is the fulfilling of the law.—Rom 13:8–10

I have wondered whether a distinction exists in verse 8 between "one another" and "the neighbor," a distinction between relations within the Christian community and relations with outsiders. Such a distinction would cause Rom 13:8 to summarize the two parts of Rom 12:9–21. But to find such a distinction may be to overinterpret a verse which may do no more than to repeat the summary twice using two sets of terms.

We have already seen that Rom 13:8–10 concludes the argument Paul began in 12:3 and that it restates the thesis of that argument: that the criterion of Christian sober judgment is the command to love your neighbor as yourself. We have also seen at the beginning of the discussion of Rom 12 and 13 that the love command functions in two ways: as a key to interpreting Old Testament law (verse 9) and as the criterion for ethical behavior (verse 10). It may now be said that the mental activity called sober judgment in 12:3 has two equally intellectual aspects: interpretation of the Bible and analysis of the ethical life. For both mental operations there is a single criterion: "You shall love your neighbor as yourself."

Conclusion

This survey of the love command in the New Testament reveals that Jesus' quotation of two Old Testament texts was repeated and interpreted in different ways by different New Testament authors. Each of the interpretations legitimately seizes some meaning that is actually present in the text. I am conscious that in explaining the usage I have relied on many of the exegetical methods familiar to Biblical scholars: source criticism, form criticism, redaction criticism, rhetorical criticism, composition analysis, canonical criticism. While I have used recognizable methods of interpretation, I have called them "literary" because they share certain characteristics: (1) the patient pursuit of tiny distinctions of meaning, (2) the good sense to value the variety of meanings in a text, and (3) permission for meaning to spill over from one text, such as the love command, to another associated text, such as Rom 12–13. The example of Jesus' command to love God and neighbor illustrates all three characteristics of "literary methods."

I have proposed that the ways of interpreting the Bible which I have called "literary" meet the criterion of humility that Alexander Campbell set out in his rules for interpreting Scripture. The person who uses these literary approaches "stands under" the text, attentive to what the text is saying in all its resonances and echoes. Attentive listening of this kind produces deep engagement with the text which may perhaps place interpreters and those with whom they speak within what Alexander Campbell called "the understanding distance." Whether or not an interpreter actually stands within "the understanding distance" and actually hears God's voice remains, in the final analysis, a miracle and a gift of God's grace.

This kind of interpretation has several implications for today's church:

(1) People who come within "the understanding distance" of a text do not always agree. Can you imagine a discussion between the author of the Good Samaritan and the author of 1 John concerning the meaning of the love command? It could be a real donnybrook! The use of literary methods legitimates a pluralistic church—not a tolerant "one-opinion-is-as-good-as-another" church, but rather, an arguing, advocating church. The advocacy of one interpretation of Scripture and the critique of another is not immoral. The struggle over what the Bible means for us today is a struggle mandated by the character of the text itself.

(2) The use of "literary methods" to set hearers within "the understanding distance" of the text promotes a democratic church. The literary approaches that I have advocated do, indeed, require some expertise. But standing within "the understanding distance" is not the sole prerogative of the specialist. What ordinary people see in a text is likely to be a story, a multi-layered story filled with meanings which spill over, out of and into other stories. If lay people can stand within "the understanding distance," then lay people can be trusted to relate to the Bible, to apply it, and to make decisions based on it.

(3) If, as I have proposed, "literary methods" give promise of bringing hearers within "the understanding distance," then it can be said that literary methods of interpretation facilitate church renewal. To *find* oneself in a text in the Bible is to be addressed by God.

What advice would I give to interpreting Disciples, especially to ministers who preach?

(1) Read and preach from many parts of the Bible. A lectionary will help locate texts that aren't old favorites and that may have associations not previously thought of.

(2) Read long passages. If, as I have argued, texts have more than one meaning, then meanings also have more than one textual locus. To preach on peacemaking, read Ps 46 and Is 2:1–5, as well as Matt 5:9.

(3) Tell stories. People don't always get the point when from hearing a biblical story in one part of the service. Don't be afraid to tell it again in the sermon. (I have a vivid memory of a very funny sermon consisting almost entirely of anecdotes about Samson, the man who botched every job God gave him.)

(4) Choose a good translation. Paraphrases are not translations; they are Bible-story books without pictures. As such their usefulness is severely limited. The Revised Standard Version is still best in many ways. It tends to use the same English word to translate a Greek or Hebrew word each time it occurs, it retains the syntax and parallelism of the original quite well, and it is available in a wide variety of printings at various prices.

(5) Don't be afraid to look at the plain meaning of the hard sayings like "take up your cross." If the Bible seems to approve the lifestyle or the ideas which come naturally, then the chances are good that one is outside "the understanding distance."

(6) Beware the "topical sermon." When the idea and the text don't quite fit, you know you aren't "standing under" the text. And that means you lack, for the moment at least, the humility required for coming within "the understanding distance."

Notes

[1] For a survey of the newer methods of biblical study see David Bartlett, "Biblical Scholarship Today, a Diversity of New Approaches," *Christian Century* 98/34 (Oct. 28, 1981): 1090–94.

[2] The literature on the command to love God and neighbor is enormous. Try Victor Furnish, *The Love Command in the New Testament* (Nashville: Abingdon, 1972), Luise Schottroff et al., *Essays on the Love Commandment* (Philadelphia: Fortress Press, 1978), Pheme Perkins, *Love Commands in the New Testament* (Ramsey, New Jersey: Paulist Press, 1982), and Mary W.

INTERPRETING DISCIPLES

Patrick, *The Love Commandment* (St. Louis: Christian Board of Publication, 1984).

[3] In addition to commentaries, see Dale Patrick, *Old Testament Law* (Atlanta: John Knox, 1984).

[4] H. R. Niebuhr, *Christ and Culture* (New York: Harper and Press, 1951) is a familiar analysis of the various ways in which loving God and loving one's neighbor are related to each other.

[5] The parable of the Good Samaritan is the subject of the several essays in *Semeia*, vol. 2 (Missoula: Scholars Press, 1974), where further bibliography may be found. My interpretation is influenced by that of R. W. Funk, *Language, Hermeneutics and Word of God* (New York: Harper and Row, 1966), as well as his contributions to the *Semeia* volume.

[6] The most recent commentary is by Raymond E. Brown, *The Gospel of John*, Anchor Bible vols. 29 and 29A (New York: Doubleday, 1966, 1970).

[7] The most recent commentary on the epistle to the Romans is Ernst Käsemann, *Commentary on Romans* (Grand Rapids, Mi.: W. B. Eerdmans, 1980). The places other than 1 Cor 13 and Rom 12–13 where Paul makes use of Lev 19:18b are Gal 5:14, 6:2, and 1 Cor 9, especially verses 19 and 21.

[8] It would be better to render the phrase in Rom 12:6—translated in the Revised Standard Version "if prophecy, in proportion to our faith"—literally: "if prophecy, according to the analogy of faith." Then "analogy of faith" would be another way of saying "criterion of faith," and an appropriate paraphrase would be "if prophecy, according to love."

[9] Winsome Munro, *Authority in Paul and Peter, The Identification of a Pastoral Stratum in Pauline Corpus and 1 Peter*, Society for New Testament Studies, Monograph Series 45 (Cambridge: Cambridge University Press, 1983), esp. pp. 56–67.

"Vox Populi Vox Dei":
Toward a Definition of Preaching

NEAL KENTCH

W HEN A DISCIPLES OF CHRIST minister stands in a pulpit on a Sunday morning, he or she usually sees two things from that vantage point: an old pulpit Bible opened to the text of the day and, beyond that, the faces of the members of the congregation. It is within this context—in the relationship between that Bible and those faces—that I will attempt to define the act of preaching in the Disciples of Christ tradition.

My purpose here is not to make the task of saying something from that pulpit any easier. So be forewarned. Of late, in my judgment, it has become all too easy to stand before a congregation and either repeat what one has heard others say—be they other preachers or theologians or biblical commentators— or just to say whatever is on one's mind. I realize that other things vie for a minister's time and that some are "just as important as what a minister says from the pulpit." I have heard other ministers say these things, and I know firsthand what they are talking about. But I am of the conviction that contemporary Disciples of Christ need to reconsider the nature of preaching and its centrality in the minister's work.

The Context

To understand the role of preaching in the contemporary Disciples of Christ community, we must first examine the community's biblical framework. In 1 Cor 12:12f and in Rom 12:4–8, the apostle Paul speaks of the community of believers as the body of Christ. According to Ernst Käsemann,[1] to understand what Paul meant by the term "body of Christ" requires us to recover the social and historical milieu in which Paul thought, paying careful attention to what he thought without too quickly "demythologizing" it into the framework of "modern" thought.[2] One discovers that Paul was not merely using an image when he spoke of the community of believers, united through word and sacrament, as the body of Christ. Paul meant just what he said: the community of believers is the body of Christ, the earthly body of the risen Lord.

According to Käsemann, there are similarities between Paul's notion of the body of Christ and Stoic philosophy's "cosmic organism," which permitted one to understand human community as a cosmic body. There are also similarities to Judaism's "corporate personality," in which one person, usually a patriarch or tribal head, was thought to embody the personality of a community. Stoicism's organism and Judaism's corporate personality were not merely images but were thought to be existing realities. The same is true, Käsemann asserts, in Paul's discussion of the body of Christ[3]: when one is baptized or when one participates in the Lord's Supper, one is incorporated into the actual body of Christ, an actual existing reality.

Cosmic bodies and corporate personalities aside for the moment, it becomes more evident that Paul meant just what he said about the community of believers being the body of Christ when one carefully examines his anthropology and soteriology. Again, according to Käsemann, Paul did not think human beings sprang forth into the world with an "essential human nature." Contrary to Bultmann's interpretation, Paul's theology did not recognize an eternal human nature, somehow existing within all human beings in all times and in all places, definable apart from one's relations with the world and other human beings—i.e., apart from one's corporeal or "bodily" relations. Rather, Paul saw one's being determined precisely by those corporeal relations—social, cultural, political, economic, or whatever. Who we are as human beings is given shape and form in our relations with corporeal reality.

Since it is the will of God to redeem all corporeality—ourselves and the reality to which we are related—it is within these relations that God seeks to effect salvation among human beings. God deals with the human race in its corporeality, creating a corporeal sphere of communication through which humanity, in its immersion in the powers that determine its existence, can be shaped and formed by God's grace.

But the question is, "Through what corporeal agency is God able to work salvation?" The earthly ministry of Jesus has been completed, and now, as the risen Lord, Christ can have no communication with the corporeal except through the agency of an earthly or corporeal body; the earthly ministry of Christ cannot continue unless the risen Christ has a corporeal body. For Paul, the community of believers united by the Spirit of Christ is the earthly body of Christ, through which his ministry continues. Through that community, the risen Lord maintains a sphere of communication with corporeal humanity, through which humanity will come under the force and power of salvation.

Since the milieu for such notions as cosmic organisms and corporate personalities no longer exists, modern theologians must question how much of Paul's understanding of the Christian community can be recovered. Although this is not the place for an extensive discussion of what Paul's thought could mean for us, two implications from his thought are still helpful in understanding the contemporary Christian community. First, the Christian community, empowered by the Spirit of Christ, is a means of grace to the world, through which the "forces and powers" of this world are to be transformed by God's grace. Second, the Christian community, empowered by the Spirit of Christ to form and shape our character, is a means of grace to its own members.

Within the first implication—that the church is a means of grace to the world—are two ideas which Disciples of Christ should find very comfortable. The first is the Christian community's participation in the lowly, earthly service of Christ to the world. The body of Christ, an eschatological community anticipating Christ's sovereignty over the world, must remain a part of the world's everyday life since Christ seeks to redeem the world through that community. Only by remaining a part of the world can the Christian community be a means of grace. Second, the idea that the ministry of the Christian community is a ministry of all believers may have been more comfortable for early Disciples than it is for us today. All members of the community have been given gifts of the Spirit, which vary from member to member and which are to be exercised in their everyday lives in the world. Only if the Christian community facilitates the priesthood of all believers can the community be a means of grace to the world.

Paul's second implication—that the church is a means of grace to its members—is very important for understanding the contemporary situation of the Disciples of Christ. One can become a member of the body of Christ only because Christ communicates with corporeal humanity through that body, imparting the Spirit to the member so that the member becomes a "reflection" of the Lord in his or her corporeality. With these two implications in mind, let us now turn to the thought of that movement in which we find our origins.

The pioneering work of Ernst Troeltsch established a sociological typology that distinguishes Christian communities with "church-like" characteristics and Christian communities with "sect-like" characteristics.[4] Although very few Christian communities can be considered purely church-like or purely sect-like, this distinction turns on the question of what is considered "holy" or "sacred" about a Christian community. When a Christian community considers its possessions (its scripture, sacraments, offices, etc.) as sacred or holy, that community is thought to have church-like characteristics, while a Christian community which considers that which is holy or sacred to lie in the heart and mind of the believer is thought to have sect-like characteristics. Communities with a preponderance of sect-like characteristics tend to emphasize early Christianity's radical ethic and, in varying degrees, to make a distinction between their members, who hold to a Christian ethic, and those outside their communities, who hold to a secular ethic. These communities are holy insofar as their members are holy. By contrast, those communities with a preponderance of church-like characteristics consider the institution of the church itself as holy and emphasize early Christianity's universal tendencies. They tend not to distinguish between a Christian and a "worldly" ethic; one need not necessarily be "pure of heart" to be a member, although participation in the sacred institution may engender a Christ-like character in its members as it offers them means of salvation.

The early Disciples movement, although it bore a mixture of church-like and sect-like characteristics, was sect-like in considering the church's sacred elements to lie in the heart and mind of the believer. Two propositions from Thomas Campbell's *Declaration and Address* illustrate this orientation:

> PROP. 1 THAT the church of Christ upon earth is essentially, intentionally, and constitutionally one; consisting of all those in every place that profess their faith in Christ and obedience to him in all things according to the scriptures, and that manifest the same by their tempers and conduct, and of none else as none else can be truly and properly called Christians. . . .

> 12. That all that is necessary to the highest state of perfection and purity of the church upon earth is, first, that none be received as members, but such as having that due measure of scriptural self-knowledge described above, do profess their faith in Christ and obedience to him in all things according to the scriptures; nor, 2ndly, that any be retained in her communion longer than they continue to manifest the reality of their profession by their tempers and conduct.[5]

If one were to ask Thomas Campbell whether the church itself were sacred, he would likely answer: "No, not the church itself. How could it be? The church consists of those who have received the grace of Christ and who, by that grace, confess their faith in

INTERPRETING DISCIPLES

Christ and manifest that faith in their tempers and conduct. These *people* are the church. It is true that the church is essentially, intentionally, and constitutionally one, but that unity is not to be found in a creed or dogma. The unity of the church is to be found in a common confession of Christ and in a common way of manifesting that confession in the way one lives."

This belief—that what is holy about the church lies in the heart and mind of the believer—becomes more evident in Alexander Campbell's writings about church offices. Campbell identified three offices of the church: evangelists, deacons, and bishops, and those in each office were to be ordained by the laying on of hands. But the early movement did not consider the authority of those offices to reside in the offices themselves; there was no "hereditary official grace." If asked whether these offices were, in themselves, sacred, Campbell might have responded: "No. Whatever authority is granted to those who hold these offices is granted to them by the people of the church, and they must answer to the people of the church. The voice of God is not the voice of any 'sacred office,' or of one who might happen to hold that office. Rather, the voice of God is the voice of the people of the church. As I have stated elsewhere, those who hold these offices have the authority of God by the authority of Christ's people, not by virtue of holding an office."[6] Among the early Disciples, those who filled the offices of the church were chosen by a holy people because they, among other things, exhibited that holiness themselves.

With regard to the ordinances (sacraments), Alexander Campbell held a more "church-like" position.[7] According to Campbell, the Lord's Supper and baptism by immersion were instituted by the Lord and were practiced by the New Testament community and therefore must be the practice of the restorationist movement. But, according to Campbell, these ordinances were not practiced merely because of a New Testament injunction. They were an essential part of the new "dispensation" of the church through which God worked to effect salvation and to order human life—a means of God's grace to human beings. This is a "church-like" understanding; although the grace of the sacraments is dependent upon the inward disposition of the believer, that grace is in no other way available for the believer's "enjoyment." Campbell considered the ordinances to be sensible "facts," like those witnessed in the New Testament, and in Lockean fashion, he thought these facts impressed themselves upon one's understanding, thereby evoking appropriate affections within the believer to produce appropriate action or conduct. To quote Campbell,

> When these facts are understood, or brought into immediate contact with the mind of man, as a moral seal or archetype, they delineate the image of God upon the human soul. All the means of grace are, therefore, only the means of impressing this seal upon the heart,—of bringing these moral facts to make their full impression on the soul of man.[8]

Here, again, is the theme of personal holiness, or the obedience of faith. Although the Lord's Supper and baptism were holy in and of themselves, the participant would experience a change of conduct through the working of God's grace.

The early Disciples of Christ movement tended to make a distinction between its members, who exhibited the obedience of faith, and those outside the community, who did not. While the early Disciples did not make this distinction as radically as other groups, the early movement did maintain itself as a distinct Christian community over and against the world by locating its distinguishing, or Christian, characteristic in its ethic or morality—a sect-like rather than church-like characteristic.

It is important to note this distinction about the movement in which we find our origins because, according to Langdon Gilkey, there has been a shift—perhaps subconscious—in American Protestantism's understanding of the Church.[9] Gilkey argues that American Protestant groups in general once distinguished themselves as Christian communities by a particular ethic that their members held, but in the contemporary form of American

Protestantism this is not the case. American Protestant groups can no longer distinguish themselves from the world on the basis of an "unworldly" ethic because, Gilkey argues, the American Protestant laity has adopted the ethics and worldview of the contemporary secular world:

> [W]e can say that the predominant form of the American church is the denomination, and that this is best understood as the *sect* type *within* culture—a new amalgamation of the historic church-type and sect-type churches, raising therefore quite new problems.[10]

Since these Protestant groups (the Disciples of Christ among them) can no longer distinguish themselves from the secular on the basis of a distinct ethic, they are faced with the question, "What is it about us that is holy or sacred or Christian?" Gilkey sees contemporary American Protestantism as taking either of two options in response to this question. Conservative groups choose the first option, distinguishing themselves as Christian communities by preserving the community's possessions over and against the world. For instance, these groups may assert the doctrine of scriptural infallibility versus modern science or may preserve a Christian ethic or morality by appointing the minister, not themselves, as its custodian. Liberal groups choose the second option. They tend to blur the distinction between themselves and the world even further by choosing, whether consciously or not, to identify the highest values of a culture as Christian values. The first option may maintain the community's identity as a Christian community, but it does so at the expense of the community's relevance. The second option may maintain the community's relevance, but at the expense of its identity as a Christian community. The problem, then, facing American Protestant groups—and by implication the Disciples of Christ— is one of maintaining their identity as Christian communities and, at the same time, of remaining relevant to the world in which we live.

But the nemesis of contemporary American Protestantism—

that Protestant groups can no longer distinguish themselves from the secular on the basis of a distinct ethic held by their members—can also be viewed as an asset. Implicit in Paul's understanding of the church as the earthly body of the risen Lord is the idea that the church is a means of grace to the world. Each member is to participate in the lowly earthly service of Christ by exercising his or her gifts in the world. Contemporary Disciples of Christ congregations are definitely in the world and are not separated from it by an "unworldly" ethic.

James Gustafson has characterized the contemporary Protestant congregation as a "voluntary association" whose membership is noncompulsory; church polity is congregational, and activity for moral or evangelical purposes is emphasized.[11] In other words, membership is by *consent* and the decisions regarding what the community ought and ought not do *and the reasons for those decisions* are arrived at through processes, whether conscious or not, of *consensus* within the membership of the community. The church is unique among voluntary associations, according to Gustafson, because it is related to certain transcendent values revealed in a particular tradition. In these consensual processes, members of the community can explain the transcendent values revealed in the community's scripture and traditions in a way relevant to the world. Out of these processes emerges a certain understanding of the self, the world, and God, which enables the community to discern and act upon its responsibilities in the world. Such action can be considered God's grace to the world.

Such a concern for the world is not at odds with the thought of the early Disciples movement. This movement, while differentiating between those who were of the church and those who were of the world, did not make this distinction as radically as some communities. The early Disciples movement was too much a product of the Enlightenment to harbor either disdain or indifference toward the world. Rather, if Alexander Campbell's thought on social ethics is any indication, it expressed a great interest in the transformation of the world's social order. Clark

Williamson offers the following as at least the subconscious belief of the Disciples of Christ:

> Here I shall venture a suggestion: Disciples theology is a quintessentially American theology of sanctification, the goal of which is to baptize or transform the worldly into the spiritual. It shares the theocentric vision of Puritanism, seeking not to build the Kingdom of God in this world but to prepare this world for the coming of that Kingdom. . . . The goal of this theology is not another world; it is the world, other.[12]

Given the notion of the church as a voluntary association, preserving the transcendent values revealed in the community's scripture and traditions in a way relevant to the world depends upon the commitment of the church's members and leaders to those values. Where such a commitment is lacking, those values are lost, and the consensual processes will take place on the basis of other values held by the community's members. Hence, our nemesis returns. What is needed is a conscious recognition that the church is a means of grace to the believer, that the church's scriptures, traditions, and sacraments are capable of creating or evoking within the believer a certain understanding of the self, world, and God. Who one is in relation to the world and to God—one's character—depends directly on how one understands those relations. If the Christian community's scriptures and traditions evoke this understanding in a manner both powerful and true, then they can instill within the believer a commitment to those transcendent values which scripture and tradition reveal. In this way, the contemporary community becomes a means of God's grace to the believer.

Preaching as an Interpretive Act

Within the context just described, it is imperative, if the contemporary Disciples of Christ are to maintain their identity as a Christian community, that the community's scriptures and traditions be preserved in a manner relevant to the world. If the manner is irrelevant, then the Disciples of Christ have nothing to say to their own members or to the world. But if the traditions are not preserved, then the Disciples of Christ have nothing to say that is not said elsewhere; they have nothing "Christian" to say. Thus, what is said from the pulpit is of paramount importance.

What occurs in those consensual processes in which the community's scripture is brought to bear upon the world? To understand the significance of preaching to contemporary Disciples, imagine several members of your congregation sitting down in one of the church's classrooms to figure out, in all sincerity, what a particular passage in scripture means for them. They come to that room with their own understanding of themselves, their world, and God to listen to the witnesses of Christians and Jews now long gone. They come asking, "Is this passage true? If so, in what way?" To answer those questions, they must do two things: they must interpret that passage in terms of their own understanding and thereby render the passage intelligible, and they must interpret their experience of themselves, their world, and God in terms of that passage. They cannot do the one without also doing the other; both movements of this interpretive act occur simultaneously. By asking questions concerning the truth of the scriptural passage, the members evaluate the truth of the passage relative to their own experience. But at the same time, they are asking whether or not the passage can meaningfully and truthfully interpret their experience. In the one instance, they understand the relevance of the passage in terms of their own experience. In the other instance, the passage is allowed to reinterpret their experience and, more than likely, challenge and transform their understanding of that experience. If both movements of this interpretive act are maintained, then the meaning of the passage is preserved, and preserved in a manner relevant to the world. In this way, the community can come to a consensus regarding the ability of scripture to interpret its experience truthfully and meaningfully and to produce a fresh understanding of the self in its relations to the world and to God. If the understanding of those relations is meaningful and true, then those members may well be transformed themselves.[13]

It is a rare moment when something like this occurs in the church, but this scenario provides us with a model for understanding the act of preaching in a contemporary Disciples of Christ community. The task of the preacher is to mediate between the old Bible in the pulpit and the faces he or she sees in the pews; interpreting the text of the day in terms of the congregation's understanding of its experience of self, world, and God renders that text intelligible to the congregation. At the same time, the preacher must allow the meaning of the text to interpret the congregation's understanding of its experience of the self, world, and God, thereby rendering that experience intelligible. The sermon should thereby create or evoke a meaningful and true understanding of that experience.

The "meaning of a scriptural text" is a complex matter which can be understood on two levels. The first is the "meaning of a scriptural text" which is to be preserved by the community. That preserved meaning is what a text meant to the community in which the text was written, or the meaning "objectified" in the scriptural text. The second level is what the text means to the present community interpreting the text, or the "subjective" meaning of the text.[14]

The meaning objectified in a scriptural text is, in some ways, like the fossilized bones of an extinct dinosaur which a paleontologist uncovers. Fossilized within a scriptural text are the remains of what that text meant to the community in which the text was produced. The problem is to recover those remains and reconstruct, in skeletal form, what that text could have meant to the community in which it was produced. Historical, form, and especially redaction criticism can be of great help to the preacher in reconstructing what a text could have meant. Form criticism works on the insight that a variety of preexisting traditions are embedded in the scriptural texts we now have. Collections of stories and interpretations of the event of Jesus Christ, often employing interpretations of Jewish texts and traditions, predate the editor's or redactor's work of composing a written text. The redactor presupposes and transforms these old materials to interpret the event in light of the redactor's situation, but also allows the traditional material to interpret that situation. The result is the written gospel or epistle. Thus, once historical and form criticism have reconstructed these preexisting traditions, redaction criticism is able to attend to the particular ways the redactor or editor reinterprets them in a particular situation. Redaction criticism allows the preacher insight into the particular understanding of the self, world, and God represented by the finished text.[15] This understanding is the objectified meaning of a text, or what the text *could have meant* to the community in which it was produced.

The dinosaur analogy also demonstrates the subjective meaning of a text. The sight of a reconstructed skeleton of an extinct dinosaur makes one wonder what such a creature would look like fleshed out, with blood flowing through its veins. From what we know of animal life, we are able to imagine a living creature with that kind of bone structure. Similarly, the preacher's task is to give flesh to the fossilized understanding of the self, world, and God from a scriptural text and to make it live again, using this skeleton as a framework on which to fit the "flesh" of our experience. It is impossible to know if the resulting "animal" is the same one which lived so many years ago, but since it is built on the same framework, it will bear some resemblance. At least it is a living "creature" meaningful to us. To state the matter plainly, a scriptural text provides the framework on which our present experience is to be arranged and rendered intelligible, and, by doing so, that framework itself becomes intelligible to us. In this way, the scriptural text becomes alive once again for us and means something to us.

Once the preacher understands the objectified and subjective meanings of a text, he or she should not *merely* preach on the abstracted understanding of the self, world, and God without returning to the text. Such a "sermon" would more closely resemble a lecture on theology. Instead, however much such abstractions are necessary, the preacher's sermon should always return to the

INTERPRETING DISCIPLES

text. The Bible, with all of its myths, stories, flights of rhetoric, and the like does not follow a lecture format. As critical studies of the Bible now recognize,[16] the ability of a scriptural text to have conveyed an understanding depended upon the literary form of the text. To understand what a text could have meant, one must understand its literary form, the vehicle used to convey that meaning. Scripture, so understood, is more an evocation than a simple setting-forth of meaning. This suggests that one's sermon should, itself, be *evocative*, calling upon the congregation to "imagine" an understanding. Since the power of a text to have conveyed meaning depends upon its literary form, it seems to follow that the form of the sermon, in order to evoke, should parallel the literary form of the text, capturing, as much as possible, its literary dynamics. A sermon should verge on the poetic.[17]

Although a sermon should be imaginative and call upon the imaginative resources of the congregation, not every whim or fancy is the Gospel. Rarely is the *truth* of what is said from the pulpit addressed. What does it mean when a parishioner shakes the pastor's hand after a Sunday morning worship service and exclaims, "What you said this morning is *so true*"? In what way can a sermon be true? The nature of an interpretive act provides some criteria. A sermon must faithfully interpret the objectified meaning of its text and of the congregation's experience, but this is not sufficient in itself. A sermon is true if it meets these criteria *and* if the members of the congregation can consent to the understanding of the self, world, and God expressed in the sermon. It is possible for an interpretive act to provide an understanding that proves untrue, or meaningless. Sometimes the text may simply not be capable of generating meaning in the context of a particular congregation's experience. At other times the preacher's understanding of the congregation's experience is inadequate, and another attempt should be made. To understand the self in its relationship with the world and with God, the sermon must be true in relation to what the congregation experiences. This statement obviously raises the question of who is to judge whether or not a sermon is true. The truth of what is said from the pulpit is a judgment that belongs to the congregation. If a sermon's particular understanding of the self, world, and God is true, the congregation should be able to give its consent to its truth; as Alexander Campbell once said, "Vox populi vox Dei." (Although it is a valuable consideration, determining what would constitute a consensus is beyond the scope of this discussion.)

But a sermon should not merely mirror, or confirm, a congregation's understanding. As already stated, one's understanding of experience is *transformed* in an interpretive act; something new about one's experience is disclosed. It follows, then, that the sermon should disclose something new about what the members of a congregation experience in their relations with the world and with God. This disclosure must still be true to their experience, but to a part of that experience of which they may not have been aware or fully conscious. And the congregation is still the judge of the truth, whose disclosure will receive the consent of the congregation, if it is true.

My aim in this essay has been to define the act of preaching within the context of the contemporary Disciples of Christ community. In arguing that preaching is to be understood as an interpretive act, I have attempted to address what I think are that community's very real problems and very real possibilities. Understood as an interpretive act, the act of preaching mediates between the community and its scripture by rendering those scriptures intelligible in terms of the community's experience and by rendering the community's experience intelligible in terms of its scripture. What is said from the pulpit is a means of God's grace to the members of the community. Those words can give shape to the members' character by evoking a certain understanding of self, world, and God. From that understanding the members will be able to discern their responsibilities in the world and act appropriately. In this way, the community is a means of grace to the world.

Notes

[1] Ernst Käsemann, "The Theological Problem Presented by the Motif of the Body of Christ," in *Perspectives on Paul*, trans. Margaret Kohl (Philadelphia: Fortress Press, 1971), pp. 102–21.

[2] Cf. Rudolph Bultmann's interpretation of Pauline anthropology in *Theology of the New Testament*, 2 vols., trans. Kendrick Grobel (New York: Charles Scribner's Sons, 1951), vol. 1, pp. 190–227. For a critique of Bultmann's interpretation of Pauline anthropology, see Käsemann, "On Paul's Anthropology," in *Perspectives*, pp. 1–31.

[3] Käsemann, "The Theological Problem," p. 104.

[4] Ernst Troeltsch, *The Social Teaching of the Christian Churches*, 2 vols., trans. Olive Wyon (New York: Harper and Bros., 1960; reprint, Chicago: University of Chicago Press, 1976), vol. 1, pp. 331–43.

[5] Thomas Campbell, *Declaration and Address* (Corapolis, Pa.: Record Publishing Company, 1909), pp. 16–17.

[6] This conjecture is based on statements by Campbell, quoted in Royal Humbert, ed., *A Compend of Alexander Campbell's Theology* (St. Louis: Bethany Press, 1961), p. 171.

[7] W. Clark Gilpin, "The Doctrine of the Church in the Thought of Alexander Campbell and John W. Nevin," *Mid-Stream* 19 (1980): 417–27.

[8] Cited in Gilpin, "Doctrine of the Church," p. 422.

[9] Langdon Gilkey, *How the Church Can Minister to the World Without Losing Itself* (New York: Harper and Row, Publishers, 1964).

[10] Ibid., p. 4.

[11] James M. Gustafson, "The Voluntary Church: A Moral Appraisal," in *The Church as Moral Decision Maker* (Philadelphia: Pilgrim Press, 1970), pp. 109–35.

[12] Clark Williamson, "Theology and the Forms of Confession in the Disciples of Christ," *Encounter* 41 (Winter 1980): 53–71.

[13] Those familiar with the works of Josiah Royce and H. Richard Niebuhr will recognize their thought in my understanding of interpretation. For further reading see Josiah Royce, *The Problem of Christianity* (New York: Macmillan Co., 1918; reprint, Chicago: University of Chicago Press, 1968), and H. Richard Niebuhr, *The Meaning of Revelation* (New York: Macmillan Publishing Co., 1941; Macmillan Paperbacks ed., 1960).

[14] James M. Gustafson, *Treasure in Earthen Vessels* (New York: Harper and Bros., 1961; reprint, Chicago: University of Chicago Press, 1976), pp. 42–45.

[15] For the type of redaction criticism which I find most helpful, see the following: Werner Kelber, ed., *The Passion in Mark* (Philadelphia: Fortress Press, 1976); Werner Kelber, *The Kingdom in Mark* (Philadelphia: Fortress Press, 1974); David L. Tiede, *Prophecy and History in Luke-Acts* (Phila-

dephia: Fortress Press, 1980). Although redaction criticism is restricted primarily to the gospels, other works of biblical scholarship are helpful to the preacher in discerning processes of interpretation, similar to the ones at work in the gospels, in other biblical texts. For instance, on Paul's epistles, see J. Christiaan Beker, *Paul the Apostle* (Philadelphia: Fortress Press, 1980), and J. Christiaan Beker, *Paul's Apocalyptic Gospel* (Philadelphia: Fortress Press, 1982).

[16] See the works of Kelber and Tiede cited in note 15 and Norman Perrin, *Jesus and the Language of the Kingdom* (Philadelphia: Fortress Press, 1976).

[17] The understanding of preaching I have delineated here has much in common with that of Leander Keck. See Leander Keck, *The Bible in the Pulpit* (Nashville: Abingdon Press, 1978).

Teaching the Faith-Story:
The Practice of Religious Education

CYNTHIA GANO LINDNER

THE PRACTICE OF RELIGIOUS EDUCATION among the Disciples of Christ, like any other facet of our life together, cannot be easily characterized or absolutely prescribed, nor should it be. One of the strengths of our church is that we do not dictate the ways and means by which congregations educate their people. By retaining the flexibility to teach in a variety of settings and circumstances, we witness to that dynamic love of God at work throughout all creation. An equally valid strength of the Christian Church (Disciples of Christ), however, is its insistence that its laity be thoroughly knowledgeable about their faith and capable of using the resources of scripture and tradition to minister to one another. Thus, while actual religious education curricula might be negotiable among Disciples congregations, that such education exists—and exists with intelligence and vitality—cannot be left to chance.

It is unfortunate that few Disciples hearts will skip a beat when the words "Christian education" are mentioned. In recent memory, Christian education is not something General Assemblies have argued about, nor have congregations split over it. If you want to set a church board meeting ablaze, introduce infant baptism or once-a-month communion. But if you are anxious to go home early, a motion advocating stronger youth programs will always get you there, for "nobody doesn't like" Christian education.

That observation must say something about Disciples and

about our practice of Christian education. On the bright side, it says that we recognize and affirm the importance of Christian education; on the other hand, it probably also indicates that we could still be more thoughtful as we plan for the education of our congregations. We know that education is important, and we assume that it is better to educate than not to educate. But just why it is important to us Disciples and just how we ought to think about it are questions which might help us clarify our particular vision for religious education.

To understand the Christian Church (Disciples of Christ) and its religious education, we need to review the early development of the church and the discipline, remembering some of the concerns that characterized their early conversations with one another. Two themes—interpretation and community—recur throughout both the literature of religious education and the history of Disciples thought. They suggest themselves as focal images for understanding why Disciples educate, finding the means of education consistent with our purposes, and developing programs that recover and utilize the best resources of our tradition.

Campbell Changes His Mind

In *Big Little School,* Robert Lynn and Elliott Wright remind us that religious education as a distinct entity and specific facet of congregational life was unheard of in the early days of the restoration movement. The believers' education came primarily from the home, informed and enforced through preaching and revival meetings. During the colonial period in the United States, the only institutional, intentional religious education was offered by the local school, where biblical and moral instruction were taught alongside reading, writing, and arithmetic. As expanding culture and warring sectarianism made necessary a stricter separation of church and state, the teaching of religion was excluded from those schools, and the church was left to assume responsibility for teaching the religious knowledge it had always presumed of its people.

INTERPRETING DISCIPLES

During these same post-Revolutionary years, an English newspaperman, Robert Raikes, devised the institution known as the Sunday school. Its purpose was to educate the poor in Gloucester, England, by teaching workers of all ages who did not have the leisure to attend weekday schools. By the end of the eighteenth century, Sunday schools had been imported to America. Part of the impetus for these schools was to prevent juvenile delinquency by educating lower class children, and for this reason the teaching contained a significant moral-religious component. In 1875, for example, the Society for the Establishment and Support of Sunday Schools included in its statement of purpose: "To prevent vice, to encourage industry, to dispel the darkness of ignorance, to diffuse the light of knowledge, to bring men cheerfully to submit to their stations."[1] In the United States the young and zealous spirit of democracy made it distasteful for Sunday schools to aim primarily at keeping the poor in their stations. The schools, instead, recruited children from all social classes and, with the advent of the public school system, shifted their focus from general literacy to the teaching of the Bible and moral behavior.

William Clayton Bower and Roy G. Ross point out in *The Disciples and Religious Education* that the restorationists and the Sunday school movement were contemporaries on the frontier. The first third of the century saw Barton W. Stone preaching at Cane Ridge, Thomas Campbell issuing his "Declaration and Address," and Alexander Campbell publishing the *Christian Baptist.* Meanwhile, the Sunday school movement became an international union, established in 1824, to make instruction in faith and morals available "in every destitute place where it is practicable, throughout the valley of the Mississippi."[2] In practice, the Sunday schools became the powerful tool of frontier missionaries, which at first led Alexander Campbell and other restorationists to oppose the movement. Campbell observed that the Sunday school tended to teach the denominational catechism and fill the minds of children with partisan theology:

> If the children are taught to read in a Sunday school, their pockets must be filled with religious tracts, the object of which is either directly or indirectly to bring them under the dominion of some creed or sect. It is true that we rejoice to see the Bible spread and the poor taught to read by these means, but notwithstanding this, we ought not . . . to suffer the policy of many engaged therein to pass unnoticed, or to refrain from putting those on their guard who are likely to be caught by the sleight of men and cunning craftiness.[3]

From these early days of the religious education movement, Campbell raised what was to become one of its major issues— definition of the term "education" itself. Was it indoctrination or was it enlightenment? Was it both or neither?

Campbell also had several other reasons for his initial rejection of the Sunday school, reasons that are thought-provoking as we analyze Disciples church schools nearly two centuries later. The Sunday school, Campbell knew, involved making religious education the responsibility of a specific group within the church or fellowship body. To him, this meant shifting the locus of religious instruction from its natural and proper place, the home, where Campbell believed that religious instruction should arise, impelled by one's personal endeavor to read and understand scriptures. He reminded parents that their example and teaching were more efficacious than the most learned sermon, for it was Christian living in the home that brought the gospel to light.

> Do not be startled when I tell you that you are, by the law of nature, which is the law of God, ordained to be the only preachers of the gospel to your own offspring. You can tell them in language more intelligible to their apprehension, the wonders of creation; you can, from the living oracles, teach them the history of our race; you can preach the gospel to them better than any Doctor of Divinity that ever lived.[4]

Campbell argued for a personal faith and religious understanding that was individually initiated and relevent, untainted by institutional hierarchies and heresies. Church-based education, he thought, destroyed the individual's initiative to explore the scriptures and replaced it with dogmatism. Much, much later, twentieth-century religious educators would argue once more for such an experience-oriented approach to education, focusing on a person's integrated religious development rather than his or her affirmation of particular theological formulations. As if these arguments were not enough, Campbell also pointed out that the Sunday school society and its near-cousin, the Bible society, potentially undermined the unity of the church. Campbell and the restorationists observed that such societies were not prescribed by the New Testament: "Their churches were not fractured into missionary societies, Bible societies, education societies . . . nor did they dream of organizing such in the world."[5]

For reasons not altogether clear, Campbell's sentiment towards the Sunday school had changed radically by 1847. In a letter to American Sunday school representative A. W. Corey, Campbell admitted that "in the absence of a practical and actually existing scheme of universal education, adapted to the genius of human nature in all its intellectual and moral characteristics, the Sunday school system is one of transcendent importance, having claims upon every friend of God and man in the whole community."[6] Campbell attributed his earlier objections to the sectarian abuses of the Sunday school movement, acknowledging that "our brethren, as the burned child dreads fire, dread sectarianism. But this is, I doubt not, carried too far—especially when it prevents them from cooperating in teaching in Sunday schools. I hold it to be rather cowardice to keep away from Sunday school cooperation."[7] From these comments it appears that Campbell's objection was not to religious education per se but to the institutionalization of that education in an imperfect world. However, he could not deny the success of the Sunday school movement as a tool for education as well as evangelism. We might assume that as he faced the realities of preaching and teaching the Bible on the unschooled, unchurched frontier, he himself came to acknowledge the need for such an organization. Disciples were a Bible people, committed to the concept of a Christianity united by the example of the New Testament church. This vision of Christian unity required that all persons be able to read and understand the Bible for themselves—and the Sunday school's emphasis on biblical literacy lent itself well to these Disciples aims.

In keeping with the early Disciples passion for both local autonomy and Christian unity, the first Disciples Sunday schools were organized along that characteristic pattern of American Protestantism that stressed both separation and cooperation. The Sunday schools were clearly a local phenomenon, encouraged by Disciples leaders but not required by constituent congregations, established and maintained independently of any central supervision within the brotherhood. At the same time, these schools understood themselves to be units of the American Sunday School Union and later of the International Sunday School Association, often using the standard primers distributed by these organizations and supporting their rallies and conventions. Yet as the various denominations established constituencies on the frontier, emphasis on separatism and denominational identity grew stronger. By 1910 the Disciples had established their own Department of Religious Education, as other denominations had done. This development, which seemed so directly to contradict Campbell's concern for the unity of congregational life and work, was deemed necessary for the smaller, homogenous Disciples brotherhood to strengthen the educational programs of local congregations and to highlight distinctive Disciples history and points of emphasis.

The first third of this century saw the heyday of religious education among Disciples, as the Department of Religious Education worked closely with Disciples colleges to make the Sunday school an effective educational agency. To this end, chairs and departments of religious education were established in all four-year Disciples colleges, an achievement that Bower and Ross consider unmatched by any other Protestant denomination. Aca-

INTERPRETING DISCIPLES

demia began to have its impact on the philosophy and method of religious education: "modern" educational theory led to the implementation of "graded lessons" and to the organization of children's education by classes and levels. "Age-level experts" and departmental officers developed curricula, trained teachers, and experimented with highly innovative weekday programs.

The horizons of religious education—and of the entire mission of the church—were broadened by the theological and psychological interpretations of such educators as William Rainey Harper of the University of Chicago and William Clayton Bower, himself a Disciple. Following their lead, the various societies within the Disciples came to understand their work as a unified endeavor with a common goal, and they joined one another to form the United Christian Missionary Society. In terms of the Disciples movement as a whole, this meant cooperation among religious educators, mission educators, and congregational developers, which all hoped would result in a broader understanding of the identity and work of the church. In terms of religious education, this broader vision helped to articulate an educational philosophy that was at once radically new yet well-founded in basic Disciples commitments. Instead of the presumption that the end of Christian education was literacy, and most especially biblical literacy, the philosophy of religious education which began to emerge during the 1920s and 1930s was one in which religion and religious education embraced all of life's experiences. As Bower describes this philosophy of Christian development, "the end of education is the *development of Christian personality* through assisting growing persons to become conscious of the situations which they face in their relations to the real and present world, to understand and weigh their experiences in dealing with these situations with the resources of historic Christian experience contained in the Bible."[8]

Articulation of this understanding marked the beginning of modern religious education among Disciples; today's educators may well recognize themselves in this quotation penned more than fifty years ago. Christian education among Disciples since

Teaching the Faith-Story

that time has paralleled that in most Protestant denominations. Lynn and Wright note that schools of religious education, curriculum development, and experimental programming were all dramatically affected both by the shortage of funding during the Depression and by the faith-shaking events of World War II. In the war's aftermath, the theology, psychology, and methods of "progressive education" seemed naively optimistic and suffered from a lack of popular appeal. The "experiential approach" to teaching and learning required more time, energy, and understanding than the volunteer Sunday school teacher could give; it was, by and large, the approach of certain educational professions and thus was expensive and not easily accessible to the local church. And so, along with much of mainline Protestantism, for the past thirty years we have teetered back and forth as we try to strike a balance between the experiential approach, which appeals to our pervasive commitment to the personal appropriation of faith, and the traditional classroom curriculum approach which addresses our emphasis on biblical literacy and adapts itself to our promotion of lay leadership.

The most recent Disciples efforts in the area of religious education have likewise reflected the cuts in staffing and budget that continue to afflict many Protestant denominations. Few Disciples colleges have chairs of religious education, our seminaries retain minimal resources in the field, and educational endeavors are for the most part local or regional, with the denomination's national organization emphasizing cooperative curriculum development. Working with the United Church of Christ, the United Methodists, several Presbyterian and Reformed groups, and the Episcopal Church, Disciples educators have attempted to develop a "four-track" curriculum to address the spectrum of religious education philosophy, offering material that ranges from a Bible content emphasis to a process (action-reflection) approach. In some quarters, this material is widely used and applauded, usually by those Disciples from larger congregations staffed with religious education professionals.

But from other quarters the curriculum receives criticisms

strikingly similar to those about its interdenominational prede-
cessors published by the nineteenth-century Bible societies: it
may be too general to meet the needs of small, homogeneous
Disciples congregations; it is, perhaps, too technical for implementation by the local church; and it seems too broad to capture
the flavor of the Disciples witness. The latter comment relates to
a question often overheard when Disciples discuss education:
What does it mean to be a Disciple, anyway? It is a significant
question for all of us, and especially for educators. There have
been many changes in Disciples religious education over the last
few decades: changes in the general structure that provides for
religious education; changes in the youth movement, once such a
visible part of our general program; changes in curriculum design. All of this gives Disciples educators ample reason to ask:
How do Disciples educate? What does our tradition offer? What
guidance can be gleaned from religious education theory to make
Christian education among Disciples a more deliberate, more
effective endeavor?

Education and the Interpreting Community
    The themes and problems identified in our historical over-
view are not unique to Disciples nor to religious education theory. But as we encounter them in Disciples experience, these
characteristics become particularly descriptive and may provide a
better understanding of their identity, their context, and their task.
    Perhaps the clearest instance of such a theme can be identi-
fied in the Christian anthropology that runs throughout our history and has a profound—although often implicit—influence on
Disciples religious education. Alexander Campbell writes in *The
Christian System* that "man is an animal, intellectual, and moral
being. *Sense* is his guide in nature, *faith* in religion, *reason* in
both."[9] He describes both humankind and religious experience as
essentially rational in nature, exemplifying the early Disciples'
mixture of Lockean philosophy and nineteenth-century American frontier Christianity. He was a child of the Enlightenment,
and his constituency was that western frontier where liberty was

protected fiercely and unity was deemed essential. This intellectual and cultural environment is reflected in Campbell's rejection of sects, creeds, and divisive systems of belief—all fallible human ideas that deny freedom and encourage intolerance. By contrast, Campbell asserted that the Bible itself "contains a full and perfect revelation of God and his will, adapted to man as he now is."[10] Furthermore, the Bible is a source of revelation that is completely accessible, because

> the words of the Bible contain all the ideas in it. These words, rightly understood, and the ideas are clearly perceived. . . . When God spoke to man in his own language, he spoke as one person converses with another—in the fair, stipulated, and well-established meaning of the terms. This is essential to its character, as a revelation from God: otherwise it would be no revelation but would always require a class of inspired men to unfold and reveal its true sense to mankind.[11]

According to Campbell, then, the hallmarks of authentic Christianity were reasonable faith and faithful reason. Truly mature Christians were those who could understand the scriptures for themselves and apply the wisdom therein to their life experience. Although Campbell's attempts to democratize religion sometimes gave the impression that reading the Bible was solely a matter of individual apprehension, he actually enlisted a rather sophisticated critical method that assumed a knowledge of biblical history and languages. Although it might appear that the Disciples' dismissal of creeds and theology and their emphasis on the popular accessibility of scripture deny the place of formal instruction in the church, in actuality the opposite is true. The importance Disciples place on individual discernment in our reading of the scriptures and our appropriation of the Christian tradition presumes careful and informed study. Campbell's Enlightenment vision of the life of faith calls for Enlightenment methods; his concern for an individual's appropriation of faith is a mandate for a church that teaches, a church that understands teaching to be an obligation central to its life and witness. And by "teaching" we do not mean simply the dissemination of facts. In order to prepare folk for their calling as discerners, as believers who can read and appropriate for themselves, religious education must include education in its purest Latin sense. The Latin root *educare* describes a continuous process of "leading out," in which knowledge of our Christian heritage and understanding of ourselves in the present can be brought to bear on our understanding of what we are to be and do as Christians.

This definition of Christian education is not peculiar to Disciples theory or practice, but it does address characteristic issues and tensions in Disciples religious education. As a way of talking about the process of Christian thought and growth, it strives to articulate the relationship between knowledge of the Bible and life experience, and it reconciles the exaggerated polarity that appears again and again in the history of Disciples religious education. As we have noted, the description of that relationship has been an ongoing task for Disciples: it was central in the restorationist's concern for New Testament Christianity and was at the heart of the early twentieth century's religious education movement, in which the Disciples figured prominently. Contemporary educators often use the word "interpretation" to talk about this connecting of life and faith: the "faith-story (Biblical tradition)," write Jack Seymour and Donald Miller, "is a tool to interpret and test one's existence, in the same way that experience helps one to understand the faith anew in different cultural epochs with different cultural needs." [12] Although it is clearly presumptuous to claim that the Disciples founders envisaged this very process in their own understanding of life and faith, we may justifiably understand our contemporary concern with interpretation as an extension and elaboration of the nineteenth-century fascination with reason, which was so seminal to the Disciples movement. Alexander Campbell anticipated this trend when he developed principles of interpretation that attempted to describe the interaction of reader and text. Thus, Christian education that intentionally facilitates interpretation embodies and clarifies an essential thrust of Disciples life and thought.

Describing the prominent historical theme of interpretation makes visible a second Disciples theme, that of a personal and communal religious life. The story of religious education among Disciples reminds us that as a people we understand ourselves not in terms of theologies and creedal formulations, but in terms of actual history of persons and places, events and organizations. Many of us who grew up in Disciples churches find it almost impossible to separate the memories of our religious development from the development of relationships and communities. Indeed, we Disciples often look to our life together when we are asked to articulate a system of beliefs: "We celebrate communion often, we baptize believers, we invite everyone to the table, we share the ministry." We are, as Clark Williamson observes, a pragmatic people, concerned most with "how things are done, and what one does."[13] Much of our "received tradition," then, is implicit in the "Disciples *form of life* as we have experienced it and been shaped by it."[14] This "Disciples form of life" is practiced by a community—a congregation or cluster of congregations who share common understandings about the life of faith, or who at least share a committed and informed tolerance of their differences. It is from living and worshiping in the Disciples congregation that one "gets a sense" of what issues are important to us—ecumenism, baptism, communion—and of how we resolve them, most often without hearing any explicit *statement* about their significance. Far beyond the church school class or any formalized instruction, then, the locus of education for Disciples, the place where the interpretations take place, is the whole of congregational life.

It seems to me that this phenomenon of the tradition-bearing community is a critical truth in our midst, and we should not overlook it if we are involved in religious education among Disciples. Our congregations function as communities of interpretation. They mediate the faith-story—the gospel and its surrounding tradition—in the context of contemporary culture, and

INTERPRETING DISCIPLES

they provide one another both encouragement and opportunity to appropriate the stories and to minister to their communities and culture. This is the interpretive process, the movement that takes place in our congregations as persons hear and wrestle with God's word, decide on its significance for themselves, and are thus empowered by that word to serve as committee members, teachers, diaconate, and neighbors in the global community. Indeed, in our emphasis on congregational polity and the priesthood of all believers, we rely on a strong interpretive process, yet this process may go unnoticed and unnurtured when we define the task of Christian education only in terms of classrooms and curriculum.

Telling the Story

There are more than a few contemporary writers in the field of religious education who downplay the importance of the Sunday school, curricula, and classrooms; that is not the intent of this article. The sheer persistence of that institution, despite both tremendous cultural odds and the ambivalence of many religious educators, suggests that the Sunday morning classroom does indeed meet a need among our people. I would urge Disciples educators, however, to examine more closely the *function* of the church school: what need, exactly, does it fulfill? what needs are not appropriately addressed there? what other resources in our life together as congregations, in our communities of interpretation, can also educate our people?

In our own history as educators, we Disciples have contributed to the general confusion that surrounds the church school in so many American Protestant congregations. The church school began as a fairly simple Sunday morning Bible class, in a day when that book was read and taught rather straightforwardly. But the Bible class's modern cousin is a diversified church school with an extremely complex set of expectations derived from recent sociological, psychological, and philosophical understandings of religious development. As we have become more aware that the life of faith is a continuous process of growth and change, over and above the intellectual acceptance of a set of propositions about the nature of reality, we have uncritically assigned to the church school the task of guiding this entire interpretive process. This is quite an assignment for a class that meets for an hour a week in one room with limited resources and a volunteer teacher; needless to say, not even the more creative curricula can fill the gaps created by this unlikely pairing.

This question of coherence between theory and practice in religious education has been addressed in a most promising fashion by Jack Seymour and Donald Miller in their anthology, *Contemporary Approaches to Christian Education*. They suggest that one cause of the frustration and ineffectiveness among contemporary practitioners of religious education is the pluralism of theories and techniques produced by the church's dialogue with the secular disciplines. Seymour and Miller present five types or models of Christian education that may help us both to clarify the philosophies implicit in our present methods and to identify the methods that might best realize the particular visions of Christian maturity we embrace. These five primary approaches are religious instruction, faith community, development, liberation, and interpretation, and Seymour and Miller do not argue for the superiority of any one method; they contend only that "a better understanding of the perspectives by which Christian education is being organized will contribute to the shaping of a more comprehensive and coherent practice of Christian education."[15]

The *religious instruction approach* draws its images and methods from the discipline of education. Its goal is the transmission of Christian religious beliefs from the teacher to the learner. The locus of learning is the classroom; important figures are the teacher and the curriculum.

In the *faith community approach*, the locus is expanded to include the whole community. This is a socialization model in which learning takes place chiefly through participation in congregational life and rituals. Such communities are usually small, and community members intentionally share commitments and lifestyles.

The *development model* shifts the focus from a body of knowledge or a community to the religious quest of the individual. This approach relies on the insights of developmental psychology to help students understand and articulate their faith experience.

The social context of life beyond the individual or church community is the setting for the *liberation model* of Christian education, which cites human suffering and oppression as the agenda for the church's educational efforts. This approach uses social analysis and a vision of justice through the Kingdom of God to inform and inspire the mission of the church; the emphasis is on action.

In comparison with the others, the fifth approach, the *interpretation model*, is less easily defined because its locus is less prescribed. It calls attention to an interrelated process of understanding the Christian tradition and to one's present experience in relationship to one another. The concern here is for method, for *how* we make connections between theology and experience, between self and world.

This typology should be especially intriguing to Disciples, given our legacy of pluralism. Undoubtedly, there are congregations that exemplify each of these five models. Seymour and Miller are quick to point out, however, that the five approaches are never really mutually exclusive: if we are careful in our analysis of the educational character of a congregation, we will usually find that a combination of these types operates in each one. Nonetheless, this typology allows us to focus on the unique combinations of approaches that foster the concept of the Disciples of Christ as a community of interpretation.

Most obviously, the approaches of "faith community" and "interpretation" enhance our earlier description of religious education as a process of interpreting the faith-story, a process informed by life in a particular community of believers. In describing the faith community, the typology suggests an important corrective: for effective religious socialization, the community must be intentional about its reason for being and must articulate and pass along the values and beliefs which make it unique. True community doesn't simply happen, nor does it perpetuate itself without plan. Disciples often acknowledge the centrality of community, but the community may have untapped power for understanding what it is to be Disciples and for educating one another and our young. The interpretation model of Christian education reinforces the Disciples emphasis on individually appropriating theology through experience, and it points to the importance of the teacher's role as fellow pilgrim and guide through the educational process. Seymour and Miller observe that such a model requires careful mutuality, as well as maturity: "both teacher and learner are challenged to give up the 'superior' feeling in order to participate in the self-understanding of the other." [16]

Finally, the five approaches help us understand the phenomenon of the church school among Disciples. Seymour and Miller's argument against the complete sufficiency of any one approach demonstrates instead that each relies on others to provide a balanced and complete understanding of education. So it is among Disciples: our strong interest in making meaning for our lives in the community of faith does indeed demand the foundation provided by another approach, the "religious instruction" model. Church schools exist among Disciples churches neither as tools of evangelism, as in the days of the Sunday school movement, nor as scenes of self-realization, as at the height of the religious education era of the thirties. Church schools survive among Disciples today because they tell stories of our faith heritage, and indeed this is a crucial contribution to any community of interpretation.

There is indeed a very important role for the church school among Disciples who are careful and reflective about religious education, provided that we allow the church school to do what it has always done best: to make Christian scriptures and Christian history available to all ages and stages of the faithful. We have erred in the name of psychological understanding as we have tried to make the church school a vehicle of every sort of religious development. As a result, the church school has lost sight of the powerful role it might play in the religious instruction of Christians. Sara Little has argued that religious instruction is a little-understood, much-abused facet of our life as Christians. It is not indoctrination, but neither is it simply an inductive process that proceeds exclusively from life among the faithful. Rather, it is "the process of exploring the church's tradition and self-understanding in such a way that persons can understand, assess, and therefore respond to the truth of the gospel for themselves."[17] Religious instruction tells of the faith-stories that are crucial for the survival of Christian community and for the individual appropriation of faith. Religious instruction is what Campbell wanted for the church when his desire for Disciples to have Bible knowledge outweighed his distrust of the Sunday school movement.

Thus I do not write against the church school among Disciples. But I do advocate a stronger, more self-conscious church school that abandons the concern for "immediate relevance" and entertaining gimmicks and concentrates instead on telling the stories—of the Old and New Testaments, of Christian history, of the Disciples heritage—with integrity, power, beauty, and love. The church school can become powerful again. It has history, experience, and the distinction of being one of the few places in contemporary congregational life where the laity teach the stories of their faith. Religious education theory has spent far too much time and energy deriding the church school; a careful analysis of its power and a real commitment to building on its strengths are long overdue.

We have seen that one reason for the church school's decline was the mistaken assumption that all religious education must happen in that setting. But the concept of a community of interpretation recognizes that religious development—the making and appropriation of meaning, informed by both faith-story and life experience—takes place in all aspects of life and is especially nurtured in the ongoing relationships and rituals of the local congregation. If we are to concentrate on religious instruction as the function of the church school, then we must also be intentional about applying and interpreting the faith-story in the wider church. Those responsible for local Disciples Christian education programs can seize opportunities for education throughout the church's ministry, interpreting all that goes on in the life of the congregation and its members in relation to Christian meanings.

"The educator asks: where in the church's ministry is the pilgrim acquiring an understanding of the Christian texts and faith story? where is the student's personal experience being addressed? where is the cultural experience of each learner being confronted? where is the ministry of each person being supported, encouraged, and assessed?"[18] An outreach committee may become the forum for a discussion of the biblical imperative to social action. An anniversary celebration may become the opportunity for an examination of the workings of God in the history of that congregation and for a discovery of God's purpose for the present. Worship on Sunday morning may involve members of a lectionary study group who have discussed the biblical texts for the day and planned the liturgy or who will respond to the sermon. Intergenerational festivals highlighting the seasons of the church year—Advent, Lent, and Pentecost, for example—may provide the tradition and history to make the community especially meaningful to children.

As I mentioned initially, we cannot prescribe a method for religious education among the Disciples of Christ: our strength often lies in our diversity, and many times our message is about the variety and mystery of our God. Instead, I advocate an attitude of rigorous dialogue, a continuing conversation between our Disciples thinkers and professors, educators and laypeople. Frequently when religious educators of any persuasion talk about method (how we *think* about religious education), we are really talking about technique (how we *do* it), and when we talk about technique we talk about professionals and programs. Those are significant conversations, for we have a job to do, and sharing those resources helps us to do it. But in order for any of us to understand the milieu in which we work and the theological and historical resources with which we can build, we must open up the discussion. The great resources for the theory and practice of religious education are to be found in the struggles of laypersons in our congregations—those who read the Bible and seek understanding, who profess faith and seek understanding, who live in a complex culture and seek understanding, and who participate, sometimes vigorously, sometimes lethargically, in the life of a local faith community. How we reflect on our religious heritage in the light of our experience is the unique creation of each individual's pilgrimage and of each congregation's identity. Disciples have historically been wary of using methods for method's sake and have been guided instead by reason and experience. These are the characteristics of a teaching church—and of a church that has much to teach the discipline of religious education.

Notes

[1] Robert Lynn and Elliott Wright, eds., *The Big Little School* (New York: Harper and Row, 1971), p. 6.

[2] Ibid., p. 18.

[3] William Clayton Bower and Roy G. Ross, *The Disciples and Religious Education* (St. Louis: Bethany Press, 1936), p. 26.

[4] Ibid., p. 27.

[5] Ibid., p. 25.

[6] Ibid., p. 28.

[7] Ibid.

[8] Ibid., p. 42.

[9] Alexander Campbell, *The Christian System* (reprint, Nashville: Gospel Advocate Company, 1874), p. 3.

[10] Ibid.

[11] Ibid.

[12] Jack Seymour and Donald Miller, eds., *Contemporary Approaches in Christian Education* (Nashville: Abingdon, 1982), p. 124.

[13] Clark Williamson, "Theology and Forms of Confession in the Disciples of Christ," *Encounter* 41 (Winter 1980): 57.

[14] Ibid., p. 71.

[15] Seymour and Miller, *Contemporary Approaches*, p. 11.

[16] Ibid., p. 136.

[17] Ibid., p. 41.

[18] Ibid., p. 142.

Moral Praxis and Pastoral Care: A Disciples Perspective

K. BRYNOLF LYON

ONE MIGHT JUSTIFIABLY BE SUSPICIOUS of an essay that purports to deal with pastoral care from a "Disciples perspective." There is certainly little within the Disciples practice of pastoral care that could be considered unique to the Disciples tradition. Indeed, the inappropriateness of such discussion has been tacitly recognized by the Panel of Scholars volumes, which contain no articles addressed exclusively or primarily to pastoral care, and by the major histories of pastoral care, which most frequently do not even mention the Disciples. This situation may strike some as unfortunate, requiring rectification, but one should not, I think, look for an argument where none exists. On the whole, the Disciples have done the same things in pastoral care as other mainline Protestant denominations.

This much should not strike us as particularly surprising. The issues which led to the formation of the Disciples were not, for the most part, those of pastoral care, but they *were* concerns of practical theology. In other words, the matter of Christian divisiveness was not primarily a systematic or even foundational theological concern, but rather a concern about the appropriate meaning and form of Christian praxis.

Praxis, in this context, refers to the mutually formative relationship between what we do and who we are, and the ways in which we reflect on ourselves and our world. *Moral* praxis designates the moral dimension of all praxis; in pastoral care, it is the moral character of the relationship between what we do and who we are, and the ways in which we reflect on ourselves and our world in the processes of pastoral care.

The factors that led to the formation of the Disciples movement certainly have implications for understanding the basic focus and inherent tensions of pastoral care. Rather than attempt to deal with pastoral care as a whole, I will focus on one particular theme that is receiving increased attention today: the relationship of pastoral care and ethics. The basic context of this relationship is the Christian community, which has traditionally been concerned with understanding, interpreting, and living the religiously and morally good life, yet has also perceived as one of its tasks the pastoral care of Christian individuals and human beings generally. What, we may wonder, is the relationship between certain religious and moral ideals and the wish to care for persons? To what extent, in other words, do these two tasks conflict with or reinforce one another?

Ethics and Pastoral Care

There are at least four ways to conceptualize the relationship of ethics and pastoral care: an exclusivist approach, a reductionist approach, an external relations approach, and an internal relations approach. Each merits some definition in the context of contemporary Christianity:

The *exclusivist approach* assumes that there is no necessary relationship between ethics and pastoral care, though there may be some mingling in practice. Although those who adhere to the exclusivist approach may claim that the Christian community's moral ideals (for example, a concern for the health or emotional maturity of persons) may provide the initial impetus in pastoral care, the exclusivist approach itself is characterized by separating moral praxis and the pastoral care process. Such a conception of pastoral care frequently rests on certain psychotherapeutic disciplines that are themselves understood, in their theoretical dimensions, as value-free science. Thus, the exclusivist approach is grounded in a philosophy of the human sciences whose aim is value-neutrality. This approach is often pursued with the best intentions, given the quite proper concern with moralistic intrusions into the pastoral care given. Yet it is becoming increasingly clear both that psychotherapeutic theory is not ethically naive and that a value-neutral philosophy of the human sciences merely obfuscates the value-commitments such sciences actually entail.[1]

The *reductionist approach* goes to the other extreme by claiming that pastoral care is and can be nothing but ethics. What we are doing in pastoral care is simply trying to impose a new moral framework or attitude, i.e., imposing the moral praxis of the pastoral caregiver upon the subjects of pastoral care. Those who hold this position consider the human sciences stance as nothing but subjective/emotive moral pronouncements under the guise of objectivity. Although the reductionist approach highlights the inevitable moral praxis of the pastoral care process, it threatens to devolve into a radical moral relativism or to become a merely moralistic tool—to become exactly what the exclusivist approach seeks to protect against.

The exclusivist and reductionist approaches highlight important dimensions of the relationship of ethics and pastoral care. Each, however, seems too one-sided. The other two approaches seek a mediating ground between these two extremes. The *external relations approach*, for example, perceives pastoral care as facilitating the growth and development of moral decision making in an individual, group, or community. While pastoral care itself is seen as having no particularly ethical stance, it aids ethical decision making by enabling the individual or group to become more aware of personal needs and the needs of others. I call this an external relations approach because pastoral care is a means to an end which has a purely formal ethical or moral character.

There is much to recommend the external relations perspective in pastoral care. Certainly, this approach attempts to safeguard the pastoral care process from simple moralism and allows us to take seriously the particular needs of the individual or community. There are indeed times with certain individuals and groups when we can appropriately conceive the *telos* of pastoral care as better moral decision making. Yet the external relations

INTERPRETING DISCIPLES

approach asks us to understand that what we do in pastoral care is only tangentially related to ethics, when in fact, the type of development and growth that our pastoral care facilitates is the formation of moral praxis itself. In other words, it is not simply the end result that has moral substance, but the very process itself, since within that process, character is formed, reformed, or transformed.

Thus, I believe a more adequate understanding of the relationship of ethics and pastoral care is to be found in the *internal relations approach,* in which pastoral care is intrinsically related to ethics, though not simply reducible to it. In other words, the moral dimension to pastoral care is always present but in no way exhausts its nature. To illustrate the internal relations perspective, it may be helpful to identify what constitutes the fundamental character of pastoral care.

Pastoral Care and Change

The nature and characteristics of pastoral care may seem intuitively obvious to many, but it is by no means easy to define concisely the variety of functions historically included under the rubric of pastoral care. Equating pastoral care and pastoral counseling has made the task all the more difficult today. Clearly pastoral care includes more than counseling or therapy. Don Browning has provided a helpful twofold definition of pastoral care: "(1) the incorporation of members and their discipline in the group goals and practices of the church, and (2) the assistance of persons in handling certain crises and conflicts having to do with existential, developmental, interpersonal, and social strains."[2] Thus pastoral care, through the effort to incorporate individuals into the "group goals and practices of the church" and to help troubled persons, is a process that facilitates change in the action of individuals, groups, and communities.[3]

The problem that arises at this point, of course, is the meaning of *change,* which can be characterized any number of ways. We could look at change in neural patterns and chemical reactions, for instance, or simply examine gross motor movement.

These would be legitimate and, in their context, appropriate ways of thinking about the nature of human change. But understanding change in its moral dimension includes recognizing the intentional nature of human action. That people have purposes, goals, and desires is fundamental to our commonsense understanding of ourselves and one another. While behavioristic approaches to the study of action have wished to eliminate such intentional language, it not only persists in popular usage but has received renewed emphasis in both human science and philosophical interpretations of action.[4] To understand how intentional action and human wants affect pastoral care, it will be helpful at this point to make a few preliminary comments on the general nature of wants, those basic human motivations that we seek out and act on. The notion of a "want" does not refer simply to what we *experience* ourselves as desiring. While wants may be more or less directly biological, they are also multiple: we have not just one or two fundamental ones, but rather a whole host of wants which may at times conflict one with another.[5]

As we develop, our wants become structured in certain ways. First, they may be arranged in some hierarchy on the basis of biological, psychological, and sociohistorical importance to our development. Thus, for example, certain sociohistorical factors, such as ethnicity, may press toward the expression of some wants more urgently than others. Likewise, some basic developmental factors, such as sexuality and aging, may bring certain wants to the fore at particular moments in the life cycle. At any rate, wants may be structured in terms of their relative importance or their relative strength.

Wants may also be structured according to particular forms in which we experience them; they are not always experienced simply in and of themselves. The forms our wants take depend upon biological, psychological, and sociohistorical factors. For example, we do not just want food, we want, say, pizza; we do not just want a relationship, we want a relationship with a particular type of person.[6]

Finally, the structuring of wants can be understood as the

INTERPRETING DISCIPLES

characteristic *patterns* we develop to gain our wants. These patterns form not only the overt action, but also the predisposing experience which leads to action. While certain patterns are conscious (we know and recognize they are there), many are unconscious and may at times be expressed in maladaptive or harmful ways. Just as wants can assume hierarchies and particular manifestations, so they can be patterned on the basis of biological, psychological, and sociohistorical factors. For example, early interaction with parents or significant others may influence our patterning of wants, and cultural differences will influence economic, political, and technological characteristics which channel the individual pattern.

Change occurs when these wants are restructured through a reordered hierarchy of wants, a shift of particular wants to something new or different, or some modification of the characteristic patterns for fulfilling wants. The underlying function of pastoral care is to facilitate the restructuring of wants in one or more of these ways.[7]

Moral Praxis and Change

There may seem little that could reasonably be called a moral or ethical element in the process of change characterized here. This is due in part to the dominant contemporary understanding of morality as abstract, contractual rules governing social or community interchange. This approach to ethics, often called "contractarianism,"[8] claims that the legitimate domain of ethics is limited to these contractual rules of social order and justice. If the nature of morality is, in fact, so limited, then surely the process of change can only be related to it tangentially. Yet there is every reason to believe that contractarianism, while an important aspect of ethics, is not the entirety. Another tradition in ethics is concerned not simply with the morally neutral contractual rules under which humans may live, but with the content, nature, and character of human living itself. This approach, often called "perfectionism,"[9] claims that morality is concerned not only with the rules governing social organization, but with the completion, fulfillment, and *telos* of life itself and with the ways we organize our lives to those ends. Although philosopher Kai Nielson argues convincingly that both conceptions of ethics form important aspects of the whole,[10] the perfectionist issues and concerns are more closely related to the moral praxis inherent in pastoral care.

Perfectionist issues have an important bearing on the structuring of wants.[11] Whether clearly or confusedly, consciously or unconsciously, all structuring of wants expresses certain organizing principles that are concerned with human purpose and fulfillment. Thus the structuring of wants inevitably has a moral dimension.[12] When individuals, groups, or communities participate in pastoral care, they are engaged in a process of change that has an inherent moral dimension.

This does not mean that pastoral care always requires change in the organizing principles of the individual, group, or community; frequently it attempts to uphold, support, and strengthen organizing principles already present. Likewise, pastoral care must deal with situations where the beliefs and commitments implied in their organizing principles conflict with individuals' actual structuring of wants. It is no news to anyone, for example, that people do not necessarily act as nobly as they speak, and organizing principles cannot necessarily be inferred from an individual's or group's stated values or commitment (concerning love and justice, for example). Indeed, becoming aware of the conscious and unconscious aspects of one's organizing principles and their relation to the structure of wants is an important task in the pastoral care process, and the difficulties of this task greatly increase the complexity and moral seriousness of pastoral care.

The process of change underlying pastoral care can be seen as a moral enterprise, although change is not exhausted by or reducible to its moral dimension; there are psychological, sociological, biological, and spiritual dimensions as well. Thus, pastoral care ideally represents an internal relations approach, in which moral considerations are intrinsic to the process of change but are only one aspect of that process. The individual or group giving the pastoral care must carefully and emphatically choose where to focus attention. For example, focusing on the psychological dimension of change does not erase the moral dimension which functions concurrently with it. Whatever the explicit focus of attention, pastoral care is always and inevitably immersed in the moral praxis of life.

To bring the matter back to the Disciples, it is not clear whether it is justifiable to speak descriptively of *the* Disciples moral praxis. Disciples tradition and contemporary Disciples thought and practice appear too pluralistic to attempt to do so. More importantly, there is a characteristic tension in the Disciples tradition which has much to tell us of the moral praxis of pastoral care from a Disciples perspective.

W. E. Garrison has described the socioreligious context within which the Disciples community was formed:

> Protestant individualism had been fully developed on the side of division and separation. That this could not be endured as a permanent condition was evidenced by the many unsuccessful attempts to restore unity. . . . The need of the hour was for the discovery of a principle of synthesis by which, without restricting the liberty of any man, a practical and effective union of religious forces might be obtained. The problem was to transcend religious individualism by finding a basis for religious solidarity.[13]

In short, Disciples attempted to find a ground upon which a principle of individualism and a principle of community could coexist in mutual enrichment.

Perhaps not too surprisingly, given Alexander Campbell's indebtedness to the philosophy of John Locke and Covenant Theology, Campbell's resolution of this issue bore many of the marks of contractarian theory. As Garrison has noted, Campbell suggested that the "unity of the church is to be found by making the terms of ecclesiastical fellowship as nearly as possible coincident with the conditions of citizenship in the Kingdom of God."[14] Of central importance, then, was what constituted those conditions. I need not rehearse at this point Campbell's resolution of these questions; they have been much discussed and criticized elsewhere and did not provide the final basis on which these issues could be adjudicated. Just as the problem of the individual's relationship to the community has continued and intensified on the general sociocultural level, so it has continued to vex the Disciples community. Clark Williamson has observed that "our struggle has been to prevent liberty from degenerating into individualism, to keep it in tension with a principle of community."[15] Ralph Wilburn has also remarked on this tension:

> This emphasis on liberty, however, must not be confused with individualism. Christian freedom is not the self-will of a stalwart individualist. From the beginning the Disciples of Christ have been aware of the need to hold this principle of individual freedom in creative balance with the principle of community.[16]

The problem of Christian unity and the attempt to resolve it along contractarian lines (that is, by allowing great latitude of interpretation with respect to "noncontractual" issues) is only one aspect of the Disciples tradition that bears on the issue at hand. Indeed, the focus on the problem of unity certainly has not meant that Disciples have been interested only in contractual rules of community order or "ecclesiastical fellowship." One certainly finds a concern with perfectionist issues (that is, understanding the most desirable way of life) throughout Disciples history. As Ernest Tuveson has noted, "Campbell's theology might be called socioreligious . . . abstract issues of 'justification,' 'calling,' and the like yield to practical preparation of 'social and religious happiness.'"[17]

That both contractarian and perfectionist concerns should operate side by side in Campbell's thought should not strike us as particularly surprising. While Campbell thought the problem of unity required resolution beyond mere human consent, by appeal to the nature of the New Testament church, he believed that the major part of morality could be discerned by the "enlightened conscience of man."[18] While clearly differing with Robert Owen on the ability of humans to make moral progress on their own, Campbell nonetheless felt that Christianity "contemplates the reformation of the world upon a new principle," presenting "new principles of human actions."[19] This strain in Disciples thought did not end with Campbell. As Williamson has argued: "Disciple theology is a quintessentially American theology of sanctification, the goal of which is to baptize or transform the worldly into the spiritual."[20] Whether one wishes to classify this concern for perfectionist issues under the rubric of a theology of sanctification or not, Disciples have certainly been intensely interested in and argued a good deal about these issues, both with others and amongst themselves.

In the main, however, the desire has been to keep these issues of perfection and sanctification separate (or at least as separate as possible) from the more strictly contractarian issues. In other words, Disciples tend to view interpretive pluralism as the most desirable way of life within the general context of Christian fellowship. This may help explain in part how it is possible for so many Disciples to be politically liberal on the one hand and socially conservative on the other.[21] Yet Disciples history has illustrated that the attempt to separate contractarian and perfectionist issues is fraught with ambiguities. The usual course has been to resolve these ambiguities on the side of individualistic contractarianism. Thus, for example, it is often heard (though nobody would ever claim the statement) that the Disciples can believe anything they want to believe. The ethical corollary of this would be that Disciples can do anything they want to do. Although this corollary is no doubt appealing to some, it threatens to collapse a conception of the good life as such into ethical egoism, and the good life of the community into simple chaos.

With respect to pastoral care, this ambiguity is particularly acute since it relates to the very goals of our work. What do we understand to be the *telos* of pastoral care? Is our emphasis on the expansion of individual liberty or on the incorporation of individuals into community? If, as one might hope, it is both of these, how do we understand their synthesis? Since pastoral care inevitably has a moral dimension, this is no matter of idle curiosity.

Certainly one of the most important problems in understanding the moral praxis of pastoral care has been the concern over moralism. This concern arose historically from the awareness of the potential tyranny of conscience—the ways in which moral pronouncement to persons experiencing emotional pain can intensify rather than provide an appropriate means of dealing with that pain. The insight is crucial in our effort to recover the moral seriousness of pastoral care. Indeed, the Disciples tradition can certainly help us avoid monolithic moral standards which fail to recognize the vitality and strength arising from interpretive pluralism, even at the level of moral praxis.

Sensitivity to the dangers of moralism, however, does not make the moral praxis of change go away. The problem is not to deny moral praxis, but rather to meet and "be with" the individual, group, or community in accordance with their needs and capacities; our pastoral care must be developmentally appropriate.[22] It would be a mistake to suggest *a priori* that the needs and capacities of others will always preclude any and every response on the level of the moral dimension (that is, addressing the organizing principles of the structuring of wants).

More than this simple awareness, however, is needed. Given the inevitable moral praxis of change, we must have some vision of what would constitute "meaningful" or "adaptive" change or growth within the variety of existential dilemmas people experience. Although our pastoral care may not necessarily be concerned at every point with the "reformation of the world," we must maintain some idea of those "new principles of human actions" that form and underlie the Christian vision. Indeed, a sensitive practical theology, developed in dialogue with contemporary psychological, sociological, and ethical perspectives, may help move us toward such useful and coherent visions.

If this is true, the tension in the Disciples tradition between individualism and community may be understood less as two competing modes of understanding ethics than as two principles within a broader perfectionist ethic. The Disciples tradition of individual liberty and social embeddedness affords us two emphases to adjudicate in understanding the structure of wants. The problem, of course, is to keep faith—and thereby to create tension—with principles of both individualism and community. While any practical theological vision guiding our pastoral care would lean too much in one direction or the other, constructing such a vision would not end discussion but rather reorient its context. Since closing our eyes to the inevitable moral praxis of pastoral care will not make it go away, the greater sin would be a failure to address critically the challenge it presents us.

The tension within Disciples moral praxis should alert us to a tension in the practice of pastoral care. Although the Disciples tradition offers us no easy resolution of this tension, it does make us aware of the necessity for both a principle of community and a principle of individualism. One need not ask more of our denominational heritage in this regard than that it provide us with these two anchors in the shifting waters of our world.

Notes

¹See, for example, Richard Bernstein, *The Restructuring of Social and Political Theory* (Philadelphia: University of Pennsylvania Press, 1978).

²Don S. Browning, *The Moral Context of Pastoral Care* (Philadelphia: Westminster, 1976), p. 20.

³This is true, I think, even in most cases where ostensibly one is only trying to support individuals or communities (as in bereavement, for example).

⁴See Bernstein, *Restructuring*, and Daniel Dennet, *Brainstorms* (Cambridge, Mass.: MIT Press, 1981), for interesting examples.

⁵This discussion is deeply indebted to the recent work of Don S. Browning; see in particular his *Religious Ethics and Pastoral Care* (Philadelphia: Fortress Press, 1983). See also Mary Midgley, *Beast and Man* (Ithaca, N.Y.: Cornell University Press, 1978), pp. 177–200.

⁶One must bear in mind here the notion of a "want" as I am using it.

A want is a conceptual abstraction of foundational motivational elements and must, therefore, be distinguished from its particularizations in experience. This highlights all the more clearly the necessity for a *critical* theory of wants (as in, for example, Marx, Freud, and Habermas). The intent of such a critical theory is precisely to open up the potential objectifications of (Marx), or fixations on (Freud), certain particularizations of wants for appropriate transformation. For a discussion of a variety of issues related to this point, see Raymond Geuss, *The Idea of a Critical Theory* (Cambridge: Cambridge University Press, 1981). Theological foundations for the necessity of such a critical theory of wants may be found throughout much liberation and political theology. Rubem Alves has discussed some of these issues under a different rubric in his "Personal Wholeness and Political Creativity: The Theology of Liberation and Pastoral Care," *Pastoral Psychology* (Winter 1977): 124–36. The recent work of John Cobb and Schubert Ogden has implications here as well, from a process theological perspective; see, for example, Cobb's discussion of "creative transformation" in *Christ in a Pluralistic Age* (Philadelphia: Westminster Press, 1975) and his more recent *Process Theology as Political Theology* (Philadelphia: Westminster Press, 1982).

[7] This, of course, does not differentiate from other activities whose underlying function might also be to facilitate change (e.g., religious education, secular psychotherapy). Pastoral care differs from these other activities in the perspective and context within which it approaches its task, rather than in the underlying function.

[8] The classic contractarian literature is Locke's *Second Treatise of Government*, Kant's *Foundations of the Metaphysics of Morals*, Rousseau's *The Social Contract*, and Hobbes's *Leviathan*. The most significant contemporary contractarian theory is John Rawls, *A Theory of Justice* (Cambridge, Massachusetts: Harvard University Press, 1971).

[9] The classic work in perfectionist ethics is Aristotle's *Nichomachean Ethics*. Contemporary positions heavily indebted to this orientation include Stanley Hauerwas, *Character and the Christian Life* (San Antonio, Texas: Trinity University Press, 1975) and Alasdair MacIntyre, *After Virtue* (Notre Dame, Indiana: University of Notre Dame, 1981).

[10] Kai Nielson, "The Choice between Perfectionism and Rawlsian Contractarianism," *Interpretation* 6 (May 1977): 139.

[11] For a fuller explication of the issues involved here, see Don Browning's discussion of the five levels of practical reasoning in *Religious Ethics and Pastoral Care*, pp. 53–71.

[12] The relationship between organizing principles and the structuring of wants is a fully dialectical one. That is, organizing principles form and

are formed by the structuring of wants. There have been several fascinating historical studies of the ways in which various organizing principles have been understood directly to structure or restructure human wants. Albert Hirschman's *The Passions and the Interests* (Cambridge: Cambridge University Press, 1977) and Arthur O. Lovejoy's *Reflections on Human Nature* (Baltimore: Johns Hopkins Press, 1961) provide wonderfully instructive accounts on these matters in seventeenth and eighteenth century social, psychological, economic, and political thought. For a discussion that illustrates these matters in religious thought, see Philip Greven's intriguing *The Protestant Temperament: Patterns of Child-Rearing, Religious Experience, and the Self in Early America* (New York: Alfred A. Knopf, 1977).

[13] W. E. Garrison, *Alexander Campbell's Theology* (St. Louis: Christian Publishing Company, 1900), pp. 67–68.

[14] Ibid., p. 161.

[15] Clark Williamson, "Theology and Forms of Confession in the Disciples of Christ," *Encounter* 41 (Winter 1980): 58.

[16] Ralph Wilburn, "Disciple Thought in Protestant Perspective: An Interpretation," in *The Reconstruction of Theology*, ed. Ralph Wilburn, Vol. 2 of *The Renewal of Church: Panel of Scholars Reports*, ed. W. B. Blakemore (St. Louis: Bethany Press, 1963), p. 307.

[17] Ernest Lee Tuveson, *Redeemer Nation* (Chicago: University of Chicago Press, 1968), p. 218.

[18] Garrison, *Alexander Campbell's Theology*, p. 177.

[19] Tuveson, *Redeemer Nation*, p. 80.

[20] Williamson, "Theology and Confession," p. 65.

[21] I am indebted for this remark to Dennis Landon.

[22] This is most decidedly *not* to say that pastoral care is simple gratification of the wishes people consciously or unconsciously hold. While gratification of wishes may at times be appropriate, even in these circumstances this must be understood within the context of a critical theory of wants (see note 6, above).

The Church Exists by Mission As a Fire Exists by Burning

L. DALE RICHESIN

EMIL BRUNNER WROTE that "the question of the Church is indeed *the* unsolved problem of Protestant theology."[1] It is a question that can be posed in a number of ways. What is the church? is essentially an ecclesiological question. What does the church do? is also ecclesiological but relates to issues of practical theology. Why does the church do what it does? is a theological question, with implications for ecclesiology.

The nature of the church, like the nature of Christ, is complex. The church can be understood as wholly of God and wholly of humanity, and both at the same time. When we address the question of *what* the church does and *why*, we can see a similar complexity. Does the gathered church worship on Sunday morning because of religious imperative (e.g., God commands us to worship) or because of a human need (e.g., we feel incomplete until we worship)? Similarly, does the gathered community of faith serve others in need because of a religious imperative (e.g., God commands us to serve others through the example of Jesus' love) or because of a moral imperative (e.g., human good requires acts of self-sacrifice and love), or some combination of both?

Poets have struggled to give words to the mystery of love. Musicians have attempted to embody profound questions of the soul in music. Philosophers have sought to examine the rationalities and irrationalities of life in their philosophies. Yet the poet's words can be tested only by speech; the musician's compositions can be enjoyed only by playing; the philosopher's ideas

INTERPRETING DISCIPLES

can be examined only in argument. And the church's ideals of love, grace, faithfulness, and reconciliation can be realized only in its activities of worship and mission. Through worship the religious imperative is spoken and received; through mission it is made manifest in a broken world. And yet what are the theoretical and practical issues of mission faced by the local church and the church at large in the world?

For Disciples congregations with their strong tradition of local leadership and authority, the concept of mission is linked with a broader understanding of the church itself. If the church is seen solely as the local congregation, then mission becomes only the activity of the local congregation in the local community. If the church is understood more generally as the larger regional and general structures of the denomination, then mission becomes only the activity of those larger units in the larger society. Thus when we claim that the church is both the local congregation and the larger structures of the denomination, we can affirm that mission must be undertaken in both local communities and the larger society.

This concept of mission does not ignore or minimize the other functions of the local congregation—namely worship and nurture. To the contrary, these three functions are essentially related. The congregation as church is a gathered community of faith, united in the worship and service of God through the proclamation of Christ's death and resurrection and through an authentic ministry that witnesses to the power of God's reconciling love in the world. *Worship*, through liturgy and preaching, prepares us for such activity by grounding our faith in humbleness toward God. *Nurture*—through Christian education, fellowship, and pastoral care—unites us as a gathered community of faith empowered by the Spirit to serve God. *Mission* then is the church's active witness of Christian love in the world by outreach, service, and prophetic voice against injustice.

As we honestly look about us—viewing our uneasy neighbors in the cities, our impoverished neighbors throughout Africa, Asia, and Latin America, and our local neighbors silently suffering in the midst of our own communities—we must begin to listen to their voices, their cries of suffering and pain. We must recognize that we, as the church, are called to serve God by giving witness to his reconciling love. We are called to love our neighbors.

Such love demands authenticity in our acts of mission. It cannot be a minor priority. If our congregations seek to serve God as witnesses of love and reconciliation in the world, then our practice of worship should nurture and educate us and inspire us to witness to such empowering love through service and outreach to those in need.

Early Patterns of Mission

In the period between the original merger of the Christians and Disciples in 1832 and the founding of the National Benevolent Association in 1886, Disciples activity in the area of mission was primarily understood as Christian education and proclamation—forming churches, founding schools and seminaries, publishing journals and religious newspapers. Many individuals were active in other issues like prohibition, suffrage, or abolition, or were generous donors to hospitals and children's homes, but by and large the church was not involved, as an institution on the congregational or general level, in such service and witness. As the Disciples movement gained strength and numbers, it began to change and to address such issues. The first two major concerns to emerge were in the area of foreign missions and of education to settlers on the American frontier. This shift can be seen in the founding of the Christian Woman's Board of Missions in 1874, the Foreign Christian Missionary Society in 1875, and the growing popularity of the Sunday School movement. Our church as an institution began to respond in direct and corporate ways to the needs of service and mission.

One of the primary influences on the Disciples at this time was the Social Gospel movement, which was an active response of ministry to the basic needs of poor people, especially in the cities. The Social Gospel movement, which cut across denominational lines throughout North America, drew inspiration from contemporary social and economic theories and was manifest in such grassroots service as the Settlement House movement (begun at Jane Addams's Hull House in Chicago in 1889) and the Salvation Army (formed in 1880 to serve the poor in urban areas). In a general sense, the Social Gospel was part of the larger progressive movement in our society, which included the labor movement, socialism, anarchism, prohibition, and the suffrage movement. Some of the more progressive churches and ministers in American cities embraced the Social Gospel as the normative understanding of the Christian faith during the period from about 1880 to 1945, but among Disciples, general acceptance of the Social Gospel was always mixed. Clergy and laity alike feared the extremes of the labor movement and were uncertain about mixing politics, economics, and religion. Nevertheless, with the founding of the National Benevolent Association in 1886, the church began to assume a direct responsibility to serve the needy and disadvantaged through homes for the aged and children's homes.

Several Disciples ministers were active in the Social Gospel movement during this time: Frank G. Tyrrell, first founder of the *Christian Century* and the *Christian Oracle;* Alva W. Taylor, prolific writer and preacher; James H. Garrison, editor of the *Evangelist* and the *Christian-Evangelist;* and Charles Clayton Morrison, second founder and editor of the *Christian Century.* By 1915 many more Disciples clergy were influenced by the Social Gospel movement as the church's concern for the crisis of poverty and suffering began to deepen.

The Social Gospel preachers certainly perceived the imminence of the crisis, but they often failed to implement an effective strategy to convey the crisis to the laity. One of the weakest aspects of the Social Gospel movement was the failure of its mission workers and preachers to recognize the essential problem of evil. The limitations of human nature and the sinfulness of the human spirit were seldom acknowledged, and human effort seemed fully adequate to vanquish evil. Social Gospel workers often believed that all that was needed to eradicate suffering and poverty was a dedication to service and charity, and they saw advancements of civilization in technology, education, working conditions, child labor laws, and especially the prohibition of alcohol as positive steps to the achievement of a perfect world.

There were, however, those working within the Social Gospel movement who sought to clarify its social understanding and methods. Theologians such as Walter Rauschenbusch of the Baptists and Charles Clayton Morrison of the Disciples saw the dangers of an unreflective response of simple Christian altruism to the problems of human suffering and injustice. These theologians granted the urgency of the crisis, but they believed that the Social Gospel should be grounded in the language and images of Christian tradition. For such theologians, the strength of the Social Gospel was in its claim that a social ministry is part of the original spirit of Christianity. According to Morrison:

> If the new gospel were a new religion, it would proceed, as new religions have always done, to create its own cultus. But the social gospel is not a new religion; it is a modern development within historic Christianity. . . . Before we are done I hope it will be clear that it is not just a new gospel but the oldest form of the Christian faith. The social gospel belongs to the genius of Christianity. It was Jesus' own gospel, and our modern conviction concerning it is derived primarily from our rediscovery of his mind.[2]

Morrison viewed the Social Gospel as a continuation of the original Disciples emphasis on Christian primitivism which claimed a first century authority. The Social Gospel pointed to the founding ideals of the faith, which were ultimately social. Other theologians of the Social Gospel also attempted to draw upon more traditional images of evil in order to ground the movement in the Kingdom of God, rather than in simple human altruism. Rauschenbusch tells us that "a theology for the social gospel would have to say that original sin is partly social. It runs down the generations not only by biological propagation but also by social assimilation."[3] Rauschenbusch called for the recovery of the traditional Christian understanding of Sin and the mythological concepts of Satan and a Kingdom of Evil, and Morrison called for a return to more traditional religious language.

Models of Mission After World War II

The lasting effects of the Social Gospel upon our denomination were extensive. Our commitments to outreach, to service to the needy, and to prophetic judgment against social injustice all deepened as a result of the movement. Since 1945, Disciples have been dedicated to mission as an activity of the local church and the general church in a variety of ways. Some see the church as giving witness to Christ's reconciling love through proclamation and evangelism. Others view the activity of the general church in such projects as nursing homes, children's homes, and hospitals as a quiet and steady witness of service to those in need. Still others, as individuals and through the local congregation, see the role of the church as one of benefactor to those in need—giving money directly to the poor and to those agencies that serve the poor. Some model the activity of the church after that of the Old Testament prophets and take strong moral positions on certain issues in society—abolition, prohibition, the suffrage movement, civil rights, feminism, farm workers rights, the nuclear freeze, and others. Local churches have been involved in a wide variety of causes both in the local community and indirectly through the general church worldwide. An excellent summary of the full range of Disciples activity during this time can be found in an article by Albert M. Pennybacker entitled "The Local Congregation: Social Action Involvement":

As a part of the general movement among Christian churches, congregations of the Christian Church (Disciples of Christ) have increasingly found ways to respond to and become actively involved in social issues, especially in the nineteen sixties. This involvement has covered a wide spectrum of activities: from direct participation in controversial programs devoted to social change to more indirect and supportive activities aimed at improving the effectiveness of traditional social service systems.[4]

One sign of this activity in the local congregations is the presence, noted by Dr. Pennybacker, of between fifteen hundred and two thousand local Church in Society committees. These committees assume a variety of functions and roles ranging from addressing systematic problems of social justice (such as racism, sexism, and poverty) to coordinating the congregation's benevolence giving for traditional helping ministries (such as hospitals, nursing homes, and childrens' homes) to enabling the congregation to respond directly to local crises (fires, floods, tornadoes, and riots). The presence of these committees in local congregations alongside of Worship, Christian Education, Personnel, and other committees reinforces our understanding that mission is no less important than worship and nurture. Mission does not happen accidentally or automatically; it must become a central part of the activity of the local congregation through its structures, its self-identity, and even its understanding of purpose.

Disciples activities for mission can also be seen at the regional and general levels. Pennybacker isolates four specific areas of general and regional activity for mission:

> (1) Actions taken by the General Assembly of the Christian Church (Disciples of Christ) and its predecessor national bodies; (2) The program of the Disciples Peace Fellowship; (3) An over-all denominational response to the urban crisis known as the Reconciliation program; and (4) The work of ecumenical bodies, such as the National Council of Churches and the World Council of Churches.[5]

To these, I would also add actions of regional and district assemblies of the Christian Church (Disciples of Christ) and the work of local ecumenical bodies such as community, city, and state-wide councils of churches.

As we pause in the midst of conversations with the United Church of Christ, we Disciples cannot help but notice the similar positions that our two denominations have taken addressing many of the social justice issues of the day. Our public support of such causes as civil rights, equal rights for women, and disarmament has been virtually identical through our General and Regional resolutions and actions. For both of our denominations, however, an ambiguity persists between the liberal social justice positions of our general and regional assemblies and the more conservative community mission activity of our local congregations. This ambiguity produces an uncertain tension about the place and form of mission.

As our positions on social issues of an earlier age were informed by the Social Gospel movement, so our recent positions have been informed by a broader, international religious movement—liberation theology. Within the many ideas of liberation theology is potential for addressing this tension between the local congregation and the general church on the area of mission.

Liberation Theology and Pluralism

In the Social Gospel movement, generous wealthy and middle-class churches and individuals were calling for relief for the poor and oppressed. As long as the churches were identified as the source of assistance, rather than as the home for the rich and poor alike, true Christian reconciliation was difficult. The current movement of liberation theology reverses that perspective, for now the poor and oppressed are calling for justice with their own voices. Liberation theologians claim that the essential truth and purpose of the Christian movement is active service to and liberation of the suffering and oppressed people of the world. Those people who are in a particular position of suffering and oppression not only are the focus of Christian theology and the church's ministry but also have a privileged voice to interpret and criticize society and the church. The people on the fringes of society are particularly sensitive to the failures of the church and society, for they have seen who benefits and who suffers from the activity and inactivity of an oppressive society and a conservative, passive church.

Liberation theology has taken four general forms: black liberation theology, feminist liberation theology, European political theology, and Third World liberation theology. (Native American liberation theology, gay liberation theology, and Hispanic American liberation theology are positions on particular social justice issues which have not, at present, received fully developed theological treatment.) The perspectives of the black and feminist liberation theologians are similar and perhaps generally familiar to most of us. Black theologians point to the historic oppression of blacks in American society and trace the incipient support of the white church for such injustice. They charge the church to cast off its former passive and condescending attitudes and to affirm the importance of civil rights and social justice. Further, they challenge the church to develop structures which enable black Christians to stand proudly on their own, rather than be patronized.

Feminist theologians similarly point to the historic oppression of women in American society and trace the church's conscious and unconscious support of such oppression. While black liberation theologians readily use biblical warrants to justify their claims for social justice, feminist theologians are more hesitant because sexist justifications are more pervasive than racist ones throughout the Bible. Nevertheless, feminist Christians challenge the church to rethink long-standing attitudes about the role of women, particularly in the area of church leadership, and to present creative new visions about how women and men can work together in the church.

European political theologians present a wide range of ideas for the church and are difficult to characterize simply. Jurgen Moltman and Johann Baptist Metz present a "theology of hope" after the despair of two world wars. Dorothee Soelle, on the other hand, presents a radical critique of materialism and offers a Christian vision informed by Marxist ideas.

Third World liberation theologians present ideas which are less familiar to most Americans, and these ideas are often perceived as radical and threatening. However, some of the most challenging and creative ideas of the liberation theology movement stem from the Third World, and we would do well to consider them carefully. Like black and feminist liberation theologians, Third World theologians point to a history of oppression by the First World (Europe and North America) from the colonialism of the nineteenth century to the economic exploitation of the twentieth. They trace the church's passive and active support for such oppression and call upon the church to develop new positions of advocacy and ministry for the oppressed. Third World theologians struggle to represent what we citizens of the First World facilely affirm: justice, independence, economic security, and freedom from foreign domination of all kinds. Unlike the feminist and black theologians, however, Third World theologians call attention to the conflict and struggle dominating their societies at all levels of race, sex, culture, and ethnic background. Third World countries like Brazil find themselves in situations of strife and division on all these societal levels, and the government is simply one of many oppressive forces. By far the largest oppressing force perceived by the Third World citizens stands outside the country, beyond the reach and influence of the people— the First World domination of the Third World in the economic order that inexorably victimizes countries like Brazil. Elements of the Catholic church in many Third World countries have taken the side of the poor and the suffering as they seek to liberate themselves from such domination.

Although our government in the United States has generally not understood its duplicitous relation to these problems, the Disciples on a general level have sought to reflect meaningful sympathy and understanding. The "General Principles and Policies of the Division of Overseas Ministries" adopted in 1981 reflects a deep commitment to the perspective of the Third World.[6]

But even though this statement embodies an ideal of support and mission, the perspectives of many of our congregations are not so understanding and supportive. Again we see a tension between the local and general levels of the church. Liberation theology, however, may give us an insight that offers the whole church a fuller vision of witness and service.

One of the major fallacies of our culture in the recent past was the presumption that ours was a homogeneous society. Despite the mass-produced conformity and sameness that we see in shopping malls, fast-food restaurants, electronic arcades, television, superhighways, and the rest of our materialistic nation, we are beginning to discover that we are *not* a middle-class homogeneous society. The rapidly increasing immigration of Hispanic people and Southeast Asians into our nation has forced us to realize that we are not the melting pot of the world, and perhaps we never were. We are now beginning to see large groups of people excluded and forgotten on the edges of our society. The liberation movements remind us that our society is not homogeneous but increasingly pluralistic.

Pluralism has required some important shifts in church thinking. Today the Christian Church (Disciples of Christ) has active and growing black, Hispanic, and Asian-American caucuses to advance the particular concerns of these ethnic groups. Church Advance Now (CAN), a national program of church development initiated in 1982, has set a goal that no less than 30 percent of all new churches will be located in minority communities. The hope is that this program will be more than just tokenism, and that it will be a significant move which recognizes the givenness of pluralism in our society.

Liberation theology makes an appeal not just to the poor and the oppressed but to all levels of society. It seeks to unite the poor and the rich, the oppressed and the oppressors, and to liberate them all from the powers of oppression which dominate both sides of a society. While particular groups (blacks, women, poor) have often voiced their claims for liberation with particular

perspectives, these groups have also come to recognize a cama-
raderie among themselves. The we/they dichotomy between the
oppressed groups and the oppressors begins to break down as the
oppressed groups realize the diffuse nature of oppression. Femi-
nists confess that they have often grounded their ideas in the
comfort of middle-class materialism. Black men confess that they
have often reflected sexist tendencies. Poor men confess that they
have often abused their wives and children. This broadening of
the idea of liberation allows North American whites and males to
be included in the conversation among the oppressed. This understanding can also allow for a better unity of mission on both the
local and general levels of our church.

In *Theology in Red, White, and Black,* Benjamin Reist offers a
theological argument for ethnic and racial pluralism: "the only
theology that can function in the multilogical world of ethnic
pluralism is a theology of theologies. Put more sharply, this is to
insist that no single confession of the gospel of Jesus the Christ
can ever suffice. There can be no valid Christology unless there
are valid Christologies."[7] Reist's argument that we must acknowledge a full spectrum of theologies in red, white, black, brown,
and yellow can be expanded to the "mutual pluralism" of racial,
ethnic, sexual, economic, and religious identities. Reist poses
four criteria as essential to a healthy pluralism: (1) mutual intelligibility, (2) mutual interdependence, (3) varying rates of relatability, and (4) mutual openness to change.[8]

(1) For Reist, *mutual intelligibility* is the basic point of departure, "a matter of disciplined openness. It presupposes that time
and effort are requisite for shared understanding."[9] Mutual intelligibility involves both communicating ourselves to others and
actively listening to others as well, and this type of mutual conversation is indeed liberating.

(2) *Mutual interdependence* realizes the importance of other
perspectives and contributions. "*Promise* is also involved, the promise of reciprocal creativity. But this promise will never be known
apart from the deepest reaches of the genuine dependence of

each upon all."[10] Mutual interdependence recognizes the validity of other perspectives and our dependence upon them for valued and creative contributions.

(3) Reist's *varying rates of relatability* acknowledge the simple fact of pluralism. "But *more* than dialogue is involved. The components of a genuine pluralism relate differently, at varying rates, with fluctuating tempo being the norm rather than the exception."[11] White Christians in the Los Angeles area, for example, find themselves in contact with Hispanic Catholics, Buddhists, and Asian Christians, while white Christians in New York City might find themselves in contact with black Protestants, Hispanic Catholics, and Jews, and all relate differently to one another on different issues.

(4) *Mutual openness to change* brings these first three criteria together as an expression of the general character of a changing pluralistic society. It opens us to "the question of the uncontrollable future . . . before us with an unnerving but invigorating intensity—for all who struggle with the depths of liberation. God—not his creatures—rules tomorrow's reflection upon this ultimacy."[12] Basic to these four criteria is the acceptance of the general level of human dignity that transcends all specific racial, ethnic, sexual, economic, and religious identities and the relativities brought on by social and economic change.

The critical voices of liberation theology reveal the need for re-evaluation and re-education if we in the church are to move beyond our often limited understandings of Christian witness and genuinely identify with those who are victims. We must learn to recognize oppression in our midst and even to identify our own needs with those of the oppressed. Can we hear the voices of the oppressed and authentically respond to them without falsely rationalizing or misappropriating them into our own privileged perspectives? Can we discover and then voice our own needs for liberation from the oppression of divorce, unemployment, and the like? Can we mediate the valid social justice claims of others with our own priorities, legitimate needs, and expectations? And can we listen to the penetrating voices of liberation

INTERPRETING DISCIPLES

theology and add our own voices without disarming their vitality? These are questions that still challenge us.

A New Model for Local Christian Witness

For mainline Disciples congregations, the radical character of oppression often is not recognizable in the same fashion as angry black, radical feminist, or Third World revolutionary fervor. The crises that confront many of our people are divorce, a declining educational system, drug and alcohol dependency, wife and child abuse within a fragmenting family structure, and a perennially oppressive economy. Such problems tend to inspire frustration and individual apathy, not fervor for change. With such a diffuse agenda of problems on local and national levels, what can we draw upon to help us develop authentic witnesses of mission in local congregations?

In the past twenty-five years the Catholic church in Latin America has begun the process of liberation. One of the most important manifestations of this new movement is the development of the *Communidades eclesiales de base*, or Basic Christian Communities. These communities are small groups (five to twenty-five members) that meet as independently as a Christian Women's Fellowship group. They study the Bible, celebrate communion, worship, and above all, develop actions to respond to the social justice issues that they face in their particular community. Although these Basic Christian Communities operate within the Catholic church, they constitute a new ecclesial structure which is not seen elsewhere in the church. At present, there are over one hundred thousand such communities in Latin America, giving witness to justice and exercising self-determination grounded in faith.

Gustavo Gutierrez has shown that the church's commitment in Latin America involves it in several important changes. To a large extent the Basic Christian Communities have helped the church to change its task and focus: (1) to "fulfill a role of prophetic denunciation against specific and grave forms of injustice that are rampant in Latin America"; (2) to call the church to a role of "conscienticizing evangelization," a call to educate the people to the "awareness of being oppressed, but nevertheless of being masters of their own destiny"; (3) to reflect its commitment to liberation of the poor by becoming a poor church; (4) to consider the inadequacies of its own ecclesial structures in addressing the problems of the oppressed; and (5) to change the lifestyles of its clergy in order to reflect its commitment to the goals of liberation.[13] Commitment to these changes in the Catholic church in Latin America indicates an important new awareness of the political strength and influence of the church. The church is understood to be politically, socially, and institutionally *in* the world, but not necessarily *of* the world. These changes can also be adapted to our Disciples efforts at mission. They can become goals to help us as we struggle with our own understandings of the "church" and "mission."

Disciples understand the church, in its congregational and general manifestations, to be a nurturing fellowship of people bound together with a common faith in Jesus Christ. That faith is understood as the reconciling activity of God's love for the world through the church's proclamation of the Word, by sermon and teaching, and through its service to those in the world who need direct ministry and liberation from oppression.

This definition has several implications for the church's self-understanding and ministry. First of all, the proclamation of its faith is closely bound to the church's sense of strength as a united fellowship nurtured by faith. Second, there is a close bond between the church's proclamation of the Word and its service to those who are in need; the spiritual proclamation of the Word cannot be separated from the physical ministry of service and liberation. Such a division fails to acknowledge the unity of spirit and matter which is the Incarnation, the essence of life itself. Jesus healed broken bodies and wounded souls often with the same miracle, with the same words of liberating grace. Today food for the hungry is often accompanied by words of prayer before eating, and prophetic sermons often denounce material social evils that oppress us. Worship and nurture and mission are interrelated parts of the same witness of faith, and this witness is an essential part of the community of faith.

The understanding of ministry and of the church among Disciples has been closely tied to our emphasis on congregationalism and lay leadership, which has shifted significantly since 1945. The rise of a professional ministry in our denomination has produced considerable argument and division, because this shift demanded a rethinking of earlier positions and attitudes. Ronald E. Osborn, in *In Christ's Place*, reflects the denomination's current position when he defines ministry as "a complete and joyful acceptance of one's life in the world, a yearning and compassionate affirmation of oneness with all men in their aloneness and their need, an uncalculating and unembarrassed participation in the pleasures which affirm humanness, an equally joyful spending of oneself—even offering of one's own life—in love by standing with the world's forgotten, embittered, and oppressed."[14]

Osborn speaks of actively participating in the world with a grounding vision of the transformative power of Christ. This commitment to transformation reflects an understanding that the church is on the side of the oppressed, the downtrodden, the hungry, and the enslaved. Osborn understands the church to be a fellowship of "servant-people" who are serving those in need and proclaiming the victory of Christ to the world's victims. Christ's own ministry is the perfect model: "we can see that the genius of that ministry was his oneness with mankind."[15] Osborn wrote those words in 1967, in the midst of the social upheaval of the 1960s and before the current emphasis on liberation theology within a middle-class denomination that had just concluded its ecclesiological Restructure. Yet these words are packed with the same explosive power as any liberation theologian's of today. Osborn's emphasis on ministry *in* the world and his understanding of Christ's oneness with humanity act both as a grounding of our faith and a charge for our witness as our local churches seek to understand where ministry takes place and to whom it is addressed.

The Liberation Theology movement, like the Social Gospel

movement before it, can be seen historically as a mode of ministry that informs theological reflection. To translate theological reflection back into active ministry, Disciples have spoken of the church as the servant-people and have proclaimed faith in the reconciling activity of God's love in the world. We must now responsibly listen to the proclamations of the oppressed and commit ourselves to reconciling the pluralism of ethnic, racial, sexual, economic, and religious identities. Once we have realized the pervasive nature of oppression, we can no longer continue to affirm our faith without acting on these issues of liberation. The cries of the oppressed are growing louder. They are becoming our cries; they are God's cries.

Although there are obvious differences between the two worlds, the strategies and ideas of Latin American liberation theologies can help us in North America. Latin America is predominantly Catholic, while North America is both Catholic and Protestant and enjoys no cultural-religious consensus. Latin America is predominantly underdeveloped and poor, while North America has vast capacities for production and prosperity. But in both, forms of oppression are manifestly real in particular, local settings. For North Americans, 10 percent unemployment is not an abstraction; they experience layoffs in their plants in their own communities. Child and spouse abuse are manifested not as statistics, but as a particular child or spouse in a particular broken family. Even the more abstract forms of North American oppression, such as consumer materialism, are manifest in particular ways that can be confronted by particular communities. And because oppression is always localized, we should be able to learn something from Latin American models of liberation theology. One of the most exciting features of these models is their focus on the local level through the structures of Basic Christian Communities. Unlike most contemporary First World theology, which has some difficulty being adapted to a local congregational setting, liberation theology began at the local level and finds its greatest strength there.

Our closest analogy to the Basic Christian Community

INTERPRETING DISCIPLES

is the Christian Women's Fellowship groups in many Disciples churches. Like the CWF groups, the Basic Christian Community begins with a spiritual center of worship and prayer groups and unites itself through fellowship, education, and study that frequently focuses on how to relate the scripture to the present world. This leads the community to consider specific and immediate social issues; in Latin America today there is no shortage of such issues. Grounded in worship and united by study, the Basic Christian Community then seeks authentic ways to address the issues, bringing their faith into the world. The church then becomes political, in the context of Latin America, by criticizing the local authorities and government and demanding change and reform.

We see in this quick summary that the Basic Christian Communities emphasize all three functions of the church. Worship is important as the beginning and basic focus. Nurture comes from study and fellowship, while mission responds to the conditions of oppression in the lives of community members. Those who are familiar with Christian Women's Fellowship groups will see many similarities, or the potential for similarity, in terms of worship, nurture, and mission. Local congregations of the Christian Church (Disciples of Christ) could easily adapt this model for local Christian witness. Whether we respond to the problems of the family and the pain of divorce or to the injustices of racism, valid local Christian witness is crucial. Without such local witness, our churches become hollow buildings and the convictions of our faith false.

Leading congregations to a more authentic local Christian witness requires several steps that review the possibilities for mission and service:

(1) *Assess the congregation's particular resources* and current involvement in local community issues. Most of our churches own a building which is not used to the fullest, and most have dedicated members who have been faithful to the church for many years. Many of these members possess valuable skills and knowledge which could be used in local witness in the community; some are

retired with free time to work as volunteers if but asked. Some of our churches have a long and stable history in the community, producing a natural acceptance and familiarity for neighbors who are not members. Most importantly, our churches are grounded in an identity of faith which gives divine meaning, purpose, and direction to their activities of service.

(2) *Assess the community's resources.* What groups in the community provide what services? What other churches are working on what issues? What coalitions, if any, have been formed between churches and local groups, block clubs, community organizations, businesses, and the like? What issues have local councils of churches addressed? What issues have been addressed by the congregation?

(3) *Analyze local community problems and issues.* What are the causes of the problems? Who or what are the obstacles to a resolution of the problem? Who is affected by the problem that might work together with others to address it?

(4) *Review past and current strategies that address a particular problem.* Have they worked? Why or why not? Do we need to do more research on the problem? Do we need to enlist the assistance of more people or groups? How can we heighten the significance of this problem in order that people might become more aware of its importance? The congregation should devise new strategies which would creatively combine and integrate the resources of the congregation with the resources of other congregations and groups in the community.

(5) *Explore the issue* theologically through the educational programs of the church. Study groups, seminars, Sunday school sessions, sermons and CWF, CMF, and CYF programs can address the issue and help the congregation see it in terms of their life of faith.

(6) *Develop a core of people* who will address the particular problem at hand and draw up a specific strategy.

(7) *Implement the strategy* with maximum participation from the members of the congregation and from other congregations and groups in the community.

(8) *Proclaim a victory that acknowledges Christ* as the source of our power and of our victory. Reflect theologically upon this victory through study groups, seminars, sermons, and similar means. The circle of witness is complete. We must now begin it again as we address new issues and problems.

This congregational approach to Christian witness reflects some important possibilities. Such an approach indicates an openness to the concerns and needs of our suffering neighbors, helps us to develop insights to our own suffering, and moves us toward pluralism. It opens the congregation as a partner with the community in solving "our" problems. The church is no longer an imposing building filled with outsiders who have few roles in the community, and Christian values and concerns no longer focus only on general prayers for peace or for the suffering victims of war with accompanying offerings. When the congregation lives out those Christian values by taking a particular stand on a specific local issue, the community views the congregation as a dedicated and strong partner, able to produce a real concern on the right issues and to back that concern with dedicated working volunteers. Such witness will not be an isolated activity of a few members but an ongoing process that affects worship, Christian education, and evangelism, as well as outreach and service. Most importantly, the congregation will now see its activities in mission as part of the activity of the whole church.

Doing The Model

I grew up in rural Missouri, and my relatives often ask me, "How can you live out there?" when I chance to visit. By "there" they mean Chicago, where I studied for the ministry and served two inner-city churches for several years; by "how can you live," they question life among the burned-out buildings, crime, teenage gangs, drugs, prostitutes, bag ladies, and drunks in the alleys. In short, the image of physical and spiritual desolation in certain urban areas is a common misperception for those who take uncertain comfort from living in the "safe" areas.

As a minister in such an urban setting, I have found myself

struggling with the models of ministry and mission offered by liberation theologians and with the various pastoral roles that press on any pastor. How can I hear the voices of the oppressed, and—as a white male urbanite, transplanted from the rural Midwest, educated in a highly respected institution—understand their claims without falsely appropriating them into my own forms of privilege or even to my own "model"? How can I transmit these claims of the oppressed of my city—or of blacks, women, or Third World people generally—to those folk in middle-class congregations who hear those claims with uncertain and often unsympathetic ears and who are often blind to the forms of oppression that press upon them as well? How can I present these claims of the oppressed in a way meaningful and urgent to my congregation without disarming their vital claims?

I am convinced, of course, that in a modern city like Chicago, in places that may seem God-forsaken, the church can still bear witness to God's reconciling love. The Basic Christian Community model of liberation theology fits well with those features of Disciples congregations that are potential sources of human energy—like the CWF groups. I wish to close with a few stories which illustrate what the model might look like in action.

The western Chicago suburb of Maywood is home to one of our Disciples churches. This community, a relatively stable, blue-collar, integrated area, has faced some difficulties in terms of housing decline, educational decline, drug abuse, and unemployment. Many years ago, however, the Maywood church committed itself to serving the needs of that community and became an integrated congregation. This was not an easy decision, but one that was charged with the vision of its pastor, K. Everett Munson. The First Christian Church of Maywood reflected this commitment by actively and regularly canvassing the neighborhood to keep close contact with the needs of the community. A variety of programs were developed to address the needs of youth and young adults. Today, this congregation remains vital and strong, and many in the community claim that the relative stability of integrated Maywood can be attributed in some degree to the witness of this church.

Jackson Boulevard Christian Church is a black congregation that occupies the building of a formerly all-white Disciples congregation. Jackson Boulevard is located in one of the several all-black housing projects for the poor in the Chicago area. Unemployment and crime are high, and juvenile crime is a particular problem. Frank and Louise Reid have been co-pastors of the church for many years, and they have sought to give strong, steady witness to the important Christian themes of love and reconciliation in this place. They have concentrated particularly on witness to young people, forming all-boy and all-girl groups as well as mixed groups and young adult groups. They have provided a strong and continuous social opportunity for the young in an area where gang activity is high. They have encouraged young people to pursue their dreams and to develop interests, skills, and special talents in order to escape the desolation of the "projects." Individuals who have succeeded and moved on often continue to support the church, thereby witnessing to others that self-fulfillment is a definite possibility.

North Side Christian Church is located in the Uptown community of Chicago, one of the most cosmopolitan communities in the country. In 1982, the local high school, Senn High School, had to provide translation services to over seventy different language groups. The area is also home to most of Chicago's American Indian population, poor white Appalachian natives, and to over fourteen thousand former mental health patients. It contains twenty-four nursing homes and half-way houses; within less than one square mile is the largest concentration of nursing home beds and the second highest percentage of senior citizen housing in the country. The community has a growing problem with unemployment as well as a deteriorating housing market, and the human needs are vast. With decreasing memberships and resources, the local area churches, including North Side Christian, began several projects to address these needs. An ecumenically based tutoring project, using the Laubauch Tutoring one-on-one method, used volunteer teachers from many churches to teach English to non-English-speaking people as well as to illiterate English-speaking people. The CWF group of North Side, along with other church groups, often went on visitations to local nursing homes. In 1966, several North Side members sponsored Korean immigrants. This nucleus was to form the First Korean Christian Church that same year. That church, (which has leased space in the North Side building since 1986) has been one of the fastest-growing Disciples churches in the region for the past six years under the leadership of pastor In Duk Kang. In 1968, North Side began its ministry to the growing Hispanic population of the neighborhood by entering into a lease agreement with the Spanish Christian Church and its pastor, Ruben I. Cruz. North Side has also affirmed its witness through a continuing ministry to the hungry and has addressed a variety of local issues, including nursing home reform, energy rate reform, conservation efforts, and housing reform, through active participation with other local churches and organizations in the Organization of the North East (ONE), a local community activist organization.

University Church is located in the Hyde Park neighborhood of Chicago. Two of its early ministers, founding pastor H. L. Willet and E. S. Ames, were also professors at the nearby University of Chicago and were Deans of the Disciples Divinity House. With a legacy of theological liberalism and a strategic location amidst the city and the academy, University Church has pursued strong, local ministries of social and community action since the 1960s. A number of recent pastors and co-pastors (including Charles H. Bayer, Peg Stearn, and C. Harvey Lord) have led the church in developing innovative liturgical and pastoral styles appropriate to numerous areas of mission. The "Blue Gargoyle" is a youth agency and coffee shop run on weekdays that provides recreation, tutoring, and job training for young people of disadvantaged neighborhoods. In 1978, a number of church members purchased a large, multi-unit building in the mostly poor, black neighborhood of Woodlawn, just south of Hyde Park, and established the Covenantal Community. This group, intentionally organized as a community drawn by faith, offers a Christian option to urban community development. University Church is co-affiliated with the United Church of Christ and joins with Presbyterians in United Campus Christian Ministry programs at the university. In 1980, University Church merged with South Community Church, a predominantly black congregation, and began appropriating black liturgical and cultural resources into its weekly worship. Original music, choreography, and liturgy created by members of the congregation are also used regularly. In 1985 the church voted to become a sanctuary church and assisted a Guatemalan family through this effort; it also declared itself a nuclear weapons free zone. Resolutions on these two issues adopted at the 1985 General Assembly were sponsored or co-sponsored by University Church.

These four examples show the variety of Christian witness and mission possible at the local congregational level in an urban context some might characterize as bleak and tragic. But in the midst of such "human forsaken" places, some experience God as present and active. While I have not been able to review missions of congregations in rural or small-town areas, it should be evident that such active Christian witness is needed everywhere.

As a Disciples minister, I have tried to recognize the anger, radicalism, and fervor that can grow out of tragic and oppressive situations, as reflected in the theological expressions of oppressed, excluded groups. In effect, the churches I have described have tried to do the same and to translate their recognition of oppression into specific programs and actions. For those of us in the mainline churches of North America, local manifestations of oppression, suffering, and tragedy can point to the radical nature of sin and oppression in the world at large and can sensitize us to our own oppression. Before we can hear Christ's word of liberation from our problems of divorce, alienation, and economic stagnation, we must recognize how such problems spiritually oppress us. This is the first task of mission, for only by seeing ourselves as the oppressed, as well as oppressors, can we identify with the voices crying around us. Thus, through liberation theology we can identify white middle-class oppression as well as racist, sexist, and economic oppression. We can point to the structures of such oppression and better understand their power. The local congregation is not passive, quiet, and helpless, but empowered to act with conviction on local issues. With a full awareness of the responsibility for mission, the local church can share more genuinely in the mission of the full church. Liberation theology witnesses to a vision of Christianity which anticipates divine action but demands authentic human participation. God forgives us through Christ; in response, we must love our neighbors. It is the gift of grace, the command of love. It is that simple, and that challenging.

Notes

[1] Emil Brunner, *The Divine Imperative,* trans. Olive Wyon (Philadelphia: Westminster Press, 1947), p. 523.

[2] Charles Clayton Morrison, *The Social Gospel and the Christian Cultus* (New York: Harper and Brothers, 1933), p. 3.

[3] Walter Rauschenbusch, *A Theology for the Social Gospel* (Nashville: Abingdon, 1917), p. 61.

[4] Albert M. Pennybacker, "The Local Congregation: Social Action Involvement," in George G. Beazeley, Jr., ed., *The Christian Church (Disciples of Christ): An Interpretive Examination in the Cultural Context* (St. Louis: Bethany Press, 1973), p. 195.

[5] Ibid., pp. 206–12.

[6] See the article by Don A. Pittman and Paul A. Williams for a more detailed elaboration of the "General Principles."

[7] Benjamin Reist, *Theology in Red, White, and Black* (Philadelphia: Westminster Press, 1975), p. 186.

[8] Ibid., pp. 33–36.

[9] Ibid., p. 34–35.

[10] Ibid., p. 34.

[11] Ibid., p. 35.

[12] Ibid., p. 36.

[13] Gustavo Gutierrez, *A Theology of Liberation*, trans. Sister Caridad Inda and John Eagleson (Maryknoll, N.Y.: Orbis Books, 1975), pp. 114–18.

[14] Ronald E. Osborn, *In Christ's Place* (St. Louis: Bethany Press, 1967), p. 26. Regional ministers often present this book to newly ordained ministers.

[15] Ibid.

Mission and Evangelism: Continuing Debates and Contemporary Interpretations

DON A. PITTMAN and PAUL A. WILLIAMS

IN AUGUST 1981, a controversial document entitled "General Principles and Policies of the Division of Overseas Ministries" was approved by the General Assembly of the Christian Church (Disciples of Christ) meeting in Anaheim, California. Initiated in 1977 as a systematic study and review of the division's philosophy and practice, the document is an important contribution to the long and fervent debate within the denomination—and within virtually all Protestant communions—on the nature of world mission and evangelism. Insofar as adoption of the "General Principles and Policies" document is an expression of the denomination's present vision, the church has moved to resolve in a decisive manner the ambiguities and tensions that have characterized the Disciples interpretations of mission and evangelism since the earliest days of the reform movement in the 1820s.

The "General Principles and Policies" document is the first officially adopted interpretation of the primary biblical and theological images that have shaped Disciples approaches to mission and overseas ministries in the last quarter-century. It affirms faith in a God who has "never, in any time or place, been without witness" and in a church "empowered by the Holy Spirit to witness in word and deed to God's nature and purpose." The document highlights the problems imposed by "imperialism, colonialism, and denominationalism" and characterizes the central social, political, and economic forces in the world today that affect Christian action and mission strategy.

The controversy attending the text in some quarters of the Disciples fellowship centers on its social-action and ecumenical orientations. Many question the priority given to advocacy for social change and justice and to the call for Christians to "stand against the 'principalities.'" Many criticize the Division of Overseas Ministries' stated assumption that "the basic 'planting' of the church has been accomplished" and the corresponding de-emphasis on personal evangelism and church growth. Some are deeply troubled by the text's affirmation of church union, particularly in what critics have judged to be the virtual "surrender" of significant congregational resources overseas to various united church organizations,¹ or the "surrender" of effective control of Disciples mission funds to the National and World Council of Churches. Yet, as Kenneth L. Teegarden, then General Minister and President of the Christian Church (Disciples of Christ), wrote in 1981:

> The Principles and Policies are—first and foremost—thoroughly Biblical. They are evangelical in the sense that they reach out to all peoples everywhere. They are radical in that they pursue a fundamental change in people. They offer a world view that recognizes the Christian as servant, not master; the mission as losing one's self, not gaining. They will not be understood by everyone because the Gospel is not of this world. They are *our* principles and policies, but they represent more of a challenge than a fulfillment. Which is as it should be.²

The fundamental theological and practical issues raised in the "General Principles and Policies" document are not new. To the contrary, they were of central importance to the reform movement led by Alexander Campbell and Barton W. Stone: What is the mission of the church? How are we to define "evangelism"? How can we most effectively declare God's love for humankind? How do we act as agents of reconciliation in a world community struggling, often violently, with the meaning of justice, freedom, and human dignity? What does Christ's prayer for unity demand of us, and what should be the character of our ecumenical relationships? How is Christian unity related to world mission?

These questions were and still are divisive within the Campbell-Stone movement. Different conceptions of Christian ministry and varied responses to the rise of American missionary activities overseas in the mid-nineteenth century helped split the Stone-Campbell movement into three separate communions: the Churches of Christ, the Non-Denominational Fellowship of Christian Churches and Churches of Christ (Independents), and the Christian Church (Disciples of Christ). Indeed, the classic phrase universally adopted by the adherents of this American reform movement—"In essentials, unity; in nonessentials, liberty; in all things, charity"—has been both promise and problem for the tradition.

The debate on strategy for world mission addresses the tradition's three formative principles of interpretation, restoration, and ecumenicity.[3] The definitions of and proper strategies for mission and evangelism have been related directly to the relative importance of these three principles in a conception of the church. The three branches of the Stone-Campbell movement have generally agreed about the individual's right and responsibility to interpret scripture and essential matters of faith. However, there have been sharp differences on the character, value, and even possibility of a restored New Testament Christianity, and also on the warrants for and effectiveness of both ecumenical cooperation in mission and movements toward church union. The fact that Alexander Campbell—the tradition's founding intellectual figure—refined his position on these matters throughout his career has permitted all three branches to ground their different visions of essential Christianity, mission, and evangelism in theological and ecclesiastical principles articulated by the revered "Sage of Bethany."

Campbell reflects the unresolved tension that has distinguished much of Disciples history, as the church has struggled to satisfy a restorationist vision emphasizing correctness in doctrine and church structure and an ecumenist vision stressing cooperation and love. Therefore, before turning to a consideration of the "General Principles and Policies" document, it will be important to examine some background: the origin of that characteristic Disciples ambiguity in Campbell's own contribution to mission strategy, the development of the denomination's missionary enterprise prior to World War II, and the Disciples response to changing social, religious, and political forces in the modern technological era.

Campbell and the Early Disciples Missionary Enterprise

Even before Alexander Campbell's death in 1866, as George F. W. Kresel has remarked, his religious movement was in serious conflict over his principles of Christian mission.[4] Indeed, there was considerable confusion in the church with regard to Campbell's primary convictions in such matters. Many of his contemporaries, for example, understood his writings to express an ardent opposition to missionary efforts. However, as Joseph M. Smith has commented, Campbell's was only a provisional dissent.[5]

He did strongly oppose the mode of missionary work prevalent in his day. Christian sects, he charged, simply propagated their own distinctive systems of human thought and practice (opinion) rather than the true Gospel (essence). Campbell asserted boldly, for instance, in his 1843 public debate with the Presbyterian minister Nathan L. Rice, that "No man thinks that the world will ever be converted to Episcopalianism, Presbyterianism, or Methodism, &c, &c. All these denominations are the creatures of apostacy. Christianity was before them all, and it will survive them all."[6]

Campbell did not agree, however, with the strictly predestinarian opponents of mission, who so emphasized God's sovereignty and holy initiative in salvation that they saw all active missionary work as hopeless folly and unbelief.[7] Campbell argued from the Great Commission (Matt 28:19–20) that in the present age God works in the world by human means. God, he stated firmly, "no longer employs Angels, Prophets, nor Apostles, as his agents in the work. He has fitted and furnished the church for this ministry. If they do their duty, the work of conversion goes on; if not, it stops."[8]

Furthermore, Campbell ultimately disagreed with those Christians who opposed cooperative arrangements for mission simply for the lack of specific scriptural warrant. His early emphasis on the recovery of the "ancient order of things"—the biblical pattern for church organization and practice—was surely in accord with the conservative dictum articulated by his father, Thomas Campbell: "Where the Scriptures speak, we speak; and where the Scriptures are silent, we are silent." In his first journal, the *Christian Baptist,* he also voiced sharp opposition to the emerging Protestant missionary societies. However, as Campbell later made explicit, his primary point had been always the rather tenuous relationship of most societies to the Church. Most missionary societies were supported by both churched and unchurched individuals and were not, as independent organizations, accountable to the Church itself. The faith community, he argued, should never transfer its sacred responsibility for missionary endeavor to some extraecclesiastical society, "lest in so doing they should rob the church of its glory, and exalt the inventions of men above the wisdom of God."[9] Thus, when the missionary entity was organized in and of the church, Campbell could defend cooperative plans for mission. He began to outline this position most clearly in 1831, with a series of essays on the "Cooperation of the Churches" in the *Millennial Harbinger.*

First, Campbell and his associates recognized the need to counter an overly rigid application of the restoration principle. In 1836, replying for Campbell to a letter in the *Millennial Harbinger,* his close friend and associate editor Robert Richardson wrote:

> A thing may be unscriptural, but it does not there follow that it is antiscriptural. . . . For while nothing can

be required for which there is no divine warrant, and nothing will be tolerated which is opposed to the laws and teachings of Christ and the Apostles, the greatest liberty of opinion is permitted as it respects every thing which is not revealed. Of this kind are the order of the exercises of public worship, the manner in which the commemorative institutions are to be attended to, the kind of building which the church is to occupy; and in the same class are found the various ways and means by which the gospel is to be spread abroad— whether by the pen—the press—the tongue—by one church or a cooperation of churches.[10]

Campbell admitted that disagreements within the church would remain concerning such "circumstantials of the Gospels" that were not matters of faith or morality. Yet reminding his followers of the liberty permitted to each Christian in such non-essentials, Campbell distanced himself from religious legalism by proclaiming in *The Christian System*, "The *law of love* is the supreme law of religion, morality, and expediency. . . . This is the spirit, and soul, and body of the Christian institution."[11] Moreover, he stated, "Christianity consists infinitely more in good works than in sound opinions."[12]

Second, Campbell began to argue that there was, in fact, convincing New Testament evidence of intercongregational cooperation, even if there were no specific divine command. He cited passages in the Pauline epistles (e.g., 1 Cor 16:1; 16:9; 2 Cor 8:1; Gal 1:22) in contending that the churches of the apostolic era were organized into "districts" and that they cooperatively selected representatives or "messengers: (2 Cor 8:19) to carry out the work of the church.[13]

Third, as he began to affirm the overriding importance of the ecumenical principle, Campbell's emphasis in writing gradually shifted from a concern with the local congregation to the church universal. By 1837, in fact, Campbell was even urging interdenominational mission cooperation among all Protestant communions. He asserted:

> We would, indeed, have no objections to co-operate in these matters with *all Christians,* and raise contributions for all such purposes as, in our judgment are promotive of Divine glory or of human happiness, whether or not they belong to our churches; for we find in all Protestant parties Christians as exemplary as ourselves according to their and our relative knowledge and opportunities.[14]

One can see, then, an emerging consensus among Disciples leaders by the 1840s for (1) less rigid restorationism, guided by the law of love in responding to the human condition; (2) imitation of New Testament forms of cooperation to better accomplish the work of the church universal; and (3) more humble recognition of the sincerity of other Christian traditions and of humanity's "relative knowledge" of the mystery and majesty of God. This consensus was clearly expressed in Cincinnati in 1849, when the first "General Convention" of Disciples created the American Christian Missionary Society (ACMS) to "promote the spread of the Gospel in destitute places of our own and foreign lands." Campbell strongly supported the ACMS and served as its president from 1849 to 1866. From the beginning, however, the ACMS provoked considerable controversy between the more liberal and conservative factions of the movement. As Grant K. Lewis has pointed out in *The American Christian Missionary Society and the Disciples of Christ,* beyond the standard objections that the ACMS was usurping the Lord's prerogative in conversion and was needlessly and unreasonably expensive, there were five primary criticisms: "(a) membership is on a money basis; (b) the society does not represent the churches; (c) the society has no scriptural warrant; (d) such an organization 'apes the sects;' and (e) its president and other advocates are inconsistent with their former views on extra-scriptural organizations."[15]

Particularly sensitive to this last critique, Campbell tried to mediate between the two factions developing within the church;

in 1850 he attempted to reconcile his earliest negative views on missionary, tract, and other societies, which he had published in his first journal, the *Christian Baptist*, with his later supportive artices in the *Millennial Harbinger*. He asserted, for example:

In my early writings on the missionary and other benevolent schemes of this progressive age, I had much to object to the manner of conducting these operations. Always believing the Christian religion to be designed for the whole world and by its Divine Founder commanded to be preached to the human race, I have ever regarded the missionary spirit of the gospel and the missionary enterprize as the proper enterprize of the Christian Church.

Bible and tract, and all other auxiliary societies for diffusing Christian knowledge, are but means for carrying out more effectually, and more successfully, this grand intention of converting the world by evangelical missionaries or evangelists. In my first essay in the first volume of the Christian Baptist, I took the ground that *the church*, in her own capacity, was the only Scriptural missionary institution known to the primitive church and to christianity, as propounded by "its Founder and his prime ministers," and that no separate or distinct association, composed of other persons than its members, could be regarded as of divine authority, or in harmony with the genius and spirit of the gospel and the church.

To this view I am as much devoted to-day as I then was; and while, consenting to a missionary society as a distinct object of contemplation, and as a means of diffusing the gospel, I now regard it as I then regarded it, as the church of any given district, in council assembled by her messengers, to devise means for accomplishing this object with more concentrated power and efficiency.

The more simply, the more promptly, and the more effectually to accomplish this, is purely a matter of Christian expediency and must vary according to time and circumstance.[16]

Campbell believed in the American Christian Missionary Society because he was convinced eventually that the Disciples could "do comparatively little in the great missionary field of the world either at home or abroad without cooperation."[17] He believed in the urgency of the church's mission, asserting that it was the responsibility of the faith community to communicate in word and deed God's truth to all humanity. He emphasized that the gospel was meant for persons of all races and nationalities. "In Christ's commission to his Apostles," he wrote, "the whole world was their diocese."[18]

Campbell urged missionaries, furthermore, to emphasize not the wrath but the love of God, reminding them to respect each individual as a child of the one Creator. While remaining always firm on the unique and supreme revelation of God's will in Christ Jesus, he yet displayed sensitivity to cultural differences. He instructed Disciples missionaries, for example, not to criticize persons for practices and values that were not "directly opposed to the import and design of the ministry of reconciliation."[19] In sum, as a cooperative organization for mission, the ACMS, in Campbell's judgment, contributed significantly to the church's ability both to improve the quality of ministries performed and to extend the reach of the Good News to the ends of the earth.

Despite Campbell's effort to portray the ACMS as an institution in and of the church, legitimated both by scriptural inference and the demands of time and circumstance, many of its objectors could never be reconciled to its existence nor to the interpretations and judgments of the Disciples leaders who founded it. The religious movement by the 1860s was, in fact, in the process of shattering over this and related issues. According to William Tucker and Lester McAllister, by the time of Alexander Campbell's death a fundamental split was developing between the conservative, anti-instrumental, anti-ACMS restorationists and the more liberal supporters of organ music in worship and of intercongregational cooperation in mission work at home and abroad.[20] Disciples have struggled ever since to come to terms with ecclesiastical polity that is both congregationally autonomous and cooperatively effective, and with theological principles that are true to the New Testament and supportive of a praxis-oriented ecumenism.[21]

The American Christian Missionary Society was able to send missionaries to Jerusalem and Jamaica and planned a mission effort in Africa. Yet, actually, little was accomplished overseas. At that time, writes Robert Thomas, "It became clear that neither the planning procedures nor support network were available for overseas missionary work, and the society turned its attention to important undertakings in education and missions in the United States."[22]

In 1874, Disciples women, intent on a more energetic missionary program and encouraged by newly established women's organizations in other Protestant denominations, founded the Christian Woman's Board of Missions (CWBM). Within two years the CWBM, led by Caroline Nevelle Pearre, reopened the Jamaica mission initiated by the ACMS and was soon sponsoring mission work in India, Africa, and Latin America. Perhaps most significantly, the CWBM established the first and only graduate school in the United States specifically for the education and professional training of missionaries for overseas service to the church. The Disciples "College of Missions," from its opening in Indianapolis in 1910 until its teaching responsibilities were transferred to the Hartford Seminary Foundation in 1927–28, was widely recognized for its high academic standards and excellent training program. Additionally, the CWBM published the monthly journal *Missionary Tidings* from 1882 until 1918, when it was merged with four other Disciples publications into *World Call*. Disciples men, as well, were concerned with the world mission of the church and thus organized in 1875 the Foreign Christian Missionary Society (FCMS). The FCMS gave exclusive attention to recruiting leaders and financially assisting mission efforts in Europe, Latin America, and East Asia. Between them, the CWBM and FCMS represented the Disciples concern for sustained mission work throughout the world.

By the second decade of the twentieth century, the denomination's broad ministries in the United States and overseas were carried out by several agencies and societies and clearly needed further organization. At the time, Disciples congregations were supporting their various cooperative ministries through special day offerings and competing capital campaigns. Therefore, the International Convention of 1919 approved the establishment of the United Christian Missionary Society (UCMS), and to facilitate greater responsibility in fiscal matters, the UCMS united a number of existing Disciples organizations: the American Christian Missionary Society, the Christian Woman's Board of Missions, the Foreign Christian Missionary Society, the Board of Church Extension, the National Benevolent Association, and the Board of Ministerial Relief.[23] Creation of the new organization was possible because the Disciples had never split the church's mission into home and foreign fields of service nor developed a specific missiology.[24]

From its earliest days the leadership of the Foreign Division of the new UCMS sought effective ways to spread the Christian gospel in word and deed, while also recognizing the need to become more sensitive to the real barriers that western attitudes of cultural and spiritual superiority and imperialistic actions posed to world mission. By the 1920s, the division's leaders became convinced that while the Christianization of the world was the ultimate goal, the only appropriate and effective strategy would be to nurture fundamentally indigenous, self-supporting, self-determining, and self-propagating churches overseas. As Robert Thomas states in *Where in the World Are We Going? The Overseas Ministry of the Christian Church (Disciples of Christ)*, the leaders of the division agreed that:

> no country can be Christianized by foreign mission ("that is the work of nationals in their respective lands");

that only such institutions should be founded as could be managed and supported by the nationals "within a reasonable time"; that it is better to do a smaller work well than undertake larger work in an unsatisfactory way ("Quality is preferable to quantity as a method in reaching non-Christians"); that developing nationals and budgeting to meet the needs of *their* work is better than sending more United States personnel.[25]

By 1928, the Disciples of Christ were involved through the UCMS in thirty-eight cooperative overseas projects, and the denomination was increasing its commitment to ecumenicity in overseas ministries. However, this commitment inevitably developed conflicts in both home and foreign missions as typical Disciples ambiguities surfaced concerning the church's nature and calling.

The question of "open membership"—the reception of non-immersed Christians into congregational fellowship—became a highly divisive matter related both to ecumenical involvements in mission work and to autonomy among the "younger" indigenous Disciples churches overseas. The appropriate UCMS policy in this matter was actively debated at each annual convention during the 1920s. Through 1925, the conventions supported resolutions requiring missionaries to adhere to the practice of closed membership, though there was considerable dissent. However, in 1926, a special UCMS "Commision to the Orient" report had a major impact on Disciples policy. As Smith has remarked:

> The Commission to the Orient made perhaps its greatest contribution to the development of Disciples mission thought and practice by its insistence upon the necessity of a new spirit in the relationships of the churches in the West and those in mission lands, and by its call to a new era of confidence in the integrity and judgment of missionaries themselves.[26]

The special commission insisted, for instance, that the church of Christ in the Orient be in fact an oriental Church of Christ, that it be an indigenous "field product" rather than a North American "factory product," and that the church overseas have the necessary freedom to make its own judgments about the demands of the Christian faith. Supporting the commission's important and controversial report, A. D. Harmon, president of the Disciples' 1926 Memphis convention, argued persuasively:

> If the fathers of this movement demanded the right to examine the Scriptures and set up the church as the Spirit revealed it to them, then can we as custodians of this heritage deny the same right to India, to Japan, to China? . . . It will not suffice for us to build our foreign mission policy as if it were an inanimate something, detached from life, built in Memphis, boxed and ready to be shipped to the world. The pattern of the church for alien Christians is to be found where our fathers found the pattern—in the Spirit of God illuminating the living word as that Spirit flows through their lives—not ours.[27]

That the Memphis convention approved the commission's call for freedom for both missionaries and the "younger" churches overseas was a remarkable victory for liberal Christian pragmatism and ecumenist vision in the denomination. This striking action, Smith argues, was "a tacit reversal of the strict restorationist position taken at Oklahoma City the year before."[28] He continues:

> In facing the threat of disintegration of their organized mission effort in the struggle over "open membership," Disciples achieved a hitherto unknown degree of common commitment to an *innovationist policy* in the conduct of their foreign missions program. . . . Disciples had departed from *restorationism* in its strictest and most iconoclastic form when they entered into interdenominational comity and cooperation. Now in their recognition that the organic unity of the church itself would

INTERPRETING DISCIPLES

never be manifested by adherence to a rigid restorationist pattern they were moving one step further. It had become clear that no existing religious body could enter into fruitful partnership in the quest for unity if it assumed that it already embodied in its own existence the full answer to the quest.[29]

Ecumenically minded Disciples had applied to the new churches overseas the principles of individual interpretation, congregational autonomy, and Christian unity based more on community than correctness. This led to a wider acceptance of open membership and a new and challenging understanding of mission, engendering truly dialogical relationships between the North American Disciples fellowship and indigenous Christian churches, other cultures, and different religions overseas.

The intense debate continued, of course. Yet the dialogical, bilateral context for Christian mission began to transform every aspect of the Disciples view of themselves as a spiritual community and of their relationships with other Christian communions, cultures, and faiths. Stephen J. Corey's 1934 address as president of the UCMS clearly reflects this new perspective. He argued cogently:

Missionaries have to go, not as formerly, with strong prejudice against everything in the older religions which they find on the field, but they have to give credit for the good which they find and speak of Christianity as the fulfillment of it and the only religion that has redemption in it through a Savior. Missionaries should not attempt to take our culture to other lands, but leave persons free to continue their own culture and help make Indian Christians and Chinese Christians instead of trying to make American Christians around the world.

Nationals should be pushed to the front, given leadership and responsibility, thus bringing the churches to self-support and self-definition.

We should present, as far as possible, a solid front on the mission fields in Christian cooperation and plans of comity. We should have understandings with our neighbors, not giving up our faith commitments, but exercising, as a people who believe in Christian unity, every degree of Christian cooperation possible so that there will be no waste of time and funds and so that as many of the millions of unreached people as possible can be reached with the open Bible by every religious body.

We must go humbly, realizing our own inconsistencies, and seeing the need of our own redemption, not as a superior race, but as Christian brethren, with the common need of a Savior.[30]

The debate for Disciples crystallized around two basic understandings of mission, the homiletical and the relational. The homiletical approach has emphasized a particular kerygmatic mode of missionary activity, the deliverance and instruction of the Holy Word. This position emphasizes the church's primary task as proclaiming the Good News for the salvation of individual souls and numerically expanding the faith community. Although dialogue with and compassionate assistance to those of other faiths is certainly valuable, the weight of the homiletical view is on personal verbal witness. The church may engage in world mission in good deeds, yet that which the Christian Church has first and most supremely to give is good words.

The relational view, in contrast, has emphasized a kerygmatic mode of missionary activity distinguished primarily by *diakonia* and *koinonia*, compassionate service to others and the establishment of human community. The church's principal task is to live the Good News and to build up God's kingdom on earth. Relationships with others are central to the church's mission on three grounds: moral, because all of God's children deserve to be treated with dignity and respect; pragmatic, because the church grows only as it demonstrates God's love through acts of compassion; and theological, because God wishes that we relate to all of his children as lovingly and forgivingly as God relates to us, and because others may reveal dimensions of God that we may not have fully understood or appreciated. Therefore, while the church indeed proclaims ultimately true words to describe the potentially saving relationship of humanity to God and God's creation, the relational approach to mission evangelizes through actions that embody the kerygma rather than through proclamation in instructive homilies. Christian doctrine, in the relational view, is most properly and effectively introduced in world mission through Christian practice.

These two understandings of mission are closely related to the traditional Disciples ambiguity about the principles of restorationism and ecumenism. The homiletical view of mission developed in fundamental harmony with the *ethos* of Disciples restorationism, which claimed to know and follow the one, true pattern of New Testament church life; mission was to articulate that knowledge for others to accept or reject. To conservatives, the liberal relational approach to world mission appeared to lose the particularity and power of the gospel, the evangelical force that was at the very heart of the apostolic church as recorded in the New Testament. To the liberals, on the other hand, the conservatives had become so scrupulous in their concern with ancient form and correct order that they had lost touch with the Spirit in which all forms were grounded, the Spirit of love that ever called the universal church to wholeness, unity, and compassionate service. A 1947 editorial in the *Christian Evangelist* stated this judgment rather sharply:

> The priority of restoration over unity has disturbed our peace and obstructed our progress toward the fulfillment of our appointed destiny. . . . Restoration has been too much concerned with the mechanics and preciseness of uniformity. Unity is concerned with the spiritual and essential. One deals with our relation to one another in matters of interpretation and practice

and corporate life. The other deals with our relation to Christ and to one another through our life with him. One is anxiously scrupulous. The other is eagerly seeking new truth and new experience in the truth. . . . Ours is a plea for Christian unity, not an ultimatum. . . . Does anyone really believe that the millions of Christians and non-Christians around the world can be persuaded one by one to accept our [Disciples] position? The experience of the past 138 years ought to be convincing on that point.[31]

Struggling thus with the historical ambiguities of their tradition and divided on these two conceptions of the church's fundamental mission, the Disciples of Christ yet attempted to carry out the Great Commission's demands for mission activity. Recognizing the dilemma of becoming another well-defined denomination in the twentieth century, the Disciples still dreamed the great dreams of Campbell and Stone for a Christian faith community "essentially, intentionally, and constitutionally one." Yet, unfortunately, the fellowship encountered only further division and institutional splintering as the church confronted the significant religious, social, and political turmoil of the world community after World War II.

The "Strategy of World Mission"

Radically altered political and ecclesiastical circumstances after World War II challenged Protestant mission societies in a manner previously unparalleled in the Christian church's modern history. Not even the serious financial hardships of the Great Depression were as strong an impetus for rethinking mission as were three developments in the post–World War II era: burgeoning nationalism, world ecumenical organization, and increasingly independent church life in mission congregations overseas.

First, the European colonial regimes that had protected and promoted Christian mission operations in Asia and Africa began to crumble before popular nationalist movements of liberation.

For example, after years of widespread civil disobedience and violence, the British government conceded India's and Pakistan's independence in 1947. After a long and bloody civil war, the 1949 victory of Mao Tse-tung's Communist forces over the western-supported Nationalist Party led quickly to the expulsion of all "foreign devils" from China and the closure of Christian missions. African independence movements of the 1950s and 1960s sealed the fate of the European colonial powers ruling that continent as well.

Second, the ecumenical movement, nurtured by such prominent leaders as Disciples minister Peter Ainslie (1867–1934) and by several major world assemblies of churches, including the World Missionary Conference at Edinburgh in 1910 and the World Conference of Christian Youth at Amsterdam in 1939, led to the founding in 1948 of the World Council of Churches (WCC). An organization of Protestant, Anglican, and Eastern Orthodox churches, the WCC was established to promote Christian fellowship and to express responsible Christian life through cooperative mission efforts around the world. Predominantly Euro-American in its initial membership, the World Council represented a forum for theological debate between advocates of the Christian Social Gospel and neo-orthodoxy, theologies based respectively on the Kingdom of God and the Word of God. More importantly, the WCC represented an organizational experiment: whether, beyond all of the theological and ecclesiological differences within the council's membership, there could emerge true ecumenical cooperation in mission. Insofar as Disciples committed themselves to this unique experiment, the ecumenical work of the World Council of Churches and the International Missionary Council (IMC), which merged with the WCC in 1961, redefined the ecclesiastical context for Disciples initiatives in mission worldwide.

The third factor that prompted a reconceptualization of world mission was the recognition in Europe and North America of the vitality and growing independence of the so-called younger churches of Asia, Africa, and Latin America. Indeed, sponsoring western churches were increasingly forced by their mission congregations to consider charges of inappropriate paternalism and unilateral conrol, charges in harmony with Third World nationalist movements. Therefore, the mission congregations' pleas for the right and responsibility of Christian self-determination ultimately changed the relationship between many sponsoring and sponsored churches. As a new spirit of dialogue and mutual seeking emerged within the church, it soon became apparent that the age of the church's unidirectional witness "from the West to the rest" was clearly coming to an end.

As the Disciples responded to new nationalist movements overseas, new ecumenical organizations for world mission, and altered relationships with mission congregations, the Board of Directors of the United Christian Missionary Society was asked to consider a document entitled "The Foreign Division Faces a Decision." This 1948 document stimulated a decade of debate on the denomination's new context for efforts in mission and evangelism. Concerns for church growth with responsible social action and for denominational heritage with ecumenical cooperation continued to spark disagreements within the Disciples fellowship and to polarize the church.

Ecumenical dialogue in the International Missionary Council, the World Council of Churches, and the National Council of Churches (formed in 1950) provided the catalyst for an official reconsideration of Disciples mission policy. In particular, the 1952 meeting of the IMC at Willingen, Germany, on "The Missionary Obligation of the Church," stimulated a systematic strategy review by the United Christian Missionary Society, under the able leadership of Disciples minister Virgil A. Sly. As a result, in January 1955, the UCMS Board of Directors approved a new statement of administrative policy for its overseas ministries. That statement, "The Strategy of World Mission," was circulated among Disciples congregations for further evaluation and refinement. A revised document, "Strategy of World Mission: Basic Policy of the Division of World Mission of the United Christian Mission-

INTERPRETING DISCIPLES

ary Society," was approved in January of 1959. Later published in the *Ecumenical Studies Series* (January 1960), the "Strategy" was signed by the Division of World Mission of the UCMS, and its "Last Word" defined it as a working document subject to continual review.

The "Strategy of World Mission" made several important contributions toward addressing the challenges of nationalism, ecumenical organization, and new relationships with more independent "younger churches." The Division of World Mission, for example, announced in the text its decision to de-emphasize large mission stations that required substantial capital investment; instead, it would develop operations with greater "mobility and flexibility" to respond to changes in the field, such as population shifts or developing areas of significant growth.[32] Moreover, the division sought "closer administrative ties to the field"[33] in order to allow more initiative from the home office. Both pragmatic decisions were designed to improve communication between the missionaries and the UCMS leadership and to enhance effectiveness in the field.

The document also reflected the theological debate within the church concerning the nature of Christian unity and the meaning of evangelism. Disciples had to address the former issue when united Protestant churches emerged in the Philippines and Japan; there was considerable concern that the newly established united churches to which Disciples were contributing would not, in fact, follow traditional Disciples practices of weekly communion, believer's baptism, and New Testament standards for church life. Addressing these real concerns, the "Strategy of World Mission," like the report of the 1928 Commission to the Orient, invoked the denomination's heritage of individual interpretation and of congregational autonomy.

The "Strategy" document also confirmed the judgment of the division's leaders that "missionaries are Christian guests and advisors on the field" and "partners in obedience with the national Christians"[34]; the denomination was clearly rejecting the paternalism and patterns of autocratic control so characteristic of the

"Great Century"[35] of Christian mission (1800–1914). Accordingly, the document proposed a procedure to transfer authority to national church bodies in a gradual, three-step process: from the complete control of mission funds by the UCMS, to shared control in selected areas of church life, and finally to full national church control.[36] This progressive but cautious and fiscally oriented plan also expressly encouraged mission churches that approached autonomous administrative status to maintain significant relationships with the UCMS, with Disciples church polity and doctrine, and with the culture and society of which they were a part.[37]

With regard to the meaning of "evangelism," the "Strategy of World Mission" included some specific definitional claims:

> Evangelism is witness for Christ directed toward all men and seeking to claim for him every department of life both personal and public. This witness is given by *proclamation, fellowship* and *service.* Answering the call to evangelism, a church finds new life.[38]

The term "evangelism" is clearly not limited to proclamation alone but refers, in a broader and more fundamental sense, to the total mission of the Church: *kerygma, koinonia,* and *diakonia.* It is significant that this statement, which depends on the published report of the International Missionary Council's ecumenical conference sponsored at Willingen in 1952, is not the only point of view on evangelism in the "Strategy."

As Joseph Smith has observed, in the entire text of the "Strategy" document are two quite distinct conceptions of evangelism. Perhaps the predominant conception is that evengelism is "a technique for capitalizing upon the potential for church growth and bringing persons into the institutional church."[39] Yet, prominently stated in the definitional section is the broader, more inclusive perspective, in keeping with the Willingen report, that views evangelism as witness "given by proclamation, fellowship and service." Smith rightly interprets the "unresolved tension" in

INTERPRETING DISCIPLES

the text as a reflection of real theological differences within the Disciples community in the 1950s.

A former missionary in East Asia who was himself a participant in the debates shaping the "Strategy" document, Smith properly identifies Donald A. McGavran as the Disciples' most recognized protagonist of church growth and evangelism in the narrow sense.[40] As early as the 1930s, McGavran was working to impress on the denomination that the primary purpose in mission was kerygmatic proclamation for the salvation of souls. In his book, *Eye of the Storm: The Great Debate in Mission,* McGavran remarks, for example, "I take as basic truth that God desires the salvation of multitudes of countable persons, who will be organized into multitudes of countable churches."[41] Moreover, he argues:

> We must separate evangelism from other good Christian activities. For example, *it has no necessary connection with diakonia [humble service]*—though diakonia is a fruit of the Spirit and may on occasion commend the gospel. An intelligent Christian will notice that diakonia is often a good preparation for the gospel, but he will also note that it was never consciously so used in the early church. *Evangelism is also separate from koinonia.* Evangelism is activity undertaken with the intent of communicating the good news. Koinonia is a fellowship of Christians which does many other things than communicate the gospel. . . . *If we make everything evangelism there is grave danger that no intentional persuasion will be undertaken.*[42]

Smith acknowledges the influence of this theological perspective on the actual development of the "Strategy of World Mission," with its ultimately inconsistent usage of the term "evangelism." However, in agreement with those Disciples who have accepted the broader vision of the church's mission as *kerygma, diakonia,* and *koinonia,* Smith critiques the "church growth" advocates as basically superficial. With reference to the "Strategy" text, he questions the meaning of results:

> Nowhere is sustained attention given to what church growth means, aside from the obvious growth in numbers of members. Again, there appears no evidence of a serious grappling with the question of the nature of the church or of the gospel. Only an answer to this question can provide a theological orientation point for understanding the relationship between "service" or "good works" and "evangelism" and serve as a guide in relating strategy to "results."[43]

"General Principles and Policies": An Emerging Consensus

In the late 1950s, when the intense debate on the "Strategy of World Mission" statement within the UCMS and within Disciples congregations was actually just beginning, a burgeoning spirit of nationalism in Africa led to popular movements for independence from the European colonial powers that had long dominated the continent. Soon after the Belgian Congo achieved independence on June 30, 1960, the important Disciples mission in that country experienced considerable turmoil, as did Disciples congregations in North America. There was uncertainty about the future of the Disciples in central Africa, the largest community of Disciples of Christ outside of the United States, and it soon became clear that, once the country was no longer dominated by Belgian power, the Protestant churches in the Congo would seek their independence from the many denominational mission societies competing in the country. Indeed, as in the Philippines and Japan in previous decades, the churches in the new nation of Zaire moved to establish greater Christian unity among themselves and autonomy from their western sponsors. Ecclesiastical independence culminated in March of 1970, when members of the Congo Protestant Council founded the Church of Christ of Zaire. The new united church moved decisively to conclude unilateral foreign mission activity in the country, while also encouraging continued cooperative relationships between foreign and Zairois Christians.

Ecclesiastical change with implications for Disciples mission policy also occurred in the United States and Canada. Discussion of denominational Restructure began in earnest in 1961 with the appointment of a Commission on Brotherhood Restructure. The process culminated in 1968 with the adoption of a "Provisional Design" for the Christian Church (Disciples of Christ). The direct impact of restructure on the United Christian Missionary Society was the governing board's remarkable decision to divest itself of autonomous decision-making power and to accept the recommendation of the Disciples General Minister and President to begin functioning as two administrative units of the church. The UCMS thereafter existed only as a foundation managing endowed financial resources. Programming for the church became the responsibility of the two new divisions that were to report to and be guided by the Disciples administrative staff, cabinet, and General Assembly: the Division of Homeland Ministries (DHM), which promotes and supervises the church's ministry concerns in North America, and the Division of Overseas Ministries (DOM), which cares for the global concerns of the Christian Church (Disciples of Christ).

These structural changes allowed the new Division of Overseas Ministries to reexamine policies and procedures in world mission. The DOM staff and board began systematically reconsidering its ministries in 1977, while continuing to function according to historical precedents and the guidelines of the "Strategy of World Mission." As a first step toward a new policy statement, the division's board of trustees asked Robert A. Thomas, then president of the DOM, to draft a report on the basic assumptions of the unit. This document became the basis for extensive discussion at each succeeding DOM board meeting through 1981, when the final product of those considerations, the "General Principles and Policies of the Division of Overseas Ministries," was approved by the Anaheim General Assembly. The text provides a historical perspective on the denomination's present approach to overseas ministry, states the theological principles that inform the division's understanding of mission and evangelism, and presents policy guidelines for administrative decision making. The document is particularly significant for its thorough acceptance of a relational rather than a homiletical understanding of mission and of a broad rather than narrow definition of evangelism. That stance is evident in the policies concerning personnel appointments for service overseas, ecumenical and interfaith dialogue and cooperation, Disciples missionary concern for the whole person, and engagement in the constant "struggle for a new and just community."[44]

To begin with, the interest in "mobility and flexibility" in overseas ministries, stated in the "Strategy of World Mission," continues in the "General Principles and Policies" as the announced practice of appointing personnel to overseas service only on a specific, short-term basis. No longer will the Christian Church (Disciples of Christ) "commission" individuals for long-term careers in religious leadership overseas. Moreover, as widely judged appropriate in the modern world community, "most program initiatives come from partner churches overseas, though the DOM also initiates programs from time to time, with a collegial pattern and consultation in all cases."[45] Both of these policy decisions highlight the call in the "Strategy" document for "closer administrative ties" between the church's general offices and overseas personnel. The "Living Link" model of the 1950s and earlier decades was based on direct lines of financial support between individual missionaries and supporting North American congregations, which permitted significant independence in the field. It was replaced by a system of specified assignments for overseas personnel, arranged through bilateral discussions of need and financed through the centralized church, in order to encourage a truly responsive and responsible approach to Christian mission throughout the world.

The commitment of the Christian Church (Disciples of Christ) to ecumenical and interfaith dialogue and cooperation in mission is affirmed unequivocally in the "General Principles and

Policies." The relationships between North American Disciples and related congregations overseas, as well as between Disciples and other Christian communions at home and abroad, should be mutual and shared. The document states:

> The DOM respects the integrity of other churches in the U.S. and Canada, as well as around the world. It assumes that the basic "planting" of the church has been accomplished—that is, the "foreign missionary movement" established the church on every continent, in nearly every nation. An era of "world mission" now exists in which the churches in each country and place in the world must engage in witness and service appropriate to that place. The churches in all parts have different gifts to share with the rest of the Christian community. Finding ways to share mutually in common tasks is crucial for the future of the church and the faith. Mission is on six continents and every place is an arena for mission, including the United States and Canada.[46]

The Disciples involvement in ecumenical relationships is addressed in all three major sections of the "General Principles and Policies" document. The first section, "Historical Perspective and Context," notes both the denomination's long-standing commitment to ecumenicity and its current coordination of mission endeavors with other member communions of the National Council of Churches of Christ (U.S.A.) and the World Council of Churches. It also lists examples of church bodies with whom the Disciples are directly related, such as the Church of Christ of Zaire, the Church of North India, the United Congregational Church of Southern Africa, the United Church of Christ of Japan, the United Church of Christ in the Philippines, and the Church of Christ of Thailand, as well as many of the effective regional ecumenical organizations with whom Disciples cooperate, such as the Christian Conference of Asia, the All Africa Conference of Churches, the Pacific Conference of Churches, the Middle East Council of Churches, and the Latin America Council of Churches.

The second major section on "Theological Principles," under the heading "Commitment to Church Union," boldly affirms the Disciples' characteristic concern for both constitutional and enacted Christian unity. The text begins:

> The Church of Christ is one. All persons who confess faith in Christ are part of the one body. The divisions that historical, geographical, societal, theological and liturgical factors produce are limitations upon the proper functioning of the body. God wills that the Church be one. That does not mean all alike, but rather a community capable of accepting with joy the enrichment of great diversity. In a world where ignorance of the gospel and desperate need and oppression are massive, and where wholeness is so elusive in every dimension of life, neither a single denomination nor historic or national tradition can carry out a global mission. *Commitment to evangelism, mission and justice is inseparable from a commitment to church union.*[47]

Recognizing that the church is both a divine institution and a human organization, the conclusion affirms that the church "is an embodiment of Christ only insofar as it is obedient, faithful to Christ's will."[48]

Finally, in the third major section on "Policy Guidelines," global witness and ecumenical partnership are interpreted as correctives to the many distortions of the gospel based on sectarian pride and the identification of Christ with culture. While claiming that the primary work of the church is in its own locality, this section emphasizes that

> no true witness and service is ever merely local. . . . Without global concern, linkages and interaction, U.S. and Canadian churches will lose sight of the nature of the gospel and the nature of the church. Wit-

ness in any place is apt to be distorted by the powers of the place and culture. . . . Engagement in a variety of ministries with partner churches around the world is essential if we are to be effective in mission in our own place. Cross-cultural and cross-national exchanges are critical for the church's witness to the universality of the gospel, and an important corrective for local and national limitations and perversions of the faith. Loyalty to Christ as Lord requires us and enables us to be with each other for the sake of the world.[49]

Ecumenical conversations are certainly part of this process. Disciples participation in the Consultation on Church Union (COCU) and the National and World Councils of Churches and direct bilateral consultations with other Christian communions— such as the United Church of Christ and the Roman Catholic Church—have affected our attitudes toward other non-Christian religious traditions as well. Coupled with the Disciples' basic confidence in the constant loving activity of God in the world is a fundamental confession that "the church is not to be identified either with Christ or the Kingdom of God."[50] According to the "General Principles and Policies," the activity of God is not limited to the Christian community:

God has never, in any time or place, been without witness. One who is more fully known in Jesus Christ has been and is at work in the creation of community, the sharing of love, the seeking of freedom, the search for truth, the reactions of wonder and awe in the presence of nature's power and beauty and creativity, and the awareness of the worth of persons.[51]

That theological position implies the possibility that the Christian community, while certainly affirming that the Christ event supremely reveals God's nature and purpose, may through dialogue with other religious traditions recognize aspects of God's nature and activity that the Church has not fully appreciated thus far.[52]

While the guidelines acknowledge God's continual creative and redemptive action in the world beyond the bounds of the Christian community and the failures of the church both past and present to understand and submit to the will of God, the text nonetheless affirms the faith community's unique and sacred calling to witness. In word and deed, Christians should proclaim God's ultimate purpose in history, "the redemption of all humanity, the full completion of the whole creation."[53] Thus

> the church is the community God calls into being and enables to engage in *God's mission*. It does not exist for itself alone but for the sake of the world. At its best, the church proclaims the good news, nurtures the people of God, encourages worship, remembers and transmits the tradition, promotes social righteousness and justice, and exhibits the promise of the reign of God.[54]

The theological vision in the "General Principles and Policies" is not unlike the relational understanding of mission which emphasizes the integrity of *kerygma, diakonia,* and *koinonia.* "Christians do not have the option of keeping the good news for themselves. . . . The uncommunicated gospel is a clear contradiction."[55] Communication is incomplete, however, unless deeds match words. That thesis is reflected, indeed, in the text's very definition of "gospel," which always includes

> The announcement of God's kingdom of love through Jesus Christ;
> the offer of grace and forgiveness of sins;
> the invitation to repentance and faith;
> the summons to fellowship in God's saving words and deeds;
> the responsibility to participate in the struggle for justice and human dignity;

the obligation to denounce all that hinders . . .
   wholeness;
a commitment to risk life itself.[56]

The "General Principles and Policies" document represents a Disciples consensus not found in the earlier "Strategy of World Mission." This consensus has gradually emerged from many years of denominational debate on the meaning of mission and evangelism and, in particular, as a response to the increasing challenges of the twentieth century. The move to accept a relational approach to world mission and an inclusive definition of evangelism has been especially encouraged by the work of three prominent Disciples leaders: Robert A. Thomas, president of the Division of Overseas Ministries from 1968 to 1983; Bokeleale Itofo, president of the Church of Christ of Zaire; and Paul A. Crow, Jr., president of the Council on Christian Unity. Their perspectives prepared the way for adoption of the "General Principles and Policies" in 1981 and continue to enrich discussion on these critical issues within the church. In many ways their works highlight theological and practical convictions that now are under new attack.

Robert Thomas, a key contributor to the "General Principles and Policies" document, has called attention to two highly controversial points in that text. The first is the statement—based on Acts 14:17 and Rom 1:20—that "God has never, in any time or place, been without witness." To claim that the God who is more fully known in Christ Jesus is active and knowable in other dimensions of human experience—"in the creation of community, the sharing of love, the seeking of freedom, the search for truth, the reactions of wonder and awe in the presence of nature's power and beauty and creativity"—calls into question a sharp distinction between reason and revelation and challenges rigid positions of religious exclusivism founded on it. It is a controversial section precisely because it tends to treat the role of the church as relative in human salvation and questions numerical church growth as the key index of success in Christian mission. It challenges attitudes of arrogance and triumphalism in world mission and calls the church to a more humble spirit regarding its own interpretation of God's will and to a more hopeful vision of the compassionate and mysterious ways of God.

Thomas has also identified a second controversial area of the text: advocacy. Acknowledging that for the most part the churches in Asia, Latin America, Africa, and the Middle East are among the world's poor, the text calls on Western Christians to reorient their priorities in mission and to work actively for a new socio-political order:

> If the churches of the West are to be partners in mission in any realistic sense they must be "with the poor." The present economic imbalance is seen by Third World churches to be the result of an exploitive and oppressive system which churches in the West should work to change for the sake of the majority of the world's peoples. *Westerners are asked to dissent from present life styles, express solidarity with the poor in their struggle for liberation and justice, share resources, and help create the political will for a new international order.*[57]

During a 1981 lecture at Disciples Divinity House in Chicago, Thomas stated his own views on the social demands of the Christian gospel quite directly. Sensitive to the criticism that the DOM and the Disciples leadership had, in committing to social advocacy, abandoned the church's responsibility for kerygmatic mission, Thomas asserted,

> We're not opposed to proclamation, we're opposed to American preachers going overseas to do it. . . . Evangelism is the witness to the Lord made in relevant and creative ways that calls for some response. We, most of our staff, would be convinced that witness is only made with strength when there is *integrity between deed and word. And until the community of faith practices what it preaches,*

nobody listens. The emphasis in this is clearly chosen because what the church needs mostly is to be confronted by its perversions of the gospel. And what the whole of these United States needs to be confronted with is *the gospel,* which is now mostly hidden either by cultural religion, or hidden by a failure to understand history and the biblical material. . . . In fact, most of what is called evangelism in this country isn't.[58]

Thomas admits that those committed to this position have adopted a broad or inclusive definition of "evangelism," involving a concern for wholeness in mission, which "the churches of the Third World have helped us formulate because they have recognized long since that poverty and hunger, injustice and oppression were concerns of Jesus, and that the good news has to do with the whole man and the whole world—indeed, the cosmos."[59]

Bishop Bokeleale Itofo, president of the Church of Christ of Zaire, provides a similar emphasis on "wholeness." In his 1973 "Annual Report of the Church of Christ in Zaire," he spoke of "preaching the Gospel" in "Word, Deed, and Unity," an approach that he reiterated in his 1977 address to North American Disciples at the Kansas City General Assembly. For Bokeleale, as for Thomas, evangelism means more than proclamation. In fact, Bokeleale extends the concept beyond word and deed to include the ecumenical principle explicitly. "Word," he argues, refers to Christian education as well as to the public proclamation of the gospel. "Deed" refers to socioeconomic development and aid as well as to proper personal conduct. "Unity" recalls the important Johannine prayer of Christ that his disciples be one, that the world might believe (John 17:20–23). Thus, although the "General Principles and Policies" and Thomas emphasize "unity," Bokeleale places it along with word and deed as central elements.

According to Bokeleale, division within the body of Christ is a major stumbling block to the spread of the gospel throughout the world. Living Christian unity in our diversity, he argues, "is a way of *preaching* the Gospel."[60] Like the early Disciples, Bokeleale considers Christian unity essential to the thought and practice of the Church. The Willingen formula that was adopted in the "Strategy of World Mission" spoke of evangelism as "proclamation, *fellowship* and service"; Bokeleale speaks of "word, deed, and *unity.*" This transition from "fellowship" to "unity" reflects the awareness of many in the church that denominationalism poses a great hindrance to the Christian mission; the General Assembly showed this awareness in 1981 when it approved Resolution No. 8114, "The Report of the Commission on Theology and Christian Unity."

Unity amidst Christian diversity is also the central concern of Paul Crow, the chief ecumenical officer of the Disciples (and from 1968 through 1974 executive secretary of the Consultation on Church Union). Crow prefaces his most recent book, *Christian Unity: Matrix for Mission,* with a quotation from the *Rule of Taizé:* "Never resign yourself to the scandal of the division of Christians." The book explores four important dimensions of mission and evangelism that proceed from the Christian gospel—*proclamation, presence, service,* and *Eucharist*—but rather than address what he judges to be the divisive issue of how mission *differs* from evangelism, Crow chooses to offer a perspective on their *common* dimensions and their intrinsic relation to unity.

Crow's terms "proclamation" and "service" reiterate the church's concern for "word" and "deed," but his remarks on "presence" and "Eucharist" constitute his particular contribution to the contemporary Disciples discussions on mission and evangelism. He defines presence as "the adventure of going to live with others in the world in the name of Christ,"[61] without which there can be no effective proclamation. Presence emphasizes being with others in significant relationship, living out the gospel in the midst of others rather than simply announcing it. According to Crow, presence requires "listening before speaking," understanding others before preaching to them, sharing life meaningfully before attempting to teach doctrines about life's meaning. He writes: "The quality of life we live among others is the most dramatic credential of our witness."[62] Conservative-evangelical missiologists, he says, have judged such references to "listening" and "being with" as evidence of a fundamental "uncertainty of faith." Yet that misses the point:

> A witnessing presence is not one of total silence. Rather, the evangelistic posture includes "listening before we speak," and recognizing that sometimes the most powerful witness to Christ is made incognito, without recognition of the evangelist. Presence conveys the love of Christ through one's lifestyle as well as through one's spoken words.[63]

"Listening," therefore, leads conscientious Christians directly to "advocacy," as being with others contributes unfailingly to human understanding and a sense of solidarity in human struggles for justice and liberty.

In addition to "proclamation," "presence," and "service," Crow finds "eucharistic sharing" integral to the mission of the Church. "Eucharist," for Crow, is the central sacrament of the Christian church, separated from which "mission becomes merely a humanitarian program, 'doing good for others.'"[64] In fact, he writes,

> a missionary presence is the fruit of participation in the Lord's Supper. "Every eucharistic gathering is therefore an act of witness, which is part of mission." *The communion table is the matrix of mission,* the place where church and world intersect in the presence of Christ, the place from which Christians are sent forth to serve and to love.[65]

The eucharistic dimension of mission and evangelism reminds the church, according to Crow, of two important facts: the sacrifice involved in the ministry of reconciliation and the significant problem posed for real Christian unity by the failure of various church fellowships to permit, much less encourage, the common celebration of the Lord's Supper. Eucharistic divisions, argues

Crow, "frustrate the mission of the church in the world. The needs of a suffering world, therefore, call us to share the one bread and the one cup of the Lord."[66]

The Continuing Debate on Theologies of Mission
     The positions advanced in the "General Principles and Policies of the Division of the Overseas Ministries" and the arguments presented by these three prominent Disciples leaders represent a broad consensus on the meaning of mission and evangelism, which the Christian Church (Disciples of Christ) overwhelmingly affirmed through the 1981 Anaheim General Assembly. Within the denomination, clearly the dominant understanding of the church's mission in the world is relational rather than homiletical in character. That is, while the church universal has recognized its obligation to uphold the cardinal principles of both love and truth, the theological and practical reflections of Disciples have progressively emphasized the former. Disciples theology has been informed more by scriptural pericopes concerning God's love than by those about God's judgment and wrath, and its normative teachings, unlike those in many church fellowships, have not emphasized the notion that God saves or damns individual souls for accepting or rejecting certain essential Christian propositions and rites. Rather than highlight the image of God as judge, Disciples have characteristically focused on images of God as loving creator, sustainer, and redeemer of all life. Correspondingly, the denomination has envisioned the Christian's primary role as the "co-worker with God" in establishing the Kingdom. The disciple of Christ Jesus is teacher and preacher, but discipleship means preeminently being a compassionate servant and an agent of reconciliation. In ministries overseas, Disciples since the Commission to the Orient (1928) and especially since World War II have emphasized relationships characterized by mutual respect, justice, and forgiveness. Evangelism has been understood to include Christian modes of action and Christian modes of speech to share the gospel. A fundamental presupposition has been that living examples of service and devotion lead

potential followers of Christ to inquire about the religious and conceptual foundations of that life of selfless action in the world.

Disciples have tended to distinguish but not sharply separate *kerygma, diakonia,* and *koinonia.* In particular, they have rejected a world mission strategy that would aim primarily for verbalized and countable "decisions for Christ" without convincing witness to the radically new common life in Christ that represents true *metanoia* or "turning." They have adopted the conclusions of the 1930 ecumenical commission on mission, chaired by William Ernest Hocking, which stated:

> The Christian way of life and its spirit is capable of transmitting itself by quiet personal contact and by contagion: there are circumstances in which this is the most perfect speech. If the actual tasks of life can be shared with the people of a community, whatever power there is in the Christianity of the worker will be revealed in operation, and will do its part in transforming the spirit of individual lives who perceive it. *This also is evangelization, not by word but by deed.*[67]

The debate, of course, continues for the Christian Church (Disciples of Christ). Indeed, there is evidence that even as the "General Principles and Policies" document was being accepted in 1981, a more conservative theological and practical attitude was emerging within the denomination. To many Disciples, the relational understanding of mission, while a helpful corrective to extreme versions of the homiletical approach, has at times been advanced in a manner that neglects the church's ministry of proclamation. Many have wondered if presence does lead as a matter of course in mission to proclamation, and some have argued that the broad or inclusive definition of mission, while intended to convey the interrelatedness of *kerygma, diakonia,* and *koinonia,* has obscured the unique aspects of the Christian life to which these different terms refer in scripture and church tradition.

The signs of a slightly more conservative vision within the Disciples fellowship are evident in at least two areas. First, since the 1981 assembly in Anaheim, there has been considerable discussion concerning the denomination's need to emphasize anew, in a more aggressive and systematic manner, Christian witness and evangelism in the narrow sense. The 1983 General Assembly of the Christian Church (Disciples of Christ) in San Antonio adopted two relevant resolutions. The "Resolution Concerning Evangelism: A Continuing Priority," No. 8334, calls for a renewed commitment to evangelism "in order that the church may have an increasing number of committed disciples of Jesus Christ" and "to the establishment of new congregations as a major evangelistic concern and thrust." The "Resolution Concerning Instruction in the Theology and Methodology of Evangelism," No. 8316, asserts unequivocally that evangelism, as an essential task and responsibility, "has been *grossly neglected* in the life of the church, in the role and work of the minister, and in ministerial education"; it calls for courses in theology and methodology for evangelistic witness "in the required seminary discipline for every Disciples ministerial candidate."[68] The denomination's recent "Growth for Witness" emphasis, as well as the increasing membership and financial resources of the National Evangelistic Association, are further signs of the vitality of traditional forms and images of personal evangelism among Disciples, although these forms and images are in some tension with the "General Principles and Policies." With reference to that document, Thomas has asserted directly, "Evangelism is what it is all about!"[69] Clearly, not all Disciples have been persuaded by that interpretation.

Second, there has been increasing criticism in the last few years of some of the ecumenically determined priorities in world mission established by the World Council of Churches (WCC) and the National Council of Churches of Christ in the U.S.A. (NCCC). This is of particular significance for the Christian Church (Disciples of Christ) because of the Division of Overseas Ministries' unusually high commitment to ecumenical decision making for initiatives in world mission. While the 1983 General Assembly rejected a resolution calling for limited future participation in such ecumenical councils in favor of another resolution reaffirming the Disciples heritage of ecumenical involvements[70]—and few in the fellowship would fully assert that denominationalism providentially permits religious diversity and promotes a healthy sense of Christian competition—a considerable number of Disciples, both lay and clergy, in recent years have been highly critical of various actions and pronouncements of the WCC and NCCC. In sum, ecumenicity appears now to many as a far less attractive foundation for Christian mission in the world. The adoption in 1983 of a resolution supporting new and substantial funding for a "Major Presence in Media"—"that would make a significant *Disciples* witness to the World, that would enhance *Disciples'* identity among the public, and that would promote *Disciples'* commitment to their church and its presence on the front line of ministry"[71]—is perhaps not totally unrelated either to the renewed evangelistic spirit within the church or to a heightened sense of disenchantment with ecumenical organizations.

The ongoing debate on the meaning of mission and evangelism is an important one for the church. That the debate within the Christian Church (Disciples of Christ) continues is as it should be. The church must constantly engage in critical reflection on its commission and its proper response to the pressing human needs of the world. The church has an obligation to embody and proclaim both Christian love and gospel truth. It is to enhance and encourage critical reflection on that obligation—certainly not to stimulate further polarization within the church—that we have attempted to place our current conversations on mission and evangelism in historical perspective. We affirm the fundamental positions advanced in the "General Principles and Policies" document, convinced that its emphasis on the integrity of word and deed and on Christian unity as the proper matrix for mission contributes to a message that the church urgently needs to hear. Yet, too, we understand and affirm those who offer constructive theological and practical critiques of the relational approach to mission and the broad definition of evangelism. The church greatly needs their contribution as well. For while these issues have been important to the development of the Disciples tradition in the past, the continuing debate within the church on proper mission priorities will become even more crucial as we approach the twenty-first century in a divided, troubled, and endangered world.

Notes

[1] Most Disciples ministers received the April 1983 "I Accuse! I Plead!" letter from Donald A. McGavran attacking the Division of Overseas Ministries for its actions relative to the creation of the Church of North India. Most received, as well, the May 1983 response of the DOM written by Robert S. Bates and Robert A. Thomas.

[2] "General Principles and Policies of the Division of Overseas Ministries" (St. Louis: Christian Board of Publication, 1981), p. 3.

[3] See Larry D. Bouchard, "The Interpretation Principle," in this volume.

[4] George F. W. Kresel, "Alexander Campbell's Theology of Missions," unpublished Th.D. dissertation, Boston University, 1961.

[5] Joseph M. Smith, "A Strategy of World Missions: The Theory and Practice of Mission as Seen in the Present World Mission Enterprise of the Disciples of Christ," unpublished Th.D. dissertation, Union Theological Seminary, 1961, p. 26.

[6] Alexander Campbell and N. L. Rice, *A Debate Between Rev. A. Campbell and Rev. N. L. Rice, on the Action, Subject, Design and Administrator of Christian Baptism; also on the Character of Spiritual Influence in Conversion and Santification, and on the Expediency and Tendency of Ecclesiastical Creeds, as Terms of Union and Communion, Held in Lexington, Ky. from the Fifteenth of November to the Second of December, 1843* (Lexington: Skillman & Sons, 1844), pp. 902–903.

[7] William Richey Hogg, "The Rise of Protestant Missionary Concern, 1517–1914," in Gerald H. Anderson, ed., *The Theology of the Christian Mission* (Nashville: Abingdon, 1961), pp. 95–111. Hogg discusses the Protestant reformers' lack of a theology of missions.

[8] *Millennial Harbinger* 2 (1831): 436.

[9] *Christian Baptist* 1 (1823): 7.

[10] *Millennial Harbinger* 7 (1836): 335.

[11] Alexander Campbell, *The Christian System* (Bethany, Va.: 1835; Nashville: Gospel Advocate Co., 1874), p. 75.

[12] Ibid., p. 123.

[13] *Millennial Harbinger* 2 (1831): 235–38.

[14] *Millennial Harbinger* 8 (1837): 272.

[15] Grant K. Lewis, *The American Christian Missionary Society* (St. Louis: Christian Board of Publication, 1937), p. 13.

[16] *Millennial Harbinger* 21 (1850): 207–208.

[17] *Millennial Harbinger* 13 (1842): 523.

[18] *Millennial Harbinger* 6 (1835): 519.

[19] *Millennial Harbinger* 4 (1833): 380.

[20] William E. Tucker and Lester G. McAllister, *Journey in Faith* (St. Louis: Bethany Press, 1975), p. 248.

[21] For more on the problems and developments entailed in early Disciples intercongregational cooperation, see Dennis Landon, "Ambivalence by Design: Disciples Structures of Church," in this volume.

[22] Robert A. Thomas, *Where in the World Are We Going? The Overseas Ministry of the Christian Church (Disciples of Christ)* (St. Louis: Christian Board of Publication, 1973), p. 11.

[23] The last three organizations later withdrew from the UCMS.

[24] As the "General Principles and Policies" document maintains, this same understanding permitted the 1968 creation of the Division of Homeland Ministries and the Division of Overseas Ministries only on practical grounds, since there was no theological basis for a distinction between the "home" and the "foreign" mission of the church; see p. 7.

[25] Thomas, *Where in the World Are We Going?*, p. 15. Emphasis ours.

[26] Smith, "A Strategy of World Missions," pp. 94–95.

[27] A. D. Harmon, "A Century of Conscious Entity," *Christian Evangelist* 63 (Nov. 18, 1926): 1449–51, 1463–64.

[28] Smith, "A Strategy of World Missions," p. 98.

[29] Ibid., pp. 98–99. Emphasis ours.

[30] Quoted in Thomas, *Where in the World Are We Going?*, p. 19.

[31] *Christian Evangelist* 85 (March 19, 1947): 275.

[32] "Strategy of World Mission: Basic Policy of the Division of World Missions of the United Christian Missionary Society," *Ecumenical Studies Series* (January 1960), pp. 19–20.

[33] Ibid., p. 24.

[34] Ibid., p. 11.

[35] This phrase was popularized by Kenneth Scott Latourette in his seven-volume work, *A History of the Expansion of Christianity* (New York: Harper and Brothers, 1937–1945).

[36] "Strategy of World Mission," p. 11.

[37] Ibid., p. 26.

[38] Ibid., p. 23. Emphasis ours.

[39] Smith, "A Strategy of World Missions," p. 225.

[40] Ibid., p. 223.

⁴¹Donald A. McGavran, ed., *Eye of the Storm: The Great Debate in Mission* (Waco: Word Books, 1972), p. 65.

⁴²Ibid., p. 64. Emphasis ours.

⁴³Smith, "A Strategy of World Missions," p. 225. The climate of theological renewal and reconsideration among Disciples of this period is evidenced by the Panel of Scholars project and in the challenge that was forthcoming from the commission on the Theology of Mission. Having published a series of critical essays reviewing the "Strategy" in 1960, they prepared a report which represented a new constructive effort on thought and practice in overseas ministries, "Theology of Mission," *Ecumenical Studies Series* 4 (Jan 1960); "Report of the Commission on the Theology of Mission," *Mid-Stream* 4 (Fall 1964): 82–185. The report is a major document in the history of Disciples thought, and it bears more careful consideration than can be given here. It appears that it anticipates the "General Principles and Policies" in several significant ways. In particular, the use of *kerygma*, *diakonia*, and *koinonia* to represent the "total proclamation of the Gospel" and the insistence that *kerygma* be defined theologically marks this report with a broad or "relational" understanding of mission (see esp. pp. 149–55). Among other things, expanding the definition of *kerygma* to include sacramental acts anticipates Paul Crow's emphasis on Eucharist in mission and evangelism (see below).

⁴⁴"General Principles and Policies," p. 16.

⁴⁵Ibid., p. 35.

⁴⁶Ibid., p. 21.

⁴⁷Ibid., p. 17. Emphasis ours.

⁴⁸Ibid.

⁴⁹Ibid., p. 22.

⁵⁰Ibid., p. 17.

⁵¹Ibid., p. 16.

⁵²See an excellent discussion of this idea in Christian theology in Alan Race, *Christians and Religious Pluralism: Patterns in the Christian Theology of Religions* (New York: Orbis Books, 1982), especially Chapter 4, "Pluralism."

⁵³"General Principles and Policies," p. 16.

⁵⁴Ibid., pp. 16–17. Emphasis ours.

⁵⁵Ibid., p. 18.

⁵⁶Ibid.

⁵⁷Ibid., p. 39. Emphasis ours.

⁵⁸Thomas's presentation was transcribed by the authors. A more detailed presentation of his views may be found in *Where in the World Are We Going?*, pp. 43–51.

⁵⁹Thomas, *Where in the World Are We Going?*, p. 46.

⁶⁰Bokeleale, "The Miracle of the Church in Africa," unpublished

transcription (Department of Africa, Division of Overseas Ministries, 1977).

[61] Paul A. Crow, Jr., *Christian Unity: Matrix for Mission* (New York: Friendship Press, 1982), p. 49.

[62] Ibid., p. 50.

[63] Ibid.

[64] Ibid., p. 57.

[65] Ibid., p. 58.

[66] Ibid., p. 59.

[67] Laymen's Foreign Missions Inquiry, Commission of Appraisal (William Ernest Hocking, Chairman), *Re-Thinking Missions* (New York: Harper & Brothers, 1932), p. 65. Emphasis ours.

[68] Texts of Resolutions No. 8334 and 8316 are included in the 1984 Yearbook and Directory of the Christian Church (Disciples of Christ) (St. Louis: Christian Word Publications, 1984), pp. 229–30 and 251–52.

[69] Thomas lecture at Disciples Divinity House of the University of Chicago, October 1981.

[70] The 1983 General Assembly rejected Resolution No. 8339 and adopted Resolution No. 8341. See the 1984 Yearbook and Directory, p. 254.

[71] See Resolution No. 8362 in the 1984 Yearbook and Directory, p. 273. Emphasis ours.

A Special Calling:
Christian Unity and
the Disciples of Christ

MICHAEL KURT KINNAMON

THE STORY IS TOLD of how the great Danish philosopher, Soren Kierkegaard, was once walking down a street when he spotted a painted sign in a shop window that read "pants pressed here." The philosopher entered and began to take off his pants until the startled shopkeeper explained that he did not press pants, he painted signs.

For more than 150 years, the Disciples of Christ have painted many signs proclaiming that we have a special calling to promote the unity of all Christians. Thomas Campbell hoped that the Christian Association of Washington (Pennsylvania), which he helped form in 1809, would help "restore unity, peace, and purity, to the whole church of God."[1] Disciples, proclaimed Peter Ainslie in 1913, are "the first definitely organized movement in the history of the Church for the healing of its schisms."[2] Howard Short entitled one of his books from the 1950s *Christian Unity is Our Business*. And since Restructure, T. J. Liggett (among others) has written that the commitment to Christian unity remains "the dominant concept of our church."[3]

Yet one wonders if people coming through the door do not find that we are simply a fellowship of sign painters who, finally, do not press many pants. Disciples have participated in several union conversations, including the nine-party Consultation on Church Union and the recent covenant explorations with the

United Church of Christ, but since the merger of "Disciples" and "Christians" in 1832, we have actually done nothing but divide. Having set out to serve as a catalyst for unity, the Campbell-Stone movement has managed to contribute three new churches to the bewildering and disheartening array of sects in American Christianity. Several Disciples communities formed by mission work overseas have indeed become part of new united churches, but Disciples have rarely initiated union conversations and have generally entered them only late in the day.[4] It is true that Disciples exert an influence out of all proportion to our size in such ecumenical bodies as the National Council of Churches of Christ (USA) and the World Council of Churches (due, partly, to the existence of our permanent ecumenical office, the Council on Christian Unity). Nonetheless, the ecumenical vision, as articulated by our founders and by the modern ecumenical movement, remains foreign to many congregations, and active commitment to the movement for church unity is questionable at all levels of Disciples life. Twenty years ago we underwent an important, necessary act of restructuring designed, at least in part, to make us more responsive and responsible partners in the burgeoning dialogue among churches; yet we now face the real danger that this new structure may harden into a denominational shell that further institutionalizes our disobedience to Christ's prayer that we may all be one. Can Disciples still say with any integrity that we have a special calling as witnesses to Christian unity?

The Vision of the Founders

So many excellent books and articles have been written on unity as a theme in the history of the Disciples of Christ that it seems unnecessary to add another essay on the subject.[5] The task of "reinterpreting Disciples" does require, however, that we briefly recall some of the seminal persons, events, and documents in the history of our fellowship and ask ourselves how Disciples thinking about Christian unity has changed over the last 150 years and what motifs and lessons from our past may help us to recover that special calling as we face the new ecumenical opportunities of the future.

There is no doubt that the two documents most closely identified with the founding of the Disciples—*The Last Will and Testament of the Springfield Presbytery,* associated with Barton Stone, and Thomas Campbell's *Declaration and Address*—are both rooted in the longing for unity among Christians and their churches. "We will," wrote Stone and his companions in the Springfield (Kentucky) Presbytery, "that this body die, be dissolved, and sink into union with the Body of Christ at large; for there is but one Body, and one Spirit, even as we are called to one hope of our calling."[6] Stone was, as one biographer has put it, "a grassroots' practitioner of Christian unity" who made union the "polar star" of his ministry. "If we oppose the union of believers," he exclaimed in the first issue of the *Christian Messenger* (1826), "we oppose directly the will of God, the prayer of Jesus, the spirit of piety, and the salvation of the world!"[7]

Thomas Campbell's plea for unity was equally impassioned. His *Declaration and Address* opens with an extended description of the "dreadful consequences of those unnatural and anti-Christian divisions which have so rent and ruined the church of God."[8] There follows a series of propositions, several of which foreshadow modern ecumenical documents:

> ††"The Church of Christ upon earth is essentially, intentionally, and constitutionally one; consisting of all those in every place that profess their faith in Christ and obedience to him in all things according to the Scriptures."

> ††Local congregations, while necessarily separate from one another, ought to be in fellowship, without "schisms" or "uncharitable divisions."

> ††All who, through grace, profess their faith in Christ "should love each other as brethren, children of the same family and father."

††"Division among Christians is a horrid evil" that is "anti-Christian, as it destroys the visible unity of the body of Christ; as if he were divided against himself, excluding and excommunicating a part of himself."[9]

Several assumptions of this extraordinary document deserve special attention. Unity is seen not simply as a human creation, but as a gift of God: the Church, the body of Christ, is one. Campbell would surely have agreed with his son that unity is important for effective evangelism: "Neither truth nor union alone is sufficient to subdue the unbelieving nations, but truth and union combined are omnipotent."[10] His main point, however, is not that Christian unity facilitates more effective mission, but that, according to the Scriptures, it is an essential characteristic of the Church. For Campbell, this unity (like the Church itself) is grounded in individual believers' faith in Christ, but it must also find expression in the corporate structures of Christian community.

For such unity to be achieved or, more accurately, made visible, Campbell regarded two things as essential: (1) the restoration of the simple terms of original Christian fellowship as recorded of the New Testament church, and (2) liberty in all matters of private opinion and church practice not mentioned in Scripture. All that is necessary, he wrote, for the unity and purity of the Church is that Christians "keep close by the observance of all divine ordinances, after the example of the primitive church, exhibited in the New Testament; without any additions whatsoever of human opinions or inventions of men."[11] It was central to Thomas Campbell's restorationism that human opinion—as expressed in creeds, theological speculation, or church structures and practice—should never be a bar to fellowship in Christ, but beyond this he proposed no precise plan of restoration. There is a naiveté in Campbell's vision (quite foreign to modern ecumenism) that causes him to overlook the basic doctrinal disagreements between churches, disagreements that arise, we now realize, from informed but differing interpretations of the same scriptural texts:

It is, to us, a pleasing consideration that all the churches of Christ, which mutually acknowledge each other as such, are not only agreed in the great doctrines of the faith and holiness; but are also materially agreed as to the positive ordinances of Gospel institution; so that our differences, at most, are about things in which the Kingdom of God does not consist, that is, about matters of private opinion, or human invention.[12]

This was coupled with what we now see as a historically false assumption that the practice of New Testament churches was uniform and, thus, constitutes an easily discernible blueprint for later Christians:

Is it not as evident as the shining light that the Scriptures exhibit but one and the same-self subject-matter of profession and practice, at all times and in all places, and that, therefore, to say as it declares, and to do as it prescribes in all its holy precepts . . . would unite the Christian church in a holy sameness of profession and practice throughout the whole world?[13]

This brings us to the most influential—and, for our purposes, the most problematic—of the Disciples founders. Alexander Campbell clearly shared not only his father's passion for the restoration of primitive Christianity but also his passion for Christian unity. In *The Christian System*, after referring to Christ's prayer for unity in John 17 (a favorite source of inspiration for the Disciples founders), he exclaims, "If this be true . . . in what moral desolation is the Kingdom of Jesus Christ! Was there at any time, or is there now, in all the earth, a Kingdom more convulsed by internal broils and dissensions, than what is commonly called the church of Jesus Christ?"[14] Further, he implies in that work that restoration is a means to oneness in the body of Christ. "Nothing is essential to the conversion of the world but the union and cooperation of Christians. Nothing is essential to the union of Christians but the Apostles' teaching or testimony."[15]

In other writings, however, the younger Campbell answers the question about original (New Testament) Christian fellowship by setting forth "essential" beliefs and practices, less as opinions to be tested than as rediscovered truths to be accepted.[16] Baptism by immersion upon personal confession of faith and the weekly celebration of the Lord's Supper are only the most obvious marks of what was becoming a new orthodoxy. It was one thing to argue, as Thomas Campbell had done, for a return to the simplicity of New Testament faith and to require no more; it was quite another to claim to have restored the "ancient order of things" and to allow no less. This shift, according to Garrison and DeGroot in their history of the Disciples, "changed the character of the Christian union enterprise from an appeal to the divided denominations to unite upon common ground into an appeal to their members to leave them and unite with the Disciples upon what they stood ready to prove was the 'original ground' newly rediscovered."[17]

The weakness in Thomas Campbell's plea for union was the unwarranted assumption that most Christians could easily agree on an "essential core" of the apostolic faith. The flaw in the thinking of many later Disciples (including, at times, Alexander Campbell) was an unwillingness to recognize their own conclusions as "opinion," to acknowledge that contrary conclusions could be drawn by others who also sought a restoration of the true scriptural witness.[18]

It is not surprising, then, that the last half of the nineteenth century saw what W. E. Garrison calls a "temporary eclipse of the union ideal" among Disciples—although they continued to paint a few signs. Restoration of a particular vision of the ancient order had become an end in itself and thus a principle of division, not reunion. The rigid insistence on believers' baptism by immersion (leading to closed membership throughout the movement) made them "un-unitable" with any except Baptists, and the Baptists were not interested in other elements of the Disciples' package.

A New Ecumenical Witness

Historians usually identify 1910, the year of the great Edinburgh Missionary Conference, as the beginning of the modern ecumenical movement. It was also the year that Peter Ainslie, pastor of the Christian Temple in Baltimore, made his dramatic appeal at the General Convention for Disciples to recover their original ecumenical commitment. One immediate result was the establishment of what is now called the Council on Christian Unity, the first agency of its kind created by a denomination to promote the ideal of unity.

The new generation of Disciples ecumenists—including such prominent figures as Ainslie, W. E. Garrison, and Charles Clayton Morrison—found that new biblical and historical scholarship (not to mention the rapidly changing fabric of American society) made their context remarkably different from the frontier environment of the Campbells and Stone. As historian Clark Gilpin puts it,

> They now interpreted this sense of the given unity of Christians in the light of a much fuller appreciation of history. The church's history was no longer the record of the loss and recovery of trans-historical scriptural truth. It was rather the organic development and expression of Christian faith. The gospel was thoroughly implicated in history at every point of its explication, and the church did not imitate an immutable pattern but instead adopted forms appropriate to witness in a changing social and intellectual environment. Restorationism was no longer a viable theological option.[19]

Those groups known today as the Churches of Christ and as the Non-Denominational Fellowship of Christian Churches and Churches of Christ (Independents) continued to focus on the concept of restoration, regarding this as the preeminent concern of the founders. But the other wing of the movement now spoke less of restoring the past than of working and praying, in the light of Scripture, for that fullness of time when God will unite all

INTERPRETING DISCIPLES

things in Christ. In his book *If Not a United Church—What?*, Ainslie traces the church through three periods of organic growth: "in the second period the plant has been sending up its stem, toughening and growing in these days of Christian activity and world-wide service. . . . Some day the third period will be upon us. I know not when nor how, but God's orchards will be in full bloom and the fruit will be a united Church of Christ on earth."[20] For the Disciples, unity was—and had always been—the hallmark of the Campbell-Stone movement, and a new methodology of ecumenical cooperation and dialogue replaced the discredited restorationism.

Alexander Campbell had not avoided contact with other denominations. He welcomed the Evangelical Alliance and, at one point, proposed in the *Millennial Harbinger* that a conference of all Protestant churches be convened to seek unity on a common understanding of faith and morality. Campbell also came to support such nineteenth-century cooperative movements as the Y.M.C.A., the American Bible Society, and the American Sunday School Association. Many of his followers, however, regarded themselves as distinct from the historical "parties" of Christianity and often avoided formal cooperation lest it compromise their transhistorical vision.

The new generation still saw denominationalism as an evil (Ainslie railed against it in several of his books), but they also realized that it is an evil in which Disciples inevitably participate until unity is won.[21] This freed them, in turn, to participate fully in the exciting ecumenical developments of the first half of this century. Disciples have contributed several important leaders to the Federal Council of Churches of Christ (now the National Council of Churches of Christ), including the General Secretary from 1950–1964, Roy Ross. Ainslie was a significant figure in the founding and early years of the Faith and Order movement; Disciples churches from various parts of the world were founding members of the World Council of Churches in 1948 and have played an active role in all subsequent assemblies; and the Disciples of Christ have taken part in the Consultation on Church

Union (COCU) since its second plenary in 1962. The first general secretary of COCU was a Disciple, Paul A. Crow, Jr. (now president of the Disciples Council on Christian Unity).

A real test of this ecumenical commitment came in the 1950s, when Disciples faced the involvement of their overseas churches in schemes of union. Extensive study resulted in the document "A Strategy for World Missions," approved and implemented by the World Division of the United Christian Missionary Society. This statement affirmed that entry into a united church would cause neither loss of funds nor severance of historic ties with Disciples. Former Disciples communities are now part of transconfessional union churches in Japan, the Philippines, Thailand, southern Africa, north India, Zaire, and (most recently) the United Kingdom. Disciples in the United States and Canada, however, remain, despite all their "sign painting," a separate community.

Building on the Heritage

To help Disciples face the present range of ecumenical challenge and contribute more creatively to the search for unity in Christ, I will suggest four convictions or perspectives that have often informed our understanding of the Church and its unity. This list is, of course, far from exhaustive, and its points necessarily overlap. It should be taken simply as one attempt to interpret the Disciples ecumenical heritage in a way that may help us promote our historic vision of Christianity freed from the discord of competing factions.

Unity and Mission

I find it impossible to summarize the first conviction because it has to do with basic orientation to the Church, its nature, and its mission. We can begin to get at the issue, however, by observing that, while Disciples have certainly not lived up to the signs painted by our ecumenical prophets, our persistent emphasis on unity has meant that we have seldom been complacent about sectarianism. Our history, if nothing else, has left many of us with a guilty conscience that can be translated into ecumenical activity. We have even managed at times to share this guilt with our partners in the ecumenical movement.

Of course, most Christians would affirm that Christian unity is a worthy ideal. But it seems to me that the Disciples emphasis from the time of our founders has implied an understanding of priorities that, while not unique, is certainly controversial. There are many persons involved in contemporary ecumenical work, for example, who argue that the pressing issues of our day—nuclear disarmament, social justice, alleviation of hunger—take precedence over the merger of separated Christian bodies. These people often contend that unity, if it does happen, will not be the result of deliberate effort (e.g., theological dialogues or union negotiations) but a by-product of our common response to the demands of witness and mission.

Disciples have certainly not stood back from the struggles for peace and justice, but there has been a tendency in our church to see the division of Christians as itself a pressing issue of our day—perhaps even the *most* pressing issue. Ainslie begins his book *If Not A United Church—What?* by proclaiming that "the greatest necessity of modern times is the unity of the Church of Christ. No other issue exceeds it in importance."[22] The same idea was advanced in 1979 at the first meeting of the Disciples Ecumenical Consultative Council (a loosely structured world organization for churches of the Disciples tradition). "We believe," said Disciples delegates from twelve countries on six continents, "that there is no more urgent task before us than the reclaiming of the vision of one Church: holy, catholic and apostolic."[23]

In a world that faces so many urgent tasks, these are striking affirmations. They rest on two very significant assumptions. First, Disciples (along with many others) have usually held that unity is the true nature of the Church. We have been given a fellowship (*koinonia*) as followers of Christ that links us like the branches of one vine (John 15) or the members of a single body (1 Cor 12), and we have been called to make this unity visible in order to convince the world that Jesus Christ is truly sent from God (John 17). As Thomas Campbell put it, the church is essentially one through Christ's gracious intention—which means that our present disunity is not simply an inconvenient obstacle to more efficient social action (important as that is) but an act of disobedience to our Lord. In short, it is sin. To oppose union, said Barton Stone, is to oppose the will of God for God's people. That is surely the strongest possible foundation for ecumenism.

This understanding means, as Clark Gilpin has written, that Disciples generally view unity as a condition for authentic mission and not merely as a tactic for pursuing it.[24] But, and this is the second assumption, there has been little doubt in the minds of our ecumenical prophets that a renewed and united Church would be far better able to address the needs of the wider human community. Unity should not be sought merely for functional reasons, but it would nonetheless have obvious functional benefits. "At the crisis of 1914," said Ainslie, "organized Christianity stood helpless in every nation on the globe and was powerless to preserve the peace of the world. Surely division has its fruit."[25] Unity would enable the Church to serve more truly and effectively as a sign and instrument of God's healing presence—and this alone makes the task of unity a priority for Christians.

In actuality, however, this talk of priorities is somewhat misleading, since Disciples ecumenists from Peter Ainslie to Paul Crow have consistently protested against the attempt to split the ecumenical agenda into the search for doctrinal unity and the demands of service, into the unity of the Church and the unity of humankind. If unity is understood as structural merger, then it should indeed be subordinated to the tasks of feeding the hungry or standing in solidarity with the oppressed. But if it is understood as the renewal of the Christian community and an act of obedience to God's reconciliation of all things to God through Christ, then it will also be seen as inseparably linked with the mission of the Church. Our "being" as a united sacramental fellowship cannot be divorced from our "doing" as a community sent into the world to bear witness to God's love. I take this to be a Disciples position which we should repeat at every opportunity.

Unity and Scripture

I am convinced that our heritage of restorationism has yielded at least one essential insight: unity should not be—in fact, cannot be—achieved by lowest common denominator bargaining, but by a common return to the sources of the faith, especially Scripture. This is certainly not to disagree with the need to interpret the biblical witness in light of contemporary experience, but Christian unity will not be Christian unless it is grounded in a common basis of fundamental affirmations derived from the records of the early Church. The Church is "apostolic"; it is not reinvented for each new generation but rests on the transmitted witness of God's revelation in Christ. Our unity must not only be geographical but temporal; we seek to be visibly linked with those who have professed faith in our Lord for the past two thousand years.

This methodological principle is at the heart of recent ecumenical advances. Until the 1950s, the Faith and Order movement (from 1948 a department of the World Council of Churches) was frequently a place where churches compared their stated positions on doctrinal questions (Augsburg vs. Westminster vs. the Thirty-nine Articles). Gradually, however, the theologians in Faith and Order began to spend less time comparing the branches of the tree and more time exploring the common trunk, exploring what Scripture and church tradition have said about such things as ministry, sacraments, and the nature of the Church. This work was given a major boost at the Montreal Conference on Faith and Order in 1963, when the delegates moved beyond the old dichotomy of Scripture/tradition to speak of "the Tradition of the Gospel testified in Scripture, transmitted in and by the Church through the power of the Holy Spirit." The tradition of the gospel (the *paradosis* of the *kerygma*), the faith of the apostolic Church transmitted as a living reality through the ages, is what Faith and Order has tried to recover and express in, for example, its recent convergence text on *Baptism, Eucharist and Ministry*.[26] The modern ecumenical movement has gone beyond the

Campbells in its awareness that the New Testament is itself a part of the Church's tradition, but the desire to ground unity in a common recovery of the witness of the early Church seems clearly in line with their thinking.

At this point the mistakes of our brief history can be turned to ecumenical profit. If the early Disciples were pretty much on target with their insistence that Scripture provides the common ground for union, they were decidedly wrong to presume that they, as one part of the universal Church, could articulate the essential biblical witness for all. Should not our own struggle with a narrow restorationism help us to see that the essential ground of unity—the tradition of the gospel—comes into focus only when the churches seek to recover it together? Should not the lessons of our history cause us to insist that the historic texts and confessional statements of individual churches must be measured by the plumb line of the apostolic tradition, and not vice versa? Are we not called by our experience to remind others and ourselves that no church is, by itself, a sufficient center for future unity?

Unity and Freedom

While Disciples have continued to listen to where the Scriptures speak, we have also continued to agree with Thomas Campbell that there must be liberty in all matters of private opinion where no clear mandate is given in the tradition of the gospel. Few slogans have been more widely quoted among Disciples than the line borrowed from an obscure, seventeenth-century Lutheran theologian, Rupertus Meldenius: "In essentials unity, in opinions liberty, in all things charity."

The problem, of course, is to agree on what are "essentials." Is it a simple profession of faith in Jesus Christ? Does it involve adherence to certain sacramental practices or doctrinal understandings derived from Scripture? Does it demand a particular mode of conduct towards one's neighbors? Disciples (at our best) have given no final answer, but we have insisted that most things which Christians have claimed as causes for division—theological perspectives, ecclesiastical structures, confessional formulations, liturgical traditions—are secondary products of human invention and thus should not constitute barriers to Christian fellowship.

This emphasis on freedom in all but the essentials—which Ronald Osborn sees as the third major focus, along with unity and restoration, in Disciples history[27]—has naturally led Disciples ecumenists to champion diversity as a hallmark of the coming Great Church. Garrison has suggested that this would mean, among other things, (1) varieties of organization and structure, (2) no creedal or doctrinal test for membership or ministry, (3) liberty and variety in the use of sacraments, and (4) diversity in forms of worship[28]—a list that most present Disciples, I suspect, would endorse. But there are difficulties with such a perspective. The Disciples approach to ecumenism has been dismissed as a form of theological minimalism or relativism which sweeps genuine doctrinal differences under the carpet and fails to take sufficient account of historic disputes. Some also accuse Disciples of a naive faith in the reason or goodwill of individual Christians, a naiveté that causes us to undervalue the importance of ecclesiastical, doctrinal, and liturgical structure.

On the positive side, this emphasis on freedom and on the secondary character of theological opinion has allowed Disciples to correct or even discard our own opinions as we have grown in understanding (e.g., through the ecumenical movement). I have heard it said that this willingness to assess previous convictions and to urge others to do the same may be the Disciples' greatest gift to contemporary ecumenism.

I am also convinced that our heritage puts us in a position to encourage another very important unity development. Some churches, including the Roman Catholic, hold that agreement is needed on a whole range of theological matters before common structured fellowship is possible. Others, however, are increasingly opposed to any notion of union as an all-or-nothing, one-time achievement, preferring to see it instead as a process of gradual growth that allows the churches to deepen their commitment to each other through intermediate structures (e.g., covenant relationships). Isn't it possible, they ask, to agree on certain points and then move towards fuller unity by stages? Isn't it likely that those things which are essential for the full restoration of visible Christian *koinonia* and those which are in the realm of legitimate diversity will become clearer through the process of sharing ever more deeply our common life in Christ? The Consultation on Church Union (COCU) and the Disciples–United Church of Christ conversations are only two of several union negotiations that have adopted this more flexible and dynamic model of ecumenical growth.

A related development is the apparent willingness of more and more churches to acknowledge that some past disagreements, even if unresolved, simply do not warrant division in this day and age—if, in fact, they ever did. The main achievement of the 1981 union of the United Reformed Church in England and Wales (URC) with the majority of the Churches of Christ in Great Britain was the uniting of those observing infant and believers' baptism into one church. That union was not really based on a theological consensus but on what the negotiators called "the integrity of a mutual recognition of well-grounded convictions."[29] It is possible, in other words, to hold that the appropriate recipient of baptism is one able to make a personal profession of faith while still acknowledging that there are good grounds in Scripture and tradition for holding that it is proper to baptize the infant children of Christian believers. The important thing, one member of the URC told me, "is not consensus but trust. We are sufficiently convinced of the reality of our shared being in Christ that we can trust one another even when we have these strongly divergent beliefs and practices on a very fundamental matter."[30] It was not long ago that most Disciples regarded believers' baptism as an essential; it is therefore significant that our sister church in Great Britain has, thanks to dialogue with another tradition, openly recognized this issue to be a legitimate matter of opinion. I cannot help but think that Thomas Campbell and Barton Stone would approve.[31]

INTERPRETING DISCIPLES

Unity and the Local Church

"The Design for the Christian Church (Disciples of Christ)," first provisionally adopted in 1968, indicates that we have out-grown our former insistence on the autonomy of local congrega-tions in favor of a fuller picture of the Church and its catholicity. Most Disciples, I think, now affirm that the Church is the com-munity of all those who are in Christ and can thus accept the statement, made by the New Delhi Assembly of the World Coun-cil of Churches, that the Church's unity will be made visible when "all in each place" are brought into a fully committed, eu-charistic fellowship and "at the same time are united with the whole Christian fellowship in all places and all ages." That is part of the greatness of the ecumenical movement: it forces us to real-ize that the black Methodist woman in Ghana, the Orthodox man in Russia, and the Catholic child from the Philippine slums are all inextricably joined with us in the body of Christ. It forces all churches to realize that their concept of the Church is too small.

But Disciples, even as we move towards a more catholic vi-sion, still resist any ecclesiastical structure or ecclesiological model that denies the integrity or independence of the locally gathered community. Disciples are correct, in my opinion, to insist that the local church, in the words of Pope Pius XII, is "the Body of Christ in miniature." Each congregation is not the whole Church, but is truly the Church.

This emphasis on the local community, while affirmed in theory, needs to become more evident in the practice of the ecu-menical movement. The search for unity is now entering a new and exciting stage as theological convergences, reached by Faith and Order or by the various bilateral (two-party) dialogues, are presented to the churches for what is technically known as "re-ception." Reception should involve the endorsement of ecumeni-cal texts by official decision-making bodies, but Disciples (and others) must also insist that it be an ongoing process of communi-cation and education within a church, whereby all its members are encouraged to embrace the results of ecumenical study. "Nothing is real," said Chesterton, "until it is local." Certainly unity will remain ephemeral until the visions and plans of reconciliation make sense and make a difference to the folks in congregations around the world. More specifically, I suspect that Disciples would generally agree that unity will not be achieved until the Christians in particular locations feel themselves responsible for one another and thus under obligation to make together the decisions that direct their worship, witness, and service. At a time when some conceive of unity as the cooperation of globally organized confessional bodies, this vision of union at the local level is a significant contribution to the ecumenical movement.[32]

What Is Demanded of Us?

Yes, many people may respond, we have an ecumenical heritage that reminds us to keep Christian unity on the agenda of board meetings and study groups. Yes, we can accept a reevaluation of that heritage which moves us, in good ecumenical fashion, beyond any claim to have recovered the ancient order of things on our own or beyond our old opposition to clerics, creeds, and structures. And, yes, we certainly admire that "apostolic succession" of ecumenical leaders who keep alive the idea that unity is the Disciples mission in national and international circles. But the temptation is then to place ecumenism at the bottom of the pile, beneath the pressing issues of the day, or to leave it to those committed experts whose lives seem to be an eternal conference on Faith and Order. Yet the Disciples heritage seems to demand more of us. There are particular steps that the whole church should now be taking, not out of loyalty to Thomas Campbell or Barton Stone but out of obedience to Jesus Christ.

At the very least, our "commitment to unity" should demand that we respond imaginatively and thoughtfully to the major ecumenical challenges that now engage the Disciples of Christ in fellowship with other churches in the Church universal.

1. Perhaps the most surprising ecumenical development of recent years has been the enthusiastic American and Disciples re-

sponse to *Baptism, Eucharist, Ministry* (BEM), produced by the Faith and Order Commission of the World Council of Churches. Ecumenism, American style, has been heavily oriented toward common service and witness; the Faith and Order component of the National Council (NCCC) is relatively weak, and many local councils have avoided theological discussion altogether. *Baptism, Eucharist, Ministry*, however, has captured the imagination of these bodies and has been hailed as an unprecedented breakthrough in reconciliation of doctrinal disputes. It was sent to the Council's member churches with a request for their official response by the end of 1985, and it received such attention that the NCCC published a special brochure simply listing the secondary materials on the text that have been produced in this country. A lay study guide and collection of worship materials for baptism and the Lord's Supper were also made available to aid local congregations.[33]

Baptism, Eucharist, Ministry was commended to the churches with the charge that their local communities study the text and its implications for congregational life. This process raised definite problems for the new Disciples polity: What would "official response" mean for Disciples when, by our own admission, we have no instrumentalities for exercising a binding "magisterium"? Are we able to express the essence of what we believe on controversial issues of doctrine so that ecumenical dialogue can advance? Are we able to incorporate the voice of the universal Church in the worship and witness of local congregations? (It is an irony of our history that Disciples may have to strengthen ecclesiastical decision-making processes—thereby participating more fully in the search for "essential" formulations—if we are ever to "sink into union with the body of Christ at large."[34])

The official Disciples response to the World Council of Churches—written by the Council of Christian Unity on the basis of congregational and regional studies and approved by the General Board and 1985 General Assembly—joins "other Christians in appreciation for the significance of this document. Indeed, we see here a witness to the apostolic faith through the ages." While "some of the language and terminology in the convergence text is not familiar to our tradition," the official response views this not as a flaw but a challenge to Disciples "to grow in our understanding of the faith as it has been expressed in different traditions and histories." Disciples have come to see that it is not possible, as our earliest pioneers had hoped, to avoid doctrinal formulation in the interest of unity. Nonetheless, despite its generally positive tone, the response does point out that many Disciples will have difficulties with parts of *Baptism, Eucharist, Ministry*: its insistence that rebaptism must be avoided, its suggestion that the "three-fold ministry" of bishop, presbyter, and deacon can be an important expression of Christian unity and continuity, and its inability to reach agreement regarding the ordination of women. The document, according to the Disciples response, requires serious study and discussion long after the period of official reaction is past.

2. The year 1984 was one of great promise and decision for the Consultation on Church Union (COCU). After a decade of low profile (to put it nicely), the delegates to the 1984 Baltimore plenary took steps that might well breathe new life into this nine-party church union. First, the delegates unanimously accepted the "final" revision of COCU's theological consensus statement, *In Quest of a Church of Christ Uniting*, and transmitted it to the highest governing body in each church with the request that formal action be taken to recognize *Quest* as a) an expression of the Church's apostolic faith, b) an anticipation of the Uniting Church that these churches wish to become, and c) a sufficient theological basis for a proposed interim "covenant." Disciples will need to give this document the same study and response that they gave *Baptism, Eucharist, Ministry*.

The second major development of the 1984 meeting is a proposal that "covenanting" be the next step in COCU's search for unity. The specific proposal from COCU's Church Order Commission envisions a covenant that "will effect the very self-identity of each participating church": mutual, public recognition of members and of each other as churches, a claiming of the theological consensus, reconciliation of ministries through a mutual laying on of hands as part of the liturgy inaugurating the covenant, regular eucharistic fellowship, common acts of mission, and the formation of "councils of oversight."

This last element has been a source of considerable debate and confusion. The proposed councils are best thought of as bridge structures—locally, regionally, and nationally—between present division and future union. Consisting of lay and ordained leaders of each church, the councils of oversight will have only such authority as the churches choose to assign. It is hoped that, initially, this will include ordination, the ordering of eucharistic fellowship, and the oversight of common mission. Any final decisions about covenanting are still several years away, but Disciples will need to give serious attention to this proposal in the last half of this decade. Perhaps more important, there seems to be a growing realization that future decisions are not really about COCU but about each other as churches.

3. Conversations between Disciples and the United Church of Christ (UCC) have, in my opinion, taken a more ambiguous turn. The findings of a Steering Committee, established to explore the possibility of union during a six-year trial period (1979–1985), were less than encouraging. Despite the fact that hundreds of Disciples congregations have been involved in study with UCC partner churches, considerable apathy exists about the prospect of organic union, as does distrust of national leadership, great divergence of opinion on what "unity" means, and lingering trauma in the UCC stemming from its creation, in 1957, out of congregationalist and reformed traditions.

The trial period resulted in a Steering Committee recommendation, adopted without great enthusiasm by both churches at their 1985 general meetings, to declare a "new ecumenical partnership" involving some common mission, theological discussion (within the context of the Consultation on Church Union and Baptism, Eucharist, Ministry) aimed at "full communion," and occasional common worship. Many ecumenists in both denominations have regarded this as little more than a way of saying "no" without saying "no," but that is a bit unfair. The committee acknowledged that they were proposing "something other than a binding commitment to become one church," but, they added, "we are also proposing more than the continuation of another round of study, or that we simply join in the cooperative mission without any commitment to a common future." The conversations have generated debate (e.g., in *The Disciple*) about the Disciples' identity as an ecumenical church, and that is surely a healthy development.

4. The Disciple-Roman Catholic International Dialogue Commission has produced an "agreed account" of its first five sessions. The document, published as "Apostolicity and Catholicity," indicates a surprising degree of convergence on such issues as baptism, tradition, and spiritual life and is being shared with the parent churches for reaction. A more serious response may well be sought after a second round of discussions.

Each of these challenges presents particular problems and possibilities for the Disciples of Christ. Responsibility to our ecumenical partners surely demands that we respond not in an ad hoc way but out of a consistent and coherent vision of the Church. It seems to me, however, that even more is demanded of us than appropriate, responsible reaction to emerging ecumenical developments. Instead of waiting for or reacting to union negotiations or theological conversations to force a reassessment of our theology, ministry, mission, sacramental practice, and structure, shouldn't we be constantly anticipating the possibility of expanded fellowship? Shouldn't we, in other words, be constantly seeking to manifest the faith of the Church universal more fully in our corporate life?

Let me be more concrete. In England, the Presbyterian and Congregationalist churches gave serious attention to the merits of believers' baptism prior to their 1972 union as the United Reformed Church. Such attention made it easier to begin negotiations with the Churches of Christ after 1972. This concern for alternative understandings of baptism was not merely an act of ecumenical courtesy or ecclesiastical compromise; it was based on a growing awareness that, according to the tradition of the gospel, Christian initiation involves both our human response (i.e., a personal profession of faith) and the gift of God's grace in the sacrament. Similarly, the plan of union which has been proposed for a new united church in Ghana incorporates the historic episcopate despite the fact that none of the present negotiating churches is episcopally ordered. These churches are convinced that (to paraphrase *Baptism, Eucharist, Ministry*) the episcopate can be an important sign, though certainly not a guarantee, of continuity and unity in the body of Christ.[35]

This same principle can be brought to bear on the difficult conversations between the Disciples and the U.C.C. Instead of simply giving "mutual recognition" to our churches' quite similar ministries, would it not be more significant to explore together the relationship of our ministries to the ministry of the Church around the world and through the ages? (The ecumenical agreements that emerge would, of course, be an invaluable resource for such exploration.) The question is not "How can we merge?" but "How can we manifest visible unity in a way that best promotes further reconciliation and best effects a common witness and mission?"[36]

From time to time, Disciples have talked about our fellowship as a bridge between Protestant and Roman Catholic wings of the Church.[37] The fact that we are simultaneously in serious conversations with the U.C.C. and Roman Catholics may indicate that there is some truth in this label. It seems to me, however, that a better image is that of leaven. If we were consciously to anticipate the possibility of union through the structures and policies of our corporate life, if we were constantly to reassess our understanding of the Church in light of developing ecumenical consenses, then we might indeed become the leaven in COCU and other settings.

I come back to where we began: How can the Disciples of Christ avoid becoming a fellowship of sign painters whose proclamations go unsupported by commitment? My work with union negotiations around the world shows me that the biggest obstacle to visible unity is the fear of losing a comfortable sense of identity.[38] As Disciples, we share a particular history, a common cultural setting, a recognizable style of worship, a pleasant feeling of brotherhood. But that should not prevent us from acknowledging that our basic identity is in Christ. The various ecclesiastical identifications may be historically understandable, but that should not obscure the deplorable fact that today they undermine the Church's mission and witness—especially in parts of the world where Christians are a minority. "How," asks the great ecumenist and missionary Lesslie Newbigin,

> can Indian society recognize the name of Jesus when those who bear his name define their identity not by reference to it, but by reference to names which evoke the memory of their special religious and cultural histories? We must show by the nature of our community that the name of Jesus does stand for a reality that transcends the precious diversity of human types and which can therefore create a fellowship in which they mutually enrich one another.[39]

Our founders had learned this lesson on the American frontier, which is why they insisted on the simple designations as "Christians" or "Disciples." Today, however, our complicated name has come to denote yet another separated tradition. The genius of the early Disciples was precisely that they made the passion for unity their identity. To join other Christians in deeper and broader fellowship should not be to lose our identity but to fulfill our special calling. That is why Virgil Sly could be convinced "that the continuing identity of Disciples of Christ is not of major importance. The important thing is whether Disciples of Christ have completely identified themselves with the purposes of Christ for his world."[40] Or why Ronald Osborn could say that he continues "to believe and to labor for the hastening of that time when Disciples no longer continue as a separate people but, finding a larger freedom in a united church, may share with others their experiment in liberty."[41] Or why Paul Crow could

INTERPRETING DISCIPLES

proclaim that "[our] *raison d'etre* is to be a reconciled and reconciling community."[42]

But there we go painting signs! In the end they bring to mind the warning issued by the Lutheran theologian, Edmund Schlink, at the Lund Conference on Faith and Order in 1952:

> We cannot proclaim our unity again and again and at the same time remain divided. . . . If we do not manifest the unity which has been given to us, God's grace will become our accusation. The inspiring vision of unity will itself then place us under the judgment of God.[43]

Notes

[1] Thomas Campbell, *Declaration and Address of the Christian Association of Washington* (Washington, Pa.: 1809), p. 3.

[2] Peter Ainslie, *The Message of the Disciples for the Union of the Church* (New York: Fleming H. Revel, 1913), p. 19.

[3] Thomas J. Liggett, "Why Disciples Chose Unity," *Mid-Stream* 19 (April 1980): 228.

[4] For a summary of Disciples involvement in modern union negotiations, see Paul A. Crow, Jr., "The Christian Church (Disciples of Christ) in the Ecumenical Movement," in George G. Beazeley, Jr., ed., *The Christian Church (Disciples of Christ): An Interpretive Examination in the Cultural Context* (St. Louis: Bethany Press, 1973), pp. 274–93.

[5] See Winfred E. Garrison, *Christian Unity and Disciples of Christ* (St. Louis: Bethany Press, 1955).

[6] Quoted in Lester G. McAllister and William E. Tucker, *Journey In Faith: A History of the Christian Church (Disciples of Christ)* (St. Louis: Bethany Press, 1975), p. 78.

[7] Ibid., p. 88.

[8] Thomas Campbell, *Declaration and Address*, p. 13.

[9] Ibid., pp. 16–18.

[10] Alexander Campbell, *The Christian System* (Cincinnati: Bosworth, Chase & Hall, Publishers, 1839), p. 87.

[11] Thomas Campbell, *Declaration and Address*, p. 18.

[12] Ibid., p. 10.

[13] Ibid.

[14] Alexander Campbell, *The Christian System*, p. 85.

[15] Ibid., p. 87.

[16] In 1825, Campbell began what became a series of thirty-two articles on the "Restoration of the Ancient Order of Things" in the *Christian Baptist*.

[17] W. E. Garrison and Alfred T. DeGroot, *The Disciples of Christ: A History* (St. Louis: Bethany Press, 1948), p. 553.

[18] For a longer treatment of this problem, see Charles Clayton Morrison, *The Unfinished Reformation* (New York: Harper and Bros., 1953), p. 156, and Ronald E. Osborn, *Experiment in Liberty* (St. Louis: Bethany Press, 1978), p. 87.

[19] W. Clark Gilpin, "Issues Relevant to Union in the History of the Christian Church (Disciples of Christ)," *Encounter* 41 (Winter 1980): 20.

[20] Peter Ainslie, *If Not A United Church—What?* (New York: Fleming H. Revel, 1920), p. 68.

[21] See Gilpin, "Issues Relevant to Union," p. 21.

[22] Ainslie, *If Not A United Church—What?*, p. 11.

[23] "A Message from the Disciples Ecumenical Consultative Council," *Mid-Stream* 19 (April 1980): 239.

[24] Gilpin, "Issues Relevant to Union," p. 23.

[25] Ainslie, *If Not a United Church—What?*, p. 33, quoted in Gilpin, "Issues Relevant to Union."

[26] The best introduction to the methodology of Faith and Order is Ernst Lange, *And Yet It Moves: Dreams and Reality of the Ecumenical Movement*, trans. Edwin Robinson (Grand Rapids, Mich.: William B. Eerdmans, 1979). *Baptism, Eucharist and Ministry* is published by the World Council of Churches.

[27] This is the major thesis of *Experiment in Liberty*.

[28] Garrison, *Christian Unity and Disciples of Christ*, pp. 245–48.

[29] This position is spelled out in Martin Cressey, "Church Union and the Visible Unity of Christ's Church," in *Growing Towards Consensus and Commitment: Report of the Fourth Consultation of United and Uniting Churches* (Geneva: World Council of Churches, 1981).

[30] In a private letter to the author from Bishop Lesslie Newbigin.

[31] The URC-Church of Christ union is discussed at greater length in *Survey of Church Union Negotiations* (1979–1981), Faith and Order Paper No. 115 (Geneva: World Council of Churches, 1982), reprinted in *Mid-Stream* 22 (January 1983): 119–50.

[32] This issue is dealt with at greater length in my article, "The Creative

Edge: United Churches and the Christian World Communions," *One In Christ* 19 (1983): 155–68.

[33] William H. Lazareth et al., *Growing Together in Baptism, Eucharist and Ministry: A Study Guide* (Geneva: World Council of Churches, 1982), and Max Thurian, ed., *Baptism and Eucharist: Ecumenical Convergences in Celebration* (Geneva: World Council of Churches, 1983).

[34] I have developed this notion further in "Authority in the Church: An Ecumenical Perspective," *Mid-Stream* 21 (April 1982), especially pp. 207–12.

[35] For an expanded discussion, see the *Survey of Church Union Negotiations*.

[36] For an expanded treatment of this theme, see "Growing Together Towards the Unity of the Church," *Mid-Stream* 23 (April 1984): 189–200.

[37] See George G. Beazeley, Jr., "The Present Place of the Disciples in the Ecumenical Movement," a reprint by the Council on Christian Unity, in *Mid-Stream* 4 (April 1965): 9–12.

[38] See "Growing Together Towards the Unity of the Church."

[39] Richard W. A. McKinney, ed., *Creation, Christ and Culture* (Edinburgh: Clark, 1976).

[40] Quoted in Ralph G. Wilburn, "The Unity We Seek," in *The Reformation of Tradition*, ed. Ronald E. Osborn, Vol. 1 of *The Renewal of Church: The Panel of Scholars Reports*, ed. W. B. Blakemore (St. Louis: Bethany Press, 1963), p. 362.

[41] Osborn, *Experiment in Liberty*, p. 105.

[42] Crow, "The Christian Church in Ecumenical Movement," p. 293.

[43] In Oliver S. Tomkins, ed., *The Third World Conference on Faith and Order* (London: World Council of Churches, 1953), pp. 159–60.

About the Authors

LARRY D. BOUCHARD is Assistant Professor of Religious Studies at the University of Virginia, teaching in the area of religion and literature. He formerly taught religion and philosophy at Eureka College (1980–1983). Currently, his areas of writing and research concern religious understandings of tragedy, evil, and integrity in contemporary drama.

DENNIS L. LANDON is the Senior Minister of First Christian Church (Disciples of Christ), in Vincennes, Indiana. He has served on the staff of Disciples Divinity House of the University of Chicago, as First Vice Moderator of the Christian Church (Disciples of Christ) in Illinois and Wisconsin, and on the General Board of the Christian Church (Disciples of Christ).

FRANK BURCH BROWN is Associate Professor of Religion and Humanities at Virginia Polytechnic Institute and State University. Composer of numerous anthems, hymns, and instrumental works, he served as Music Director and Composer-in-Residence of University Church in Chicago from 1975–1979. He is the author of *Transfiguration: Poetic Metaphor and the Language of Religious Belief* and *The Evolution of Darwin's Religious Views*.

LOWELL K. HANDY is a Ph.D. candidate in Bible at the University of Chicago. His work involves the rise of monotheism as the religious basis for the centralization of community in the Old Testament.

MARY W. PATRICK, a student of New Testament and early Christianity, is working on a doctoral dissertation concerning the rhetoric of Ignatius of Antioch at the Lutheran School of Theology at Chicago. She is the author of *The Love Commandment*.

NEAL KENTCH is Associate Minister at University Place Christian Church in Enid, Oklahoma. He is also a doctoral candidate in the Doctor of Ministry program at the Divinity School of the University of Chicago.

CYNTHIA GANO LINDNER is Co-Minister at First Christian Church in Albany, Oregon. She was Associate Minister at First Congregational Church in Corvallis, Oregon (1983–1986) and Interim Associate and Campus Minister at University Church in Chicago (1982–1983) and is also a doctoral candidate in the Doctor of Ministry program at the Divinity School of the University of Chicago.

K. BRYNOLF LYON is Assistant Professor of Pastoral Care at Christian Theological Seminary in Indianapolis. He is the author of *Toward a Practical Theology of Aging* and articles on ethical issues in human development.

L. DALE RICHESIN is minister at First Christian Church in Maywood, Illinois. He has previously served as Associate Pastor of St. Paul Community Church in Homewood, Illinois, as Pastor of North Side Christian Church in Chicago, and as Student Associate at First Presbyterian Church of Chicago. He is the co-editor, with Brian Mahan, of *The Challenge of Liberation Theology: A First World Response,* as well as many articles on social ministry.

DON A. PITTMAN is Assistant Dean and Assistant Professor of History of Religions at Brite Divinity School, Texas Christian University. Formerly he served as Associate Dean and Interim Dean of the Disciples Divinity House, University of Chicago, and as Lecturer at the University of Chicago Divinity School.

PAUL A. WILLIAMS is a Ph.D. student in History of Religions at the University of Chicago Divinity School, specializing in African religions, history of Christianity, and Buddhism. He is the son of missionaries who served the Christian Church (Disciples of Christ) overseas in Zaire.

MICHAEL KINNAMON is Assistant Professor of Theology at Christian Theological Seminary in Indianapolis, having completed service in 1983 as Executive Secretary of the Faith and Order Commission of the World Council of Churches. He is an ordained minister in the Christian Church (Disciples of Christ) and received his Ph.D. from the University of Chicago in the field of Religion and Literature. He is the author of *Why It Matters*, dealing with the World Council of Churches' text, *Baptism, Eucharist, and Ministry*, and of a number of articles on ecumenism. He currently serves as a member of the Ecumenical Partnership Committee between the Christian Church (Disciples of Christ) and the United Church of Christ.

THE EDITORS would like to express their thanks to a number of individuals and institutions who contributed in many ways to this project. Thanks to Don S. Browning, Martin E. Marty, Disciples Divinity House, Divinity School of the University of Chicago, and to Jim Duke, Keith Gregory, Ken Lawrence, Nancy Stevens, and TCU Press. Thanks also to C. Harvey Arnold, Rich Dieter, Margarita Scheffel, Randall Doubet King, Preston Simons, Nancy Tanner, A. T. A. Detox, Eureka College, North Side Christian Church, the Organization of the North East (ONE), St. Paul Community Church, and Somerset House. A special thanks to Ruth Bedell for her love.